Legalines

S0-EGS-504

Editorial Advisors:

Gloria A. Aluise
Attorney at Law

David H. Barber
Attorney at Law

Jonathan Neville
Attorney at Law

Robert A. Wyler
Attorney at Law

Authors:

Gloria A. Aluise
Attorney at Law

David H. Barber
Attorney at Law

Daniel O. Bernstine
Professor of Law

D. Steven Brewster
C.P.A.

Roy L. Brooks
Professor of Law

Scott M. Burbank
C.P.A.

Jonathan C. Carlson
Professor of Law

Charles N. Carnes
Professor of Law

Paul S. Dempsey
Professor of Law

Ronald W. Eades
Professor of Law

Jerome A. Hoffman
Professor of Law

Mark R. Lee
Professor of Law

Jonathan Neville
Attorney at Law

Laurence C. Nolan
Professor of Law

Arpiar Saunders
Professor of Law

Lynn D. Wardle
Professor of Law

Robert A. Wyler
Attorney at Law

TORTS

Adaptable to Fourth Edition of Henderson Casebook

By Gloria A. Aluise
Attorney at Law
and
Carol Dilfer Whalen

THE barbri GROUP

A COMPLETE PUBLICATIONS CATALOG IS
FEATURED AT THE BACK OF THIS BOOK.

HARCOURT BRACE LEGAL AND PROFESSIONAL PUBLICATIONS, INC.

EDITORIAL OFFICES: 176 W. Adams, Suite 2100, Chicago, IL 60603

Legalines

REGIONAL OFFICES: New York, Chicago, Los Angeles, Washington, D.C.

Distributed by: **Harcourt Brace & Company** 6277 Sea Harbor Drive, Orlando, FL 32887 (800)787-8717

SERIES EDITOR
Astrid E. Ellis, J.D.
Attorney at Law

PRODUCTION COORDINATOR
Sanetta Hister

Legalines™

SHORT SUMMARY OF CONTENTS

TABLE OF CONTENTS AND SHORT REVIEW OUTLINE

I. INTENTIONAL INFLICTION OF BODILY HARM—BATTERY

A. A PRELIMINARY LOOK AT THE PROCESS

1. **Investigation.** Prior to filing a lawsuit on a tort claim, a detailed investigation must be conducted. This investigation should cover, at least, four important points.

   a. **When.** Determining when the injury occurred is a necessary first step. All tort claims must be brought within particular time periods set by statute. These statutes indicate that the action must be brought within a certain period of time after the action accrued. The typical periods set by such state statutes may be one, two, three, or four years.

   b. **Damages.** With few exceptions, tort claims may only be brought when the injured party has suffered some form of loss. The investigation should determine whether the injured party has suffered personal injury, property damage, or economic loss. If such losses have occurred, compensatory damages may be recoverable. If the act against the injured party was intentional, additional damages called nominal damages or punitive damages may be recoverable.

   c. **Valid claim.** To recover any damages, the injured party must, of course, have a valid legal claim. The investigation should determine whether such a claim exists. The primary focus of a course on torts is the basic elements of valid legal claims for injuries.

   d. **Settlement.** The trial of a lawsuit is time-consuming and expensive. During the investigation process, efforts should be made to reach a settlement.

2. **Pleadings.** Should actual court action be necessary, such an action is begun by the filing of pleadings. The plaintiff files a *complaint*, which sets forth the claim. The defendant's response, an *answer*, indicates which facts are denied and which defenses shall be raised.

3. **Trial.** The trial is a formal, structured procedure that allows both sides to present the facts as they see them. The judge then instructs the jury on the law, and the jury determines the facts, applies the facts so found to the law, and reaches a verdict. The judge then enters a judgment. The usual steps in that process are:

   a. **Opening statements.** Both parties are given the opportunity to present a brief outline of the facts they expect to prove.

   b. **Direct and cross-examination.** Each side presents its evidence, usually the plaintiff first and then the defendant; each side can also question the witnesses from the opposing side.

   c. **Closing arguments.** At the close of all proof, each side is allowed to address the jury and present a summation of what it perceives to be the major points, issues, and conclusions drawn from the evidence offered.

4.   **Appeal.** The party losing a trial may appeal the case to a higher court. It should be noted that once a jury has determined the facts of the case, the appellate courts do not review the findings of fact, except for clear error by the jury. The only errors that can be appealed are errors of law.

B.   BATTERY

1.   **Prima Facie Case.**

   a.   **Definition.** A "battery" is the intentional, unprivileged harmful or offensive contact by the defendant with the person of another.

   b.   **Elements of prima facie case.**

   1)   **Intent.** As found in the Restatement of Torts, intent is the actor's desire to cause the result of his actions (a harmful or offensive touching) or his belief that these consequences are substantially certain to result from his actions. There is no requirement that there be a hostile or malicious intent (*i.e.,* to do harm, etc.). Objective facts may be introduced to prove a defendant's subjective state of mind.

Vosburg
v. Putney

   a)   **Intentional or unlawful act--Vosburg v. Putney,** 80 Wis. 523, 50 N.W. 403 (1891).

   (1)   **Facts.** While sitting in a schoolroom, Putney (D) lightly kicked Vosburg (P) in the shin, unintentionally aggravating a previous injury. As a direct result of the kick, P lost the use of his leg permanently. P sued D, alleging assault and battery, and was awarded $2,800. On appeal the verdict was set aside and the case was remanded for retrial. In the subsequent case a judgment for $2,500 was granted. D appeals.

   (2)   **Issue.** In an action for battery, must the plaintiff prove that the defendant *intended* to cause the harm that resulted?

   (3)   **Held.** No. Affirmed.

   (a)   In an action for assault and battery, a plaintiff need only show that the defendant either committed an unlawful act or that the defendant had an unlawful intention to commit the harm produced.

   (b)   Since the kick did not occur in the normal course of play on the school ground, D may not assert the implied license of the playground that will excuse all injuries that are the result of boyish play.

    (c)   Because the kick took place during regular school hours in the school-room, D's actions were unlawful and the court will infer an unlawful intent.

    (d)   Hence, D committed assault and battery and is therefore liable for all damages which resulted from his unlawful conduct.

(4) Comment. This case also states the well-settled proposition that the tortfeasor must take his victim as he finds him; *i.e.*, the mere fact that the plaintiff is more susceptible to injury does not mitigate the tortfeasor's liability.

b) Substantial likelihood that offensive contact will occur--Garratt v. Dailey, 46 Wash. 2d 197, 279 P.2d 1091 (1955).

(1) Facts. Garrett (P) alleged that Dailey (D), a five-year-old boy, had deliberately pulled a chair out from under her as she was sitting down, causing her to fall and fracture her hip. D claimed that he moved the chair so he could sit in it himself, and upon noticing that P was about to sit down, tried in vain to move the chair back in time. On remand, the court found that when D moved the chair, he knew with substantial certainty that P would attempt to sit down where the chair had been. P appeals from a decision denying her recovery of damages for an alleged assault and battery.

(2) Issue. In an action for assault and battery, may a defendant be held liable if he did not intend to cause the resultant harm, but knew with substantial certainty that his actions would likely cause it?

(3) Held. Yes. Reversed and remanded for clarification.

    (a)   Battery is the intentional infliction of a harmful or offensive bodily contact upon another.

    (b)   An act is deemed to be intentional if it is done either for the purpose of causing the contact or apprehension thereof, or with the knowledge that such contact or apprehension is substantially certain to result therefrom.

    (c)   Since the court found on remand that D knew with substantial certainty that P would attempt to sit down where the chair had been located, he had the requisite intent to be liable for battery.

    (d)   When a minor has committed a tort with force, he is liable to be proceeded against the same as any other person.

(4) Comment. The general view of intent is that the defendant will be found to have the necessary intent when a reasonable person in the defendant's position would believe that a particular result was certain to follow his acts (even if the defendant did not subjectively intend to cause the harm). Children are charged with liability for the batteries that they commit, but the standard for their liability is commensurate with what is expected of children—considering their age, experience, and intelligence.

2) **Contact—harmful or offensive touching.** The second element of the prima facie case is that there must be some actual contact between the defendant and the plaintiff.

   a) **Kind of contact.** As the *Garratt* case indicates, direct contact between the defendant and the plaintiff's person is not required. Sufficient contact is found when the defendant touches or strikes something that the plaintiff is holding or is closely associated with, *e.g.,* the clothes the plaintiff is wearing.

   b) **Physical harm.** There is no requirement that there be actual physical harm caused by the touching or contact. If the touching is "offensive or insulting," it is actionable.

C. CONSENT

Consent of the plaintiff or the existence of a privilege (*see* D., *infra*) will exonerate a defendant from liability for an act which, on its face, would otherwise give rise to tort liability. Of course, the burden is on the defendant to plead and prove the existence of consent or a privilege.

1. **General Rule on Consent.** Under the general rule, consent by a plaintiff to an act which would otherwise give rise to tort liability will act as a bar to an action based on such act. However, the consent must be effective to act as a bar. Problems often arise as to whether the plaintiff has in fact given consent and whether the plaintiff has the capacity to give consent.

2. **Manifestation of Consent.** Consent may be express or implied. When a plaintiff, by words or conduct, intentionally indicates that he is willing to permit an invasion of his rights by a defendant, there is *express consent.* *Implied consent*, on the other hand, may be either implied-in-fact, as where the plaintiff acts in such a way as would be understood by a reasonable person to be consent to invasion of his rights by the defendant, or implied-in-law, as where circumstances are such as to create the privilege in the defendant to invade the plaintiff's rights without liability (*e.g.,* a doctor rendering emergency medical care to an unconscious person).

   a. **Silence or inaction as consent.** Silence or inaction may be consent, depending upon what a reasonable person under like circumstances would think. While it is unreasonable to think that silence in the face of a threatened beating is an implied consent thereto, it would probably be reasonable to assume that silence in response to an offered kiss from a suitor is an implied consent thereto. Of course, if the defendant knew that the plaintiff would not consent to the act, though the plaintiff remained silent, there will be no implied consent.

O'Brien
v. Cunard
Steamship
Co.

   1) **Failure to object--O'Brien v. Cunard Steamship Co.,** 154 Mass. 272, 28 N.E. 266 (1891).

a) **Facts.** Cunard (D), a steamship company, gave notice that it was offering smallpox vaccinations to its passengers on board ship so that they could avoid quarantine requirements at port. O'Brien (P) stood in line with other women who were waiting to receive vaccinations. D's employee, a doctor, vaccinated those who had no vaccination mark. When P's turn came, P held up her arm to be vaccinated, telling the doctor she had already been vaccinated. Seeing no mark, the doctor indicated she should be vaccinated again. P did not object. P sued to recover damages for battery. P appeals a directed verdict for D in lower court.

b) **Issue.** Under circumstances where a reasonable person would be expected to object if she did not consent to a battery, may a defendant infer consent from the plaintiff's nonobjection?

c) **Held.** Yes. Judgment for D.

(1) Conduct may imply consent to a battery.

(2) In certain situations failure to resist is sufficient conduct from which consent may be assumed.

(3) The court will not consider P's unexpressed feelings.

d) **Comment.** In determining whether consent has been given, the court will be guided by the overt acts and not the state of mind of the plaintiff. This case also illustrates the importance not only of the issues of substantive law (*e.g.*, what is a harmful touching?) but also of understanding the nature of the legal decisionmaking process. That is, there are *fact* questions (*e.g.*, did D actually hit P?); *law* questions (*e.g.*, what are the elements of the tort of battery?); and questions of *application* of law to the facts (*e.g.*, if D touched P, and an offensive touching is one that a reasonable person would find offensive, was the touching in this situation an offensive touching?). Generally, in a legal dispute the jury decides fact questions, the court decides law questions, and the jury decides application questions (unless all reasonable minds would agree on the outcome, in which case the judge removes such questions from the jury), but different courts may handle these issues differently in any given case.

3. **Informed Consent.** It is generally held that consent must be voluntary and informed and that mistake in the facts will vitiate apparent consent.

a. **Mistake of fact.** A plaintiff's mistake as to the nature of a defendant's conduct will vitiate the plaintiff's apparent consent. For example, where a plaintiff submits to a body massage under the mistaken belief that the defendant is treating an illness and that the massage is a necessary part of the treatment, the plaintiff will not be deemed to have consented to the defendant's offered indecent familiarities. Similarly, a person who accepts and eats candy poisoned by a defendant, without knowledge of the poison, does not consent to be poisoned by the defendant.

    b. **Mistake of law.** Consent is ineffective if given under a mistake of law, *e.g.*, submitting to arrest under belief that an arrest warrant is valid, when in fact it is not.

    c. **Fraud.** Consent procured by fraud is ineffective (*See, e.g.*, the body massage example, in a., above). However, fraud as to collateral matters does not vitiate consent; *e.g.*, where a plaintiff consents to sexual intercourse with a defendant in return for a $10 bill offered by the defendant, which is counterfeit, the fact that the plaintiff did not know the bill was counterfeit will not negate the consent if it is otherwise effective.

    d. **Duress.** Consent given in response to physical force or threats thereof against a plaintiff or a member of his family will be ineffective.

    e. **Unlawful acts.** There is a split of authority concerning whether a voluntary participant to an unlawful act can be deemed to have "consented" thereto for the purpose of barring a subsequent action against a fellow participant for damages.

Barton v. Bee Line, Inc.

    1) **Statutory rape--Barton v. Bee Line, Inc.,** 238 App. Div. 501, 265 N.Y.S. 284 (1933).

        a) **Facts.** Barton (P), a 15-year-old girl, alleges that while she was a passenger on a common carrier, Bee Line (D), she was forcibly raped by D's chauffeur. P sued D for failure to perform its duty as a common carrier to P. D defended based on the chauffeur's testimony that P consented to sexual relations. The jury was charged that P was entitled to recover even if she consented. The jury returned a $3,000 verdict, which the court set aside. P appeals.

        b) **Issue.** May a female under the age of 18 who understands the nature of her act recover civil damages for sexual relations to which she consented?

        c) **Held.** No. Order setting aside verdict is affirmed.

            (1) State criminal law provides that it is illegal for a person to have sexual intercourse with a female, not his wife, under 18 years of age, even if she consents.

            (2) The object of this law is to protect society from promiscuity.

            (3) Rewarding consenting females with civil damages will not advance this public policy but will rather frustrate it by encouraging minor females to become seducers.

            (4) P's consent, although to an illegal act, barred her civil cause of action for rape.

        d) **Comment.** Other jurisdictions would hold differently in the *Barton* case. The basic difference in theory is that the purpose of tort law is to act as a reinforcement of the criminal system. Thus, in effect, each private plaintiff acts as a private prosecutor in the punishment of the wrongdoer.

4. **Surgical Operations and Emergencies.** While a doctor is generally subject to the same rules as others with respect to invasion of another's rights, the law has developed certain exceptions. If, during an operation, a doctor discovers a condition in a plaintiff that requires immediate attention or that would require another operation to remedy, consent to the additional surgical procedure is deemed implied in law, unless the patient specifically limited the authority of the doctor prior to the operation. With respect to emergencies, the victim is assumed to consent to acts by a doctor consistent with what a reasonable person would desire under the same circumstances.

a. **Unauthorized operation--Bang v. Charles T. Miller Hospital,** 251 Minn. 427, 88 N.W.2d 186 (1958).

Bang v. Charles T. Miller Hospital

  1) **Facts.** Bang (P) complained during an office visit with a doctor (D), of the diminished size and force of his urinary stream and an increased frequency of urination. D admitted P to the hospital for further examination. P, upon D's recommendation, consented to and underwent a prostate operation, during which P's spermatic cords were severed. The severance was done to prevent infection. P alleges that he was not told that his spermatic cords would be severed and did not consent to this procedure. P sued for damage for an unauthorized operation. P appeals dismissal of his action.

  2) **Issue.** In an action to recover damages for an unauthorized operation, must the question of whether a plaintiff consented to the severance of his spermatic cords be submitted to the jury?

  3) **Held.** Yes. Dismissal reversed and new trial granted.

    a) Whether an operation was unauthorized is a fact issue to be decided by the jury.

    b) Where a physician can ascertain in advance of the operation alternative situations and where no emergency exists, a patient should be informed of alternatives and given a chance to decide among them.

    c) Failure to inform under such circumstances would result in an unauthorized operation.

    d) In this case, no emergency existed and P should have been informed of the necessity of severance and alternative possibilities.

    e) The question of whether P was informed as to the severance of the spermatic cords and consented thereto is, therefore, a question of fact for the jury.

b. **Lawful extension of an operation--Kennedy v. Parrott,** 243 N.C. 355, 90 S.E.2d 754 (1956).

Kennedy v. Parrott

1) **Facts.** Parrott (D), a doctor, while performing an appendectomy on Kennedy (P) to which P had consented, discovered in the area of the original incision large cysts on P's left ovary. D, following accepted surgical practice, punctured the cysts and in so doing cut a blood vessel, which resulted in P's developing phlebitis in her leg. P sued to recover damages for an unauthorized operation. P appeals a judgment of involuntary nonsuit for D.

2) **Issue.** May a doctor who in the course of an authorized operation discovers a diseased condition in the area of the original incision extend the operation to remedy the condition without liability for an unauthorized operation?

3) **Held.** Yes. Judgment of involuntary nonsuit is affirmed.

    a) A surgeon has a duty to extend an internal operation to remedy any abnormal or diseased condition in the area of the original incision whenever, in his sound professional judgment, this is required by correct surgical procedure, and in so doing is therefore not liable for an unauthorized operation.

    b) The basis for this rule is that the patient while anesthetized is incapable of consenting and those with authority to consent for her are not readily available.

    c) Voluntary submission to a physician for diagnosis and treatment of an ailment creates a presumption that what the doctor did was either expressly or impliedly authorized.

4) **Comment.** In this case the consent to the intentional invasion of one's person was "implied by law." Such consent is implied only where there are extreme circumstances; for example, where action is necessary to save the patient's life. Usually four requirements are necessary to find consent: (i) the person is not able to consider the matter; (ii) an immediate decision is necessary; (iii) there is no reason to believe that he would not give consent; and (iv) a reasonable person in the same condition would consent.

In re Estate of Brooks

c. **Right to refuse treatment--*In re* Estate of Brooks,** 32 Ill. 2d 361, 205 N.E.2d 435 (1965).

    1) **Facts.** Brooks (P), a married woman with no minor children, had been under a doctor's care for a peptic ulcer and had informed the doctor that her religious belief as a Jehovah's Witness precluded her from receiving a blood transfusion. P released the doctor and hospital from liability that might arise out of failure to give a transfusion. When P's condition worsened and she was admitted to the hospital, badly in need of a transfusion, the court, at the request of P's doctor and the state attorneys, appointed a conservator of the body of P to authorize the blood transfusions. The court acted without notice to P or P's husband, although both were readily available. The blood transfusions were given. P seeks the expungement of all orders in the conservatorship proceedings.

2) **Issue.** Does a competent adult without minor children have the right to refuse lifesaving medical treatment that is forbidden by her religious convictions?

3) **Held.** Yes. Orders of lower court reversed.

   a) The exercise of religious freedom may properly be limited by governmental action only where such exercise endangers, clearly and presently, the public health, welfare, or morals.

   b) When P, as a competent adult without minor children, knowingly refused medical care necessary to preserve her life because of her religious beliefs, her refusal was not an overriding danger to society. Thus, even though she is later so weakened as to be incompetent, the government may not limit her right to refuse the treatment.

4) **Comment.** This case concerned an adult plaintiff. When the patient is a child, courts are more likely to decide that the interest of the state in the health of children is sufficiently strong to allow the state to order medical treatment.

   d. **Harmful contact in sports.** Some sports, such as football, involve harmful contact with other players during the regular course of the game. Participation in the game can be held to imply consent to that contact. [*See* O'Brien v. Cunard Steamship Co., *supra*] Participation in such a game, however, does not imply consent to all contact that may occur. Where a player strikes another in a manner completely outside the rules and the expected behavior and customs of the game, the consent to contact may be exceeded.

D. PRIVILEGE

Under the general rule, if a defendant is privileged to act in a way that would otherwise give rise to tort liability, a plaintiff's action based on such conduct will be barred.

1. **Self-Defense.** One may be privileged to use force in his own defense if such force appears reasonably necessary for his protection.

   a. **Nondeadly force.** Nondeadly force (*i.e.,* force that is not likely to cause death or serious bodily harm) may be used in self-defense where the actor reasonably believes he will be caused immediate harm by the other person's conduct. The force used by the actor must be reasonable under the circumstances, and cannot go beyond the necessity of the situation. There is generally no duty to retreat or comply with the demands of the aggressor.

b. **Deadly force.** Deadly force (*i.e.,* force that is likely to cause death or serious bodily harm) may be used in self-defense where the actor reasonably believes that the other person's conduct will result in either death or serious bodily harm to the actor. Under the minority rule, the actor has a duty to retreat before using deadly force, except if (i) the actor is in his own home (or, in a few jurisdictions, place of business), (ii) retreating would be dangerous, or (iii) the actor is attempting a valid arrest.

c. **Reasonable force.** Whether force is reasonable is determined on an objective basis, *i.e.,* what force would have been used by the average, reasonable person under the same or similar circumstances.

Courvoisier
v. Raymond

1) **Mistake in belief of danger--Courvoisier v. Raymond,** 23 Colo. 113, 47 P. 284 (1896).

   a) **Facts.** Courvoisier (D), who slept in a room above his jewelry store, was awakened in the night by men who were attempting to break in. Armed with a revolver, he ejected two men from the premises, and fired shots in the air to disperse others who were outside throwing stones at him and his building. The shots attracted Raymond (P), a deputy sheriff, to the scene. P attempted to approach D. Thinking P to be one of the rioters, D shot him. P sued for damages. The jury was instructed to bring a verdict for P if they found that P was not assaulting D when D shot him. D appeals a judgment for P of $3,143.

   b) **Issue.** Where the circumstances are such as to lead a reasonable person to believe his life is in danger, is that person justified in using force against another whom he mistakenly believes to be a part of the danger?

   c) **Held.** Yes. Judgment for P is reversed.

      (1) The jury instruction had the effect of eliminating the circumstances created by the rioters from consideration by the jury.

      (2) If D would have been justified in shooting one of the rioters who approached D as P did, and if D actually mistook P for one of them, then the circumstances might have justified D's actions.

      (3) A person may be justified in using force not only against those who actually endanger his life, but against those whom a reasonable person in the same circumstances would believe endanger his life.

   d) **Comment.** The general rule also indicates that there is no duty to retreat if the actor is in his own home or he is attempting a valid arrest. There is no privilege of self-defense when the danger has passed or when excessive force is used.

d. **Retaliation.** There is no right to retaliate. If the danger has passed, the privilege of self-defense expires.

e.	**Excessive force.** In asserting his privilege of self-defense, if an actor uses excessive force, the other party then has the privilege of protecting himself against the degree of force being exerted by the actor.

2.	**Defense of Others.**

a.	**Introduction.** Under the *majority* view, one may be privileged to use force in the defense of others if (i) the other person would be privileged to defend himself, (ii) the force used is reasonable under the circumstances, and (iii) intervention is necessary to protect the other person. Under this view, the actor steps into the shoes of the third person and may be liable if he defends a third person who is actually the aggressor, regardless of how reasonable such intervention may have appeared to him. A *minority* of courts permit the use of force whenever the actor *reasonably believes* the third person is being attacked.

b.	**Scope of privilege.** At common law, one was privileged only to come to the aid of one's family or servants. Today, it is recognized as socially desirable to aid those in distress, even if they are strangers.

3.	**Defense of Property.** One is privileged to use only that force reasonably necessary to defend one's property. Deadly force generally can only be used in defense of one's dwelling, and many courts further restrict its use to situations where the invasion appears to threaten death or serious bodily harm (*i.e.,* tying it into another privilege—self-defense or defense of others).

a.	**Mechanical devices--Katko v. Briney,** 183 N.W.2d 657 (Iowa 1971).

Katko v.
Briney

1)	**Facts.** For 10 years Briney (D) owned an unoccupied farmhouse. Despite "No Trespass" signs which he posted, the house had been broken into several times. To discourage further intrusions D set a "shotgun trap" in one of the farmhouse bedrooms so that when the bedroom door was opened, the shotgun would fire at the legs of the intruder. D posted no warning of the trap. Katko (P) and a companion broke into the house to steal old bottles. P was shot in the leg and thereby suffered a permanent deformity. P sued for damages. D appeals a verdict for P of $20,000 actual and $10,000 punitive damages.

2)	**Issue.** May a person protect his property by the use of force sufficient to cause death or great bodily harm?

3)	**Held.** No. Judgment for P affirmed.

a)	According to early case law, spring guns are lawful only to prevent the commission of felonies of violence and where human life is in danger.

b)	P's breaking and entering, though a felony, was not a felony of violence.

c)	Spring guns and other traps which inflict great harm are privileged against only those upon whom the landowner, if he were present, would be free to inflict injury of the same kind.

d)   The law places a higher value on human safety than mere property rights.

e)   One may use reasonable force to protect property but not such as will take human life or inflict great bodily harm.

4)   Dissent. Judgment for P should be reversed.

a)   A person who sets a spring gun device should be liable only if he does so with the intent to kill or seriously injure, or if he does so negligently.

b)   D testified that the spring gun was set to frighten intruders.

c)   The majority holding creates absolute liability for setting a spring gun.

5)   Comment. The general rule regarding the use of mechanical instruments that could result in death is that they cannot be used unless the target is threatening human life. A person can use reasonable force, but not deadly force, to protect property if the intrusion by the other person is not justifiable, he reasonably believes such force is necessary, and prior to the use of force he demands that the intruder leave. In short, the use of a spring gun or similar instrument would seldom be appropriate.

b.   Necessity of entry. There are some circumstances where the owner of the property cannot rightfully refuse to allow a person from entering upon his land.

1)   Private necessity. If there is an emergency situation of sufficient gravity, a person has a limited privilege that allows him to enter onto another's property.

Ploof v.
Putnam

a)   **Application--Ploof v. Putnam,** 81 Vt. 471, 71 A. 188 (1908).

(1)   **Facts.** Ploof (P) was sailing on a lake with his wife and children when a storm arose which threatened to destroy the boat and passengers. To escape the storm, P moored his boat to Putnam's (D's) dock. D's servant unmoored the boat, which was then driven upon the shore and destroyed. P and his family were injured. P sued, alleging that it was D's duty to permit P to moor his boat to the dock and that D negligently unmoored the boat. D appeals a verdict for P.

(2)   **Issue.** Will necessity justify entry upon another's land that would otherwise be a trespass?

(3)   **Held.** Yes. Judgment of the lower court as to necessity is affirmed, but the case was remanded for a finding as to whether P could have moored his boat elsewhere with equal safety.

(a)   An inability to control movements inaugurated in the proper exercise of a strict right will justify entry upon the land of another.

(b) Entry upon land to save goods in danger of destruction is not a trespass.

(c) One may sacrifice property of another to save human life.

(d) Threatened loss of property or life will justify entry upon another's land. The facts of this case disclosed a necessity to moor the boat.

2) **Public necessity.** One has a privilege to enter upon another person's land if it is reasonably necessary to avert a public disaster. The necessary elements of the privilege are: (i) an immediate and imperative necessity and not just one that is expedient or utilitarian; and (ii) an act that is in good faith, for the public good.

a) **Application--Vincent v. Lake Erie Transportation Co.,** 109 Minn. 456, 124 N.W.2d 221 (1910).

Vincent v.
Lake Erie
Transportation
Co.

(1) **Facts.** Lake Erie (D), a transportation company, following Vincent's (P's) instruction, moored its boat to P's wharf so that P's cargo could be unloaded. During unloading a violent storm arose which prevented the boat from leaving the wharf. Thereafter, the storm threw the boat against the wharf, damaging the wharf. P sued to recover for the damages. D appeals an order denying a motion for judgment notwithstanding the verdict.

(2) **Issue.** May one who is forced by necessity to use the property of another do so without liability for injury to the property caused by his use?

(3) **Held.** No. Judgment for P is affirmed.

(a) The ship's master exercised ordinary prudence and care in keeping the ship moored to the wharf during the storm.

(b) In so doing he deliberately protected the ship at the expense of the wharf.

(c) The damage to the wharf did not result from an act of God or unavoidable accident but rather from circumstances within D's control.

(d) Having deliberately availed himself of P's property, as the storm gave D the right to do, D was liable for injury inflicted by his actions.

(4) **Dissent.** Judgment for P should be reversed.

(a) The master exercised due care.

(b) The injury to the dock was an inevitable accident.

(c) The owner of the dock, who had entered into contractual relations with the owner of the vessel, should bear the loss.

(5) **Comment.** The Restatement (Second) of Torts creates a privilege in favor of the actor to enter upon the land of another in order to avoid serious harm, coupled with an obligation on the part of the actor to pay for any damage done.

4. **Obeying Military Orders.** Members of the armed forces are privileged to inflict harmful contact on others if such contact is reasonably necessary to comply with a superior's lawful command (or one reasonably believed by the actor to be so). [Restatement (Second) of Torts §146]

5. **Disciplining Children.** Parents are privileged to reasonably discipline children. [Restatement (Second) of Torts §147]

a. **Battery in the classroom--Tinkham v. Kole,** 252 Iowa 1303, 110 N.W.2d 258 (1961).

1) **Facts.** Tinkham (P) was an eighth grade student who was 13 years old, five feet, two inches tall, and weighed 110 pounds. While P sat in a classroom before the class bell rang, he put on a pair of white gloves that were issued by the school band. When Kole (D), P's teacher entered the classroom as the class bell rang, he told P to remove the gloves. P started to remove the gloves, finger by finger. D told P to hurry but P continued removing the gloves in the same way. D then hit P about the head several times and continued to hit him even after P assured D that he would not do it again. Evidence also indicated that the gloves were tight and difficult to remove, that the class was disorderly and had not yet begun at the time of the incident, and that P sustained potentially permanent hearing impairment as a result of D's actions. At the close of P's evidence, D moved for a directed verdict. The court characterized the case as "foolishness" and said that in order for P to prevail, P must show the punishment was so cruel and unusual as to be beyond reason, such as chaining a child to a bed or deliberately burning his fingers. The court found D's actions reasonable and granted the directed verdict. P appeals.

2) **Issue.** Under the facts and circumstances here, was there a jury question presented on the reasonableness of the punishment?

3) **Held.** Yes. Reversed and remanded.

a) The undisputed evidence showed that D struck P several times on both sides of his head and that this was done in anger. Reasonable minds might find injury was likely to result from the manner in which the punishment was inflicted and that the punishment was unnecessary and uncalled for.

b) There is no authority that supports the standard put forth by the trial court, *i.e.,* that the punishment was "so cruel and unusual as to be beyond reason." Thus, P was given a burden he was not required to meet.

c)   A teacher is immune from liability for physical punishment where evidence shows administration of that punishment was reasonable. This requires consideration of: (i) the nature of the punishment, (ii) the nature of the student's misconduct, (iii) the student's age and physical condition, and (iv) the teacher's motive in inflicting the punishment. If there is proof that a teacher, in administering punishment, violated any one of these standards, liability will result.

II. ACTUAL CAUSATION

A. INTRODUCTION

Liability of the defendant will remain merely a theory unless the one who claims injury can establish that the harm is legally recognized and substantial enough to invoke the tort process. This section will deal with the identification of the person responsible, the nature of the harm, and the damages recoverable.

B. CAUSE-IN-FACT

The plaintiff must be able to prove that the defendant caused the injury in a factual sense by showing a connection between the defendant's conduct and the plaintiff's harm. The rule most often applied is the "but for" test (sine qua non); *i.e.,* the injury to the plaintiff would not have happened "but for" the actions or the failure to act of the defendant. The cause-in-fact question is a sophisticated one because any given cause may have several contributing factors. The cause-in-fact question really asks whether, from a common sense point of view, the fact finder (jury or court) can find a substantial connection between the defendant's conduct and the resulting injury to the plaintiff.

1. **Circumstantial Evidence.** In establishing the connection between the defendant's actions and the plaintiff's injury, circumstantial evidence is allowed. Circumstantial evidence is the existence of one fact, or group of facts, which gives rise to the inference that another fact must be true.

   Hoyt v. Jeffers

   a. **Weight of circumstantial evidence is question for jury--Hoyt v. Jeffers,** 30 Mich. 181 (1874).

      1) **Facts.** Hoyt's (P's) hotel, located 233 feet northeast of Jeffers's (D's) sawmill, was destroyed by fire. There was no direct evidence that a spark from D's mill caused the fire, but P attempted to prove such by showing (over D's objection): (i) sparks from the mill had landed in the vicinity of the hotel on many occasions, particularly when the wind blew from the southwest; (ii) other fires near the hotel had been caused by sparks from the mill; (iii) two prior fires at the hotel had been caused by sparks from the mill; and (iv) a recent 12-foot extension on the mill chimney from which the sparks were emitted had not altered the emission of sparks. Based upon this circumstantial evidence, P sued for damages to his hotel. D appeals a verdict for P, as based on improper evidence.

      2) **Issue.** Is circumstantial evidence admissible in a negligence action to prove the cause of damages?

      3) **Held.** Yes. Judgment for P is affirmed.

         a) The evidence was properly admitted and it is for the jury to determine how much weight to give it.

         b) The mill and chimney were shown to be in substantially the same condition as at the time of the other fires.

c)   The mill was operated identically at all times and the danger to property was the same at all times.

d)   Sparks continued to be emitted, landing in the area of the hotel.

e)   The above would tend to produce a reasonable belief that the fire in the hotel was caused by a spark from the sawmill.

4)   Comment. This case indicates that while there must be evidence of some direct connection between D's acts and P's injury there need not be direct eyewitness testimony. The causation was established indirectly from evidence from which the inference of cause could be drawn.

2.   **Mathematical Probabilities--Smith v. Rapid Transit Inc.,** 317 Mass. 469, 58 N.E.2d 754 (1945).

Smith v. Rapid Transit Inc.

a.   **Facts.** Smith (P) claimed that while driving on Main Street at 1:00 a.m. she was injured when she was forced to collide with a parked car in order to avoid a negligently driven bus. She could not identify the bus but attempted to prove that it was owned by Rapid Transit Inc. (D) by showing that, although other bus lines operated in the city, D operated the only buses with routes on Main Street. She further showed that D made runs at 12:10 a.m., 12:45 a.m., and 1:15 a.m. and that mathematically, it was likely that it was D's bus that had forced her off the road. P sued for personal injuries and appeals a directed verdict for D.

b.   **Issue.** May a verdict as to causation be based solely on mathematical probability?

c.   **Held.** No. Directed verdict for D is sustained.

1)   Private or charter buses might also use Main Street.

2)   It is not enough that mathematically the chances favor a certain proposition.

3)   A proposition is proved, by a preponderance of the evidence, if it appears more probable in the sense that actual belief in its truth, derived from the evidence, exists in the mind of the tribunal.

4)   Mathematical probability is, by itself, insufficient to prove causation.

d.   **Comment.** Even if there is a high correlation based upon mathematical probability that an event must have happened in a certain way, odds alone are not always enough to establish the inference for which the circumstantial evidence is presented.

3.   **Loss of a Chance--Falcon v. Memorial Hospital,** 436 Mich. 443, 462 N.W.2d 44 (1990).

Falcon v. Memorial Hospital

a.   **Facts.** Moments after Falcon (P) gave birth to a healthy baby, P suffered a sudden and complete respiratory and cardiac collapse and died soon after. An autopsy indicated that she had sustained an amniotic fluid embolism, an unpreventable complication that occurs in approximately one out of 10,000 or 20,000 births. P's administratix sued Memorial Hospital and P's physician (Ds). P's expert testified that it was negligent not to have inserted an intravenous line in P before giving her anesthesia and that if such a line had been inserted, P would have had a 37.5% chance to survive. The trial court dismissed the complaint because P failed to show that introduction of the line would have made it more probable than not that P would have survived. The court of appeals reversed.

 b. **Issue.** May a plaintiff show that the asserted negligence of defendants caused her physical harm by establishing that it is more probable than not that the defendants reduced the opportunity to avoid harm?

 c. **Held.** Yes. Judgment of court of appeals affirmed and case remanded.

  1) According to P's expert testimony, P would have had a 37.5% opportunity of surviving if Ds had inserted an intravenous line. In reducing P's opportunity of living by failing to insert an intravenous line, her physician caused her harm, although it cannot be said, more probably than not, that he caused her death.

  2) We see the injury resulting from medical malpractice as not only physical harm, but also as including the loss of opportunity of avoiding physical harm. A patient goes to a physician precisely to improve her opportunities of avoiding, ameliorating, or reducing physical harm and pain and suffering.

  3) We and a number of other courts have recognized loss of an opportunity for a more favorable result, as distinguished from the unfavorable result, as compensable in medical malpractice actions. Under this approach, damages are recoverable for the loss of opportunity although the opportunity lost was less than even, and thus it is not more probable than not that the unfavorable result would or could have been avoided. Under this approach, a plaintiff must prove, more probably than not, that the defendant *reduced* the opportunity of avoiding harm.

  4) The loss of a 37.5% opportunity of living constitutes a loss of substantial opportunity of avoiding physical harm. In this case, 37.5% times the damages recoverable for wrongful death would be an appropriate measure of damages.

Summers
v. Tice
 4. **Alternative Liability--Summers v. Tice,** 33 Cal. 2d 80, 199 P.2d 1 (1948).

 a. **Facts.** While hunting with Summers (P), Tice and Simonson (Ds) fired shotguns simultaneously in P's direction. P was shot in the eye and lip. It could not be determined which defendant had injured P or if both had. The trial court entered a verdict against both defendants. They appeal joint liability on the ground that they were not joint (associated) tortfeasors.

 b. **Issues.**

  1) When each of two persons by their acts is possibly the sole cause of

harm, has a plaintiff met his burden by introducing evidence that one of the two persons is culpable?

   2)   Does the burden then shift to the defendants to show which was the actual cause of the harm?

c.   Held.   1) Yes.   2) Yes.   Judgment for P affirmed.

   1)   When P introduces evidence that one of two people injured him, the burden of proof shifts to Ds to show which of them actually caused the injury.

   2)   It is unfair to deny the injured person recovery because he cannot prove how much injury each did when it is certain that between them they did it all.

   3)   This rule should apply whenever the harm has plural causes, not merely when the defendants act in concert.

   4)   Both defendants were negligent; the negligence of one of them resulted in injury; each has the burden to absolve himself if possible.

d.   Comment.   Since either of the defendants' actions would satisfy the "but for" test, the rules of causation are relaxed and the burden shifts to the defendants to establish who is liable for the injury. This relaxation of the causation rule should be kept distinct from the situation where there are joint tortfeasors. Here, the negligence of both defendants is clear even though only one probably caused the injury.

5.   **Res Ipsa Loquitur.**   "Res ipsa loquitur" means literally "the thing speaks for itself." In short, it applies to those situations where the injury could not have occurred unless someone was negligent, and the only source of the negligence was within the scope of the duty owed by the defendant to the plaintiff. In this situation, it is inferred that the defendant is negligent and the burden of proof shifts to the defendant to prove absence of negligence rather than requiring the plaintiff to prove the defendant's negligence. The reason for this inference is that in these circumstances the defendant has better access to the facts concerning causation and thus should bear the burden of refuting the inference of negligence.

   a.   Burden on defendants to show due care--Ybarra v. Spangard, 25 Cal. 2d 486, 154 P.2d 687 (1944).

Ybarra v. Spangard

   1)   **Facts.**   Ybarra (P) consulted Dr. Tilley, who diagnosed appendicitis and arranged for an appendectomy, which was performed by Dr. Spangard at a hospital owned by Dr. Swift. Prior to the operation, P's body was adjusted on the operating table by Dr. Reser, an anesthetist, who pulled P to the head of the operating table and laid him back against two hard objects at the top of his shoulders. P awoke the next morning attended by Thompson and another nurse. P immediately felt sharp pain between his neck and right shoulder, which spread to his lower right arm, although he had never suffered pain or injury there before. P's condition worsened after his release from the hospital, resulting in paralysis and atrophy. P sued all of

the doctors to recover damages for personal injuries due to negligent malpractice. Dr. Reser and the nurses were employees of Dr. Swift; the other doctors were independent contractors. They contended that P must show by what instrumentality he was injured and which defendant controlled it. The lower court entered judgments of nonsuit as to all defendants. P appeals.

2) **Issue.** Where a person is rendered unconscious to undergo surgical treatment and in the course of the treatment receives an unexplained injury to a part of his body not the subject of treatment, is it the burden of each of those who were charged with the patient's well-being to demonstrate that they exercised due care toward the patient?

3) **Held.** Yes. Judgment of the lower court is reversed.

a) Where a person is rendered unconscious in order to receive medical treatment and an untreated part of his body is injured, those entrusted with his care have the burden of initially explaining the cause.

b) Every defendant in whose custody P was placed for any period had a duty of ordinary care to see that he was not unnecessarily injured.

c) Any defendant who negligently injured P or neglected P so that he could be injured would be liable.

d) An employer would be liable for the negligence of his employees; a doctor in charge of the operation would be liable for the negligence of anyone who assisted in the operation.

e) Each defendant had within his control one or more instrumentalities by which P might have been injured.

f) It is unreasonable to insist that P, who had been rendered unconscious, identify the negligent defendant.

4) **Comment.** Much like the policy behind the shifting of the burden of proof in *Summers v. Tice, supra,* res ipsa loquitur is a way of "smoking out" evidence that would be completely unavailable to the plaintiff because of his unconscious condition. Since someone is negligent and the relevant information is in the defendant's possession, it is more reasonable to shift the burden in such circumstances to the defendant to explain the inference of negligence than to require the plaintiff to prove the defendant's negligence.

6. **Apportioning Damages Where Actual Tortfeasor Is Unknown.**

a. **Enterprise liability.** In *Hall v. E.I. Du Pont de Nemours & Co., Inc.,* 345 F. Supp. 353 (E.D.N.Y. 1972), the plaintiffs were injured separately in numerous separate explosions of blasting caps. The blasting cap industry was concentrated among six manufacturers which collaborated through a trade association in designing caps. The court concluded that all the defendants jointly controlled the risk and that if the plaintiffs could prove that the injurious caps were manufactured by one of the defendants, the burden of proof as to causation would shift to all the defendants.

b. **Market share liability--Sindell v. Abbott Laboratories,** 26 Cal. 3d 588, 607 P.2d 924 (1980), *cert. denied*, 449 U.S. 912 (1980).

Sindell v. Abbott Laboratories

    1) **Facts.** Sindell (P) sued several drug companies which had produced DES, a drug to prevent miscarriage. P's mother had taken DES while pregnant and P consequently developed a bladder tumor that was surgically removed. Approximately 200 companies had produced DES, and P could not prove which one produced the DES used by her mother. The lower court dismissed the complaint, and P appeals.

    2) **Issue.** May P recover from the drug manufacturers which produced a drug identical to the one which injured P without identifying the manufacturer of the precise product which caused the injury?

    3) **Held.** Yes. Judgment reversed.

        a) The "alternative liability" theory of *Summers v. Tice* (*supra*) cannot apply since P cannot identify the actual tortfeasor. Neither can the "enterprise liability" theory of *Hall v. E.I. Du Pont de Nemours & Co., Inc.,* (*supra*) apply since that theory is appropriate only where a small number of manufacturers jointly control the risk and do not have to comply with governmental standards.

        b) The rationale behind *Summers* applies here, however. Between an innocent plaintiff and negligent defendants, the latter should bear the cost of the injury, when the nature of the product delays injury so as to make identification of the tortfeasor impossible.

        c) It is reasonable to measure the likelihood that any of the defendants supplied the injurious product by the percentage of the entire production of DES attributable to each defendant. Thus, once P proves injury caused by DES, each DES manufacturer is liable to P in proportion to its individual share of the entire DES market, unless it can prove individually that it could not have produced the precise product that injured P.

    4) **Dissent.** The majority's new theory is essentially a new version of the "deep pocket" theory of liability. "Market share" liability presents grave and sweeping economic, social, and medical ramifications which are better resolved by the legislative branch.

7. **Concurrent and Successive Causation.** If a potential danger from one source has diminished the value of the loss actually inflicted, the damages may be reduced by the other contingency.

a. **Application--Dillon v. Twin State Gas & Electric Co.**, 85 N.H. 449, 163 A. 111 (1932).

    1) **Facts.** Dillon's (P's) decedent, a 14-year-old boy, had habitually played with his friends on a bridge over which Twin State (D) had strung electric wires. While seated on a girder, P's decedent lost his balance and was electrocuted when he grabbed the electric wire to keep from falling and suffering death or serious injury. P sued to recover damages for wrongful death. D appeals the denial of a motion for a directed verdict.

    2) **Issue.** If, but for a negligent injury, the injured person would still have suffered other injury, may the court in awarding damages consider the other injury and its potential effects on the injured person?

    3) **Held.** Yes. Denial of the motion for directed verdict affirmed.

        a) To constitute actionable negligence there must be damage.

        b) If, but for the wires, the boy would have fallen, then D did not deprive him of a life expectance long enough to be given pecuniary allowance and D would only be liable for conscious suffering sustained by the shock.

        c) Likewise, evidence that the boy would have been crippled by the fall should be taken into account in determining damages to earning capacity as though he had already been crippled.

        d) The above issues of fact may lead to different conclusions and therefore must be tried.

8. **Joint Tortfeasors.** If two or more persons act in concert or together are the cause of the injury to the plaintiff, the defendants are jointly and severally liable to the plaintiff for the injury.

a. **Application--Kingston v. Chicago & Northwestern Railway**, 191 Wis. 610, 211 N.W. 913 (1927).

    1) **Facts.** One fire, set by sparks emitted from Chicago & Northwestern Railway's (D's) locomotive, joined with another fire of unknown origin and together they entered and destroyed Kingston's (P's) property. The fires were of comparatively equal size and the jury found each of them to be the proximate cause of P's damage. Trial court granted P judgment in his action for damages. D appeals.

    2) **Issue.** If two separate acts constitute the proximate cause of injury, is each tortfeasor liable for the full damage?

    3) **Held.** Yes. Judgment for P is affirmed.

        a) Any one of two or more joint tortfeasors whose concurring acts result in injury is individually responsible for the damage.

b) Exceptions to the above-stated rule would arise if D's fire joined a much larger fire or one resulting from natural causes.

c) Nothing in the record suggested any natural cause of the second fire.

d) It is D's burden to show that the fire which joined his fire originated from natural causes.

e) While under some circumstances a wrongdoer is not responsible for damages which would have occurred in the absence of his wrongful act, he is responsible where two causes, each attributable to the negligence of a responsible person, concur in producing injury.

f) To permit each wrongdoer to plead the wrong of the other as a defense would permit both wrongdoers to escape and make it impossible to apportion damages.

4) **Comment.** Where each of the fires individually are substantial factors in the resultant loss, then liability can extend to both causes, and one tortfeasor is not excluded merely because another party could also be liable for the damage.

b. **Right of contribution.** At common law, there was no right of contribution between joint tortfeasors, which meant that the whole judgment could be collected from one of the defendants and the other defendants would not have to share in the cost of the judgment, either to the plaintiff or the defendant that had to pay the judgment. Modern law grants to the paying defendant the right to collect a pro rata share of the judgment paid to the plaintiff from each of his codefendants.

9. Cause in Fact.

a. **Sine qua non ("but for" rule).** If the injury to the plaintiff would not have happened "but for" the act or omission of the defendant, such conduct is the cause in fact of the injury.

Examples:

1) The omission of one driver to give a turn signal is not a cause of an auto collision when the driver of the other auto was not looking and would not have seen it even if it had been given. In such a case, the defendant was negligent, but his negligence in not signaling his intention to turn was not the actual cause of damage.

2) The failure to supply fire fighting equipment which could not have been used anyway because no water was available is not the actual cause of the plaintiff's loss because his building burns down.

b. **Proof of causation.** The plaintiff has the burden to prove that more likely than not the defendant was a substantial factor in bringing about the injury.

Ford v.
Trident Fish-
eries Co.

c.   Defendant's omission as the cause--Ford v. Trident Fisheries Co., 232 Mass. 400, 122 N.E. 389 (1919).

1)   **Facts.** Ford's (P's) decedent, an employee on Trident's (D's) fishing trawler, drowned when he fell overboard. No one saw him fall. P sued D for damages arising from the drowning, alleging as negligence that the trawler's lifeboat was lashed to the deck instead of being suspended from davits for quicker use and that the lifeboat was equipped with only one oar. The trial court granted D's motion for directed verdict at the conclusion of P's evidence. P appeals.

2)   **Issue.** Can one be held liable for injuries that his omission, although negligent, did not contribute to?

3)   **Held.** No. Verdict for D affirmed.

   a)   One may not be held liable for injuries which would have occurred regardless of his negligent omission or act.

   b)   There was no evidence to show that D's omission contributed to the decedent's death.

4)   **Comment.** This is the majority rule.

d.   Concurrent causes. In the case of concurrent causes, strict application of the "but for" rule fails if each cause, by itself, would not have been sufficient to bring about the result or if each cause, by itself, would have been sufficient to bring about the result. Conduct then is considered a cause of the injury if it is a "substantial factor" in bringing about the harm.

III. VICARIOUS LIABILITY

A. INTRODUCTION

The issue addressed in this section is to what degree one person can be held liable for the actions of another person. The liability is vicarious if the actions of the acting party can legally be extended to the named party. Vicarious liability can be found in one of several ways:

1. **Masters, Servants, and Independent Contractors.** The general rule is that a master (employer) is vicariously liable for the actions of his servants (employees) while they are acting within the scope of their employment.

   a. **Respondeat superior.** The master-servant relationship is a consensual relationship in which one person performs services on behalf of another person, and the person on whose behalf the service is rendered has control or the right to control the conduct of the person who is rendering the service. With the control of the actions goes the responsibility for the results of those actions, or legal liability. Even if the plaintiff can establish that there is a master-servant relationship, she must also be able to prove that the tortfeasor was acting "within the scope of his employment" before the master can be held vicariously liable.

      1) **Scope of employment.** "Scope of employment" can be defined in one of several ways. Generally the conduct of the employee must be of the same general nature as that authorized. Some factors that need to be considered in determining the scope of employment are:

         a) Is the action normally done by the servants?

         b) What is the employment relationship between the employer and the employee?

         c) Did the employer expect the employee's actions?

         d) What was the extent of the injury? Was the employee's act criminal in nature?

      2) **Intentional torts.** The usual rule is that intentional torts done by an employee are not within the scope of the employment of the employee, but recently there has been a movement to include some intentional torts within the vicarious liability of the employer if the employment involved use of force (*e.g.,* a bouncer).

      3) **Independent contractors.** The general rule is that an independent contractor is not the servant of the general contractor or the employer and thus the employer is not vicariously liable for the independent contractor's tortious conduct. This general rule has three very important exceptions.

a) **Neglect in employing and supervision.** Though the master will not be liable for the actions of the independent contractor, he can be liable for any negligence in selecting, instructing, or supervising the independent contractor.

b) **Nondelegable duties.** There are certain duties that the general contractor cannot divest himself of by hiring someone else to do the job (*e.g.*, excavation).

c) **Inherently dangerous activities.** For certain activities that expose the public to significant risks, the law has deemed it appropriate for those who undertake the activity to bear the cost of the accident. Those activities are usually related to blasting or the storage of explosives.

2. **Joint Enterprise.** When two or more persons join together to achieve a common purpose, the negligent conduct of each participant is imputed to every other participant. The basic elements of a joint enterprise are: (i) a contract, expressed or implied, in which the parties enter into an undertaking together; (ii) a common purpose; (iii) a community of interests; and (iv) an equality of rights and control over the agents employed.

An example of a joint enterprise is a partnership where all the partners are liable for the acts of each partner, at least where the partner acts within the scope of the partnership.

3. **Family Purpose.** The family purpose doctrine imposes liability upon the owner of a family car for harm caused to others by a family member while operating the car for a family purpose. This theory has been developed by judicial interpretation and is not available in all states. The elements of the doctrine are:

a. The automobile is owned by the defendant sought to be held vicariously liable;

b. The automobile is the family car;

c. The driver of the car which caused the accident is a family member;

d. The automobile is used for a family purpose; and

e. The car is used with the owner's permission.

4. **Successor Corporation Liability.** When one corporation buys the assets of another corporation and a person is injured by a product previously manufactured by the bought-out corporation, a question exists as to whether the corporation which bought that company should be liable for the injury. Two theories have been used to hold the successor corporation liable.

a. **Continuity of enterprise doctrine.** Where there is continuity of management, employees, business situs, and general business activity, it may be assumed that any liabilities or obligations also continued.

b. **Product line continuity.** Where the same product line continues to be produced and marketed, the successor corporation will be liable for injuries caused by earlier examples of that product line.

IV. NEGLIGENCE

A. ORIGINS OF NEGLIGENCE

Negligence is by far the most rapidly growing of the unintentional torts, and has found new room for growth in areas such as product liability and equipment operation accidents. The basic theory behind the law of negligence is the creation of an unreasonable risk of harm to others. What is meant by an unreasonable risk of harm is usually found by balancing the benefits derived from the activity with the harm or the threat of harm that the activity produces.

1. **Development of Negligence Theory.** Traditionally it was held that a person was liable for any act he committed, regardless of whether he was at fault, so long as he was the source of the injury. Slowly this concept of liability regardless of fault gave way to the theory that one could escape liability if his actions were inadvertent or involuntary.

Brown v.
Kendall

   a. **No liability unless the injury is intentionally or negligently caused--Brown v. Kendall,** 60 Mass. 292 (1850).

      1) **Facts.** Brown's (P's) dog and Kendall's (D's) dog were fighting. D, in attempting to separate the dogs, stepped backwards and raised a stick to strike at them. As he did so he accidentally hit P in the eye. P had approached the scene from behind D. P brought a trespass action against D for assault and battery. The court instructed the jury that if D's act was not necessary and if D was not duty-bound to separate the dogs, then D was responsible for the consequences of his blow. D appeals the jury's verdict for P as based on an improper instruction.

      2) **Issue.** Where the act is not intentional, can there be liability without fault?

      3) **Held.** No. Judgment for P reversed and new trial ordered.

         a) Liability must be based on fault or an unlawful intent.

         b) To recover in this case, P must show that D failed to use ordinary care.

         c) Ordinary care is the care which a prudent and cautious person would use in the same circumstances.

         d) The burden of proving a lack of due care is on the plaintiff.

      4) **Comment.** This case indicates that before a cause of action will exist, there must be some form of fault either in the form of negligence or an intentional wrongdoing.

2. **Applicable Standard in Negligence Case.** In most negligence cases the standard of care that is placed upon the defendant is that degree of care that a "reasonable person" would exercise under the same set of external circumstances. Thus, in short, the test suggests an objective standard

that falls short of any superhuman effort or second guessing after the fact by the jury. The jury also is not allowed to speculate about possible conduct on the part of the defendant, but only to consider what the reasonably prudent person would have done in his position.

a. **Recognition of unacceptable risk--United States v. Carroll Towing Co.,** 159 F.2d 169 (2d Cir. 1947).

1) **Facts.** In the afternoon of January 4, a barge owned by the United States (P) broke from its moorings and sank, allegedly because of Carroll Towing's (D's) negligence. P's employee in charge of the barge, the bargee, had been ashore for 21 hours and was not on the barge when it broke loose. The accident occurred in the full tide of war activity when barges were constantly being towed in and out of the harbor. P sued for damages. D contended that P was also negligent in that the bargee was not on the barge when it broke loose. P appeals a verdict for D.

2) **Issue.** Was P's employee, the bargee, negligent in being ashore?

3) **Held.** Yes. Judgment for D affirmed.

   a) The barge owner's liability depends upon whether his burden of adequate precautions (B) is less than (<) the probability that the barge will break away (P) multiplied by the gravity of resulting injury if it does (L). If B < PL, then the barge owner is negligent.

   b) The harbor was crowded; it was not beyond reasonable expectation that work might not be done carefully.

   c) Under such conditions, it was a fair requirement that the barge owner have a bargee aboard during working hours.

4) **Comment.** The main issue in a negligence case is whether a reasonable person would have realized the risk involved in a course of action. If so, but he still did not change his conduct, then negligence can be inferred.

b. **Unreasonable risk of harm--Washington v. Louisiana Power and Light Co.,** 555 So. 2d 1350 (La. 1990).

1) **Facts.** Washington was electrocuted when his CB radio antenna came into contact with Louisiana Power and Light Co.'s (D's) uninsulated 8,000 volt electrical wire that spanned his back yard 21½ feet above the ground. Five years before his death, Washington and his son had suffered burns when the antenna came into contact with the line while they were moving it. After the previous incident, Washington had requested D to insulate the line or move it underground; D said it would do so only at Washington's expense. Washington's adult children (Ps) brought suit. The trial court found D at fault and awarded substantial money damages to Ps. The court of appeals reversed, noting the earlier burns and Washington's extreme care thereafter, up to the day of his accident, never to move the antenna alone or toward the line. Ps were granted certiorari.

2) **Issue.** Did D breach any duty owed to Washington?

3) Held. No. Affirmed.

   a) D's duty to provide against resulting injuries is a function of three variables: (i) the possibility electricity will escape, (ii) if it does, the gravity of any resulting injury, and (iii) the burden of taking precautions adequate to avert the accident. When the product of the possibility of escape multiplied by the gravity of the harm, if it happens, exceeds the burden of precautions, the risk is unreasonable and the failure to take those precautions is negligence.

   b) Balancing these factors here, we conclude that although a risk existed that the antenna stationed in the corner of Washington's yard could be lowered and moved to within a dangerous proximity of the power line, that possibility could not be characterized as an unreasonable risk and D's failure to take additional precautions against it was not negligence.

   c) Here, the balancing process focuses our attention on the fact that the possibility of an accident appeared to be slight beforehand and on the reality that precautions against such slight risks would be costly and burdensome because such risks exist in great number and have not usually been considered unreasonable or intolerable.

Weirum v. RKO General, Inc.

c. Foreseeability of risk--Weirum v. RKO General, Inc., 15 Cal. 3d 40, 539 P.2d 36, 123 Cal. Rptr. 468 (1975).

   1) Facts. RKO General, Inc. (D) owned radio station KHJ, which held a promotional contest. The contest awarded prizes to the first person to locate a disc jockey who was driving around the Los Angeles area. Two youths in separate cars were racing on the freeway to locate the disc jockey when one of them forced another car onto the center divider, where it overturned. The innocent driver was killed and Weirum (P), the deceased's wife, sued D. The jury returned a verdict for P and D appeals, claiming that it owed no duty to the decedent arising out of the broadcast of the contest.

   2) Issue. Does D have a duty of reasonable care toward every person exposed to a foreseeable risk of harm?

   3) Held. Yes. Judgment affirmed.

   a) Each person must use ordinary care to prevent others from being injured as the result of his conduct. Foreseeability of the risk is a primary consideration in establishing the element of duty. While duty is a question of law, foreseeability is a question of fact for the jury. The jury found that the decedent was exposed to a foreseeable risk of harm, and there is substantial evidence to support that finding.

   b) D claims that since the contest had been going on for some time prior to the accident, and yet there had been no prior injuries, this accident could not be foreseeable. However, the fortuitous absence of prior injury does not justify relieving D from responsibility for the foreseeable consequences of its acts. The fact that a third party actually caused the accident does not relieve D, whose actions stimulated the dangerous driving.

    c)   Virtually every act involves some conceivable danger. Liability is therefore limited to unreasonable risks of harm, when the gravity and likelihood of the danger outweigh the utility of the conduct involved.

    4)   **Comment.** The three preceding cases use similar language and rationales yet give different final results. In each case, the appellate court is affirming the trial court, which indicates that appellate courts are reluctant to interfere with trial courts' reasonable attempts to deal with these difficult problems of foreseeability and legal duty.

d.   **Standard of care for emergency situations.** The reasonable person confronted with an emergency may act differently than he would if there was no emergency. This does not mean that a different standard is applied; it only indicates that the emergency conditions are added to the circumstances that are taken into consideration in determining how a reasonable person would act when confronted with the situation.

    1)   **Sudden emergency--Young v. Clark,** 814 P.2d 364 (Colo. 1991).

Young v.
Clark

        a)   **Facts.** Young (P) and Clark (D) were each driving on a highway when construction caused traffic to slow to between 35 and 45 m.p.h. An unidentified driver who was four or five cars ahead of P pulled out of the center lane and then abruptly swerved back into the lane of traffic, forcing all drivers to apply their brakes. D, who had looked over her shoulder while attempting to change lanes, applied her brakes but was unable to avoid colliding with the rear of P's car. P filed suit claiming D was negligent in operating the car. The trial court submitted this issue, along with the issues of P's contributory negligence and the negligence of the unidentified driver, to the jury and included Colorado's "sudden emergency" doctrine in the jury instructions. The jury found for D. P was granted certiorari.

        b)   **Issue.** Under the circumstances of this case, was it error for the court to instruct the jury on the "sudden emergency" doctrine?

        c)   **Held.** No. Affirmed.

            (1)   Colorado's pattern "sudden emergency" instruction states: "A person who, through no fault of his or her own, is placed in a sudden emergency, is not chargeable with negligence if the person exercises that degree of care which a reasonably careful person would have exercised under the same or similar circumstances."

            (2)   The jury's application of this doctrine is explicitly conditioned upon the finding that the actor was not placed in a perilous predicament through any fault of her own. Therefore, the factual dispute as to whether D was at fault was appropriately submitted to the jury by the trial court.

(3) Sufficient evidence was presented regarding the sudden and unexpected reentry of the unidentified driver into the flow of traffic to support giving the instruction. Even P conceded that he had to brake "hard" to avoid the driver in front of him and that the unidentified driver probably shared some fault in causing the accident.

B. PROOF OF NEGLIGENCE

1. **Introduction.** If persons of reasonable intelligence may differ as to the conclusion to be drawn, the issue must be left to the jury; if not, the court will decide. Generally, the burden of proof, *i.e.,* the risk of nonpersuasion, is on the plaintiff, and if the evidence she introduces is not greater or more persuasive than that of her adversary, she must lose. The burden of going forward with presenting proof, on the other hand, is established by presumptions, and the failure to rebut a presumption may result in a directed verdict. The proof of what is negligent behavior depends, in part, upon the legislative intent in enacting the statute, custom, etc.

2. **Violation of Statutes.** Statutes that affect a defendant's conduct may be either civil or criminal. If a plaintiff is provided a civil remedy under a statute, she will not have to be concerned with negligence. However, where the defendant has violated a criminal statute and in the process injured the plaintiff, she may sue the defendant for negligence, aside from the defendant's criminal liability. When a court adopts a standard of care embodied in a criminal statute, the rationale is that a reasonable person always obeys the criminal law. However, for a plaintiff to support a claim that the violation of the criminal statute by the defendant was negligence, the statute must have clearly defined the conduct or duty required and the class or individual to whom it applies. Failure of a defendant to act as required will constitute a breach of the duty. However, for a plaintiff to establish liability, she must show that she is in the class protected by the statute and that the statute was enacted to protect members of the class from the type of injury the plaintiff suffered. Depending upon the jurisdiction, violation of a statute can have several effects. The majority view finds violation of a statute to give rise to a conclusive presumption of negligence, *i.e.,* negligence per se. In California, violation is deemed to give rise to a rebuttable presumption of negligence. In still other jurisdictions, violation is deemed merely evidence of negligence. However, where a plaintiff's claim is based on violation of the statute as negligence, a defendant generally has available the defenses of contributory negligence and assumption of risk.

Martin v.
Herzog

a. **Violation of statutory requirement is per se negligence--Martin v. Herzog,** 228 N.Y. 164, 126 N.E. 814 (1920).

1) **Facts.** P's intestate was thrown from the wagon he was driving and killed when D failed to drive his car to the right of the center of the highway. The accident occurred at night. The wagon had no lights, a statutory violation. P sued D for damages resulting from his negligence. D was denied a jury instruction that the absence of a light on the wagon was prima facie evidence of contributory negligence. The trial court found for

P; the appellate division reversed and ordered a new trial. P appeals the reversal.

2) **Issue.** Is the unexcused violation of a statute negligence in itself?

3) **Held.** Yes. Order of the appellate division is affirmed.

   a) Unexcused omission of the statutorily-required lighting is negligence in itself.

   b) To omit safeguards prescribed by statute for the benefit of others is to fall short of the duty of diligence toward the rest of society.

   c) The trial court erred in giving the jury the power to relax the duty that P's intestate owed to other travelers.

4) **Comment.** This case adopts the majority view that violation of a statute is negligence per se.

b. **Purpose of statute as affecting per se negligence status--Tedla v. Ellman,** 280 N.Y. 124, 19 N.E.2d 987 (1939).

Tedla v. Ellman

1) **Facts.** Tedla (P) and her brother were wheeling carriages loaded with junk along the right edge of a highway when they were struck by a vehicle driven by Ellman (D). P was injured; her brother was killed. There were no footpaths along the highway and the pedestrians were probably carrying a light. Nevertheless, D moved to dismiss P's complaint for damages on the ground that P was contributorily negligent as a matter of law because she violated a statute which required that she walk on the left side of the highway. P introduced evidence that the traffic was very heavy on the other side of the road, but the traffic was light on the side on which she walked. D appeals a verdict for P.

2) **Issue.** If a statute sets forth a general rule of conduct (without fixing a standard of care which would under all circumstances tend to protect life), will a justifiable deviation from the general rule be regarded as negligence per se?

3) **Held.** No. Judgment for P affirmed.

   a) The legislature intended to set forth a general rule which would provide for the safety of pedestrians.

   b) Nevertheless, in this situation obedience to the rule would have subjected the pedestrians to great danger.

   c) We cannot reasonably assume that the legislature intended that a statute enacted for the safety of pedestrians must be observed when observance would subject them to more imminent danger.

   d) Negligence is the failure to exercise the care required by law.

   e) Statutes such as the one in question may be properly construed as intended to apply only to ordinary situations. Thus, the statute may be subject to an exception if disobedience is likely to prevent rather than cause the accidents which the statute seeks to prevent.

4) **Comment.** This case, like *Martin v. Herzog* (*supra*), was decided by a New York court. The court probably decided differently here because the statute in *Martin* had as its goal the prevention of accidents at night, and the plaintiff there had no excuse for not having night lights on his vehicle. Here, the statute presumably had as its goal the protecting of pedestrians from traffic. With traffic lighter on the "wrong side" of the street, a pedestrian might reasonably conclude that the side with less traffic was less of a risk. The plaintiff had a sufficient excuse to allow her case to go to the jury.

Brown v.
Shyne

c. **Violation of statute must be proximate cause of plaintiff's injury--Brown v. Shyne,** 242 N.Y. 176, 151 N.E. 197 (1926).

1) **Facts.** D was practicing without a license as a chiropractor in New York. In so doing he was guilty of a misdemeanor. P, after nine treatments from D, became paralyzed. P sued for damages resulting from D's negligent treatment. D appeals a jury verdict of $10,000, contending that it was improper to instruct the jury that they might infer negligence from the violation of the licensing statute.

2) **Issue.** May negligence be inferred from a chiropractor's violation of the statute requiring licensing of medical practitioners?

3) **Held.** No. Judgment for P reversed and a new trial granted.

a) The statute is intended to protect the public from unskilled practitioners.

b) Nevertheless, the violation of the statute was not the proximate cause of P's injuries; it has no direct bearing on the injury.

c) P must prove that D failed to exercise the care and skill that would have been exercised by a qualified practitioner. This may not be inferred from the fact that D was unlicensed.

4) **Dissent.** The judgment should be affirmed.

a) The jury was properly charged and had ample evidence with which to connect P's injury with D's acts.

b) In practicing medicine, D violated the law. The law did not recognize D as a physician; the court should not either.

c) If his act was the direct and proximate cause of the injury, he is liable irrespective of negligence.

5) **Comment.** It is the general majority opinion that violation of a licensing statute will not constitute negligence per se.

3. **Custom.** Following custom in the community or trade practice is never conclusive. Custom is merely evidence of the standard of care owed. The standard remains whether the average reasonable person would have so acted under the same or similar circumstances. A professional is held to the standard of care customarily exercised by members of that profession or trade in the same or similar community.

    a. **Proof of custom--Trimarco v. Klein,** 56 N.Y.2d 98, 436 N.E.2d 502 (1982).

        1) **Facts.** Trimarco (P), a tenant in Klein's (D's) apartment building, was injured when he fell through a glass shower door. Although it was general practice to use shatterproof glass in shower doors, D had not replaced the previously installed glass, claiming that he had no duty to do so. P sued D and secured a jury verdict. The Appellate Division reversed, finding that D had no duty to replace the glass absent notice of the danger. P appeals.

        2) **Issue.** May evidence of business custom be used to indicate a defendant's proper standard of care?

        3) **Held.** Yes. The appellate court is reversed, but a new trial is ordered on other grounds.

            a) Evidence of custom or practice is admissible because it reflects the judgment and experience of a larger group. Custom, however, is not conclusive but merely evidence of reasonable care, *i.e.*, evidence of D's conformity to the custom may show due care; evidence of D's failure to follow custom may show a failure to use reasonable care. Custom is also evidence of feasibility of a particular precaution.

            b) A custom or common practice is not necessarily conclusive—before it can be, the jury must be satisfied with its reasonableness. Here, P's evidence was enough to sustain the jury's verdict. It was also for the jury to decide whether the modest cost and ready availability of safety glass and the growing custom of using safety glass in shower doors rendered the practice of not using it no longer reasonably safe.

        4) **Comment.** There is a movement toward imposing a higher standard of care when the plaintiff knows of inherent dangers in an industry-wide custom. To decide otherwise would allow an entire industry to keep its safety standards artificially low just by refusing to raise the industry-wide standards.

    b. **Adherence to standard of industry is not absolute defense--The T.J. Hooper,** 60 F.2d 737 (2d Cir. 1932), *cert. denied*, 287 U.S. 662 (1932).

        1) **Facts.** Eastern Transportation Co. (D) owned two tugs (one of which was the *T.J. Hooper*) which were towing barges owned by the Northern Barge Corp. (P) that were carrying cargo. The tugs, like most others, were not equipped with radio receivers and the tug masters

were unaware of reports of an impending storm. The storm sank, the tugs and destroyed the barges and cargo. The cargo owners sued P, who in turn sued D for damages to the cargo and barges. There was evidence that the tug master, had he heard the weather report, would have turned back. The trial court found the tugs unseaworthy and D jointly liable with P to the cargo owners. D petitions for exoneration from or limitation of liability.

2) Issue. Is adherence to a trade custom an absolute defense to negligence?

3) Held. No. Judgment against D affirmed.

    a) The fact that most tugs were not equipped with receivers is not the final answer.

    b) An industry may not set its own tests for reasonable prudence. The court must in the end say what is required.

    c) Tugs towing several barges cannot easily maneuver and are very vulnerable to bad weather. Although the whole industry has lagged in the installation of receivers, they are required by reasonable prudence to install them.

Helling
v. Carey

c. Medical treatment--Helling v. Carey, 83 Wash. 2d 514, 519 P.2d 981 (1974).

1) Facts. Helling (P) consulted ophthalmologist Carey (D) for vision problems. Although P visited D several times, D never performed a test for glaucoma. When D did finally perform the test, P was diagnosed as having glaucoma, but had suffered permanent vision loss due to the delay in performing the test. Expert testimony established that the standards of the profession did not require the administration of the test to people under the age of 40 since the chance of glaucoma was remote under that age. D received a verdict and judgment. P appeals.

2) Issue. Although a doctor follows an accepted professional custom, may the court set a higher standard of care?

3) Held. Yes. Judgment reversed and remanded.

    a) Although the risk of glaucoma for P was slight, the test to detect the disease was simple and inexpensive. The burden to perform the simple test was substantially less than the serious illness and injury suffered. Although the professional custom may be evidence of due care, the court must ultimately set the appropriate standard.

4) Comment. Ordinarily, the test for the standard of care of a physician is that of a physician in good standing. Where the issues are complex, expert testimony is relied upon to determine what a physician should have done.

4. Expert Testimony. Often negligence cases become a battle between a plaintiff's experts and a defendant's experts. Expert testimony is admissible on any relevant point if the expert's testimony will aid the jury. However, an expert's testimony is not admissible if the matter upon which he is to testify is within the jury's realm of experience, the rationale being that the jury is competent to form opinions on matters within the realm of its experience. Note that an expert may testify directly on the ultimate fact the jury is to decide; a lay witness may not.

   a. "Expert" defined. Generally, an "expert" is anyone whose knowledge on a particular subject is greater than that of a lay person.

   b. Opinions of expert witnesses--Hines v. Denver & Rio Grande Western Railroad Co., 829 P.2d 419 (Colo. App. 1991), *cert. denied,* (1992).

Hines v. Denver & Rio Grande Western Railroad Co.

   1) Facts. Hines was hit and killed by a train while walking between the railroad tracks in a remote area. Hines's wife (P) brought a wrongful death suit against Denver & Rio Grande Western Railroad Co. (D). D's investigation of the incident showed that statements by the train's crew concerning the number of warning whistles conflicted with the train's "black box." At trial, P's expert witness opined that the crew had been negligent in braking, sounding the whistle, and keeping a lookout. The jury found for P, awarding compensatory and punitive damages, which were reduced for Hines's comparative negligence. D appeals.

   2) Issue. Did the trial court err in allowing P's expert to express an opinion that the crew's operation of the train constituted negligence?

   3) Held. No. Affirmed and remanded for errors not involving the merits of this claim.

      a) Federal Rule of Evidence 704 provides that if an opinion is otherwise admissible, it is not objectionable because it embraces an ultimate legal issue to be decided by the jury.

      b) The Advisory Committee's Note to Rule 704 states that the basic approach to both lay and expert opinions is to admit them when they might help the jury. However, the rules on expert opinion are not intended to permit experts to tell the jury what result to reach.

      c) Expert opinions should be evaluated by considering the interrelationship of several pertinent evidentiary rules: (i) the expert opinion should be relevant, *i.e.,* tend to make the existence of any consequential fact more or less probable than it would be without the evidence; (ii) the expert should be qualified to help the jury find "a solid path through an unfamiliar and esoteric field"; (iii) the expert opinion the probative value of which is outweighed by undue prejudice should be excluded; and (iv) preliminary disclosure of expert testimony's underlying data should be required so that the jury can adequately evaluate the opinion.

d) The trial court correctly evaluated the expert opinions according to the applicable law.

5. **Circumstantial Evidence.** Circumstantial evidence is the proof of one fact, or group of facts, which gives rise to an inference by reasoning that another fact must be true. Circumstantial evidence is admissible to prove negligence.

6. **Res Ipsa Loquitur.** Res ipsa loquitur, directly translated, means "the thing speaks for itself." In situations where (i) it is highly probable that the injury would not have occurred in the absence of someone's negligence, (ii) the indicated source of the negligence is within the scope of a duty owed by the defendant to the plaintiff, and (iii) neither the plaintiff nor any third party appears to have contributed to the plaintiff's injuries (and the defendant has better access to the evidence concerning the cause of the injury), an inference is permitted that the defendant was negligent, without any direct proof, and the defendant then has the burden of going forward and introducing evidence to overthrow the inference. The courts recognize res ipsa loquitur because of the existence of a needy plaintiff without access to proof of negligence.

a. **Requirements for res ipsa loquitur.** Res ipsa loquitur is applicable if:

(i) the accident is the kind that will not normally occur without someone's negligence;

(ii) the cause of the harm is in the complete control of the defendant; and

(iii) the plaintiff did not in any way voluntarily contribute to the harm.

Res ipsa loquitur is an evidentiary presumption. If the plaintiff can prove the above three elements, he need not prove actual negligence of the defendant. The negligence is simply presumed.

Boyer v. Iowa
High School
Athletic
Association

b. **Instrumentality that caused injury must be under defendant's exclusive control--Boyer v. Iowa High School Athletic Association,** 206 Iowa 1061, 152 N.W.2d 293 (1967).

1) **Facts.** Boyer (P) was a spectator at a high school basketball game. As the game ended and P and others began to leave the bleachers on which P had been sitting, which were designed to fold against the gym wall, they collapsed, causing P to fall nine feet to the ground and suffer injuries. P brought suit on two grounds: (i) res ipsa loquitur, and (ii) specific acts of negligence. The trial court dismissed the charges of specific negligence but submitted the res ipsa loquitur question to the jury. D appeals a verdict for P, contending that the res ipsa loquitur doctrine does not apply because evidence of the cause of the collapse was equally accessible to P and D.

2) **Issue.** Must a plaintiff show that evidence of causation is peculiarly accessible to the defendant before res ipsa loquitur may be invoked?

3) **Held.** No. Judgment for P affirmed.

a) The doctrine of res ipsa loquitur permits an inference of D's negligence from the happening of the injury.

b) Application of the doctrine is based on two facts: (i) exclusive control and management by the defendant of the instrumentality which causes the injury, and (ii) the occurrence would not ordinarily happen if reasonable care had been used.

c) Although the doctrine is based on the underlying reason that evidence of the true cause of injury is accessible to D but not to P, the presence of this underlying reason is not an indispensable requirement for application of the doctrine.

d) Furthermore, we are not persuaded that evidence of the cause of the collapse was accessible to P. She could not be expected to inspect the bleachers immediately after being seriously injured by them.

4) **Concurrence.** It seems unnecessary to cling to the doctrine that the instrumentality that caused the injury must have been exclusively controlled by D before res ipsa loquitur may be applied.

c. **Appropriateness of res ipsa loquitur when plaintiff has the means of proving negligence--Shutt v. Kaufman's, Inc.,** 165 Colo. 175, 438 P.2d 501 (1968).

Shutt v. Kaufman's, Inc.

1) **Facts.** Shutt (P) sued Kaufman's (D) for damages which she received when she sat down on a chair in D's shoe store, which bumped a display table and caused a metal shoe stand to topple and strike P on the head. At trial the jury found for D. P appeals based on the manner in which the court applied res ipsa loquitur to the case. P argues that because she could not foresee the accident, res ipsa loquitur should apply.

2) **Issue.** Can a plaintiff invoke res ipsa loquitur if she has available to her the means of proving the defendant's negligence?

3) **Held.** No. Judgment for D affirmed.

a) Although the accident was unforeseeable, P had the means by which to prove D's negligence; therefore, res ipsa loquitur does not apply.

b) P could have shown that the display table was unstable or that the shoe stand was in a dangerous position. These are the means by which D's negligence might have been proved.

c) The storekeeper must exercise reasonable care to insure the safety of his patrons but he is not an insurer against all accidents.

d) Although the trial court gave an erroneous instruction regarding res ipsa loquitur, P was entitled to none at all and was not harmed thereby.

4) **Comment.** As noted above, res ipsa loquitur is not applied in all cases. Due to its conclusiveness, res ipsa loquitur is applicable only if the defendant has better access to the facts than the plaintiff.

d. **Injury inflicted by someone outside of defendant's control--City of Louisville v. Humphrey,** 461 S.W.2d 352 (Ky. App. 1970).

City of Louisville v. Humphrey

1) **Facts.** Humphrey's (P's) husband was arrested for intoxication by Louisville's (D's) employees. Thereafter, he lost consciousness and was placed in the city's "drunk tank." When he failed to regain consciousness he was taken to the hospital, where he eventually died of injuries received around the left eye and forehead. P sued for and recovered damages for her husband's death on the theory that he was injured either by the city's employees or by fellow prisoners in the city's custody. There was no direct evidence as to the cause of the injuries. D appeals.

2) **Issue.** Will res ipsa loquitur apply where the injury might have been inflicted by someone not within the defendant's control?

3) **Held.** No. Judgment for P reversed.

    a) Res ipsa loquitur will not apply if the injury might have been caused by someone not within D's control. Here, there was no direct evidence as to who injured P's husband.

    b) Even if it could be proven that a fellow prisoner injured the husband, P would need to prove the city negligent in permitting the injuries by showing that it had a prior knowledge of the violent propensity of the fellow prisoner. To hold otherwise would make prisonkeepers absolute insurers of the safety of each prisoner.

    c) P did not meet the burden of proof.

e. **Defendant has given up control of instrumentality--Escola v. Coca Cola Bottling Co.,** 24 Cal. 2d 453, 150 P.2d 436 (1944).

1) **Facts.** Escola (P), a waitress, was injured when a Coca Cola bottle broke in her hand. P sued the bottling company (D). At trial she relied on res ipsa loquitur to establish D's liability for her injuries and was awarded a jury verdict. An expert testified at trial that pressure tests performed on new Coca Cola bottles were nearly infallible. D did not test reused bottles except for visible defects. D appeals application of the res ipsa loquitur doctrine to P's case.

2) **Issues.**

    a) Will the fact that a defendant had given up control of the instrumentality prior to the injury prohibit the application of res ipsa loquitur?

    b) May res ipsa loquitur apply if the accident might ordinarily occur without negligence?

3) **Held.** a) No. b) No. Judgment for P affirmed.

    a) The doctrine may be applied upon the theory that D had control at the time of the negligent act, although not at the time of the accident, if P first proves that the condition of the bottle had not changed since it left D's presence and that P exercised care in handling it.

    b) It must appear that the accident would not have occurred without negligence. The injury resulted either from an overcharge of pres-

Escola v.
Coca Cola
Bottling Co.

surized gas, which could only be the result of D's negligence, or a defect in the bottle. In light of evidence that the new bottles were not defective, a defective bottle would almost certainly be the result of D's negligence in failing to discover a defective reused bottle. Hence, the accident would not have occurred without D's negligence.

    4)   **Concurrence.** A manufacturer should be absolutely liable when an article that he places on the market knowing that it has not been inspected is defective and causes injury.

C. SPECIAL RELATIONSHIPS

1.   **Duty of Owners and Occupants of Land.** In this area duties are divided into fairly rigid and arbitrary categories depending on the type of landowner or occupier and plaintiff involved. These duties are generally the result of historical precedent and often would be considered inconsistent with what reasonable persons under the same or similar circumstances would do.

    a.   **Persons outside of the premises.** The person in possession of land is required to exercise reasonable care with regard to his activities on the land for the protection of those outside the premises.

        1)   **Natural conditions.** A landowner/occupier is not liable for damages resulting from conditions on the premises arising in a state of nature.

        2)   **Public highways or walkways.** The public right of passage on a highway carries with it an obligation on the part of the abutting landowners to use reasonable care for the protection of those on the highway.

        3)   **Artificial conditions.** Where the landowner/occupier creates artificial conditions on the land, he is obligated to inspect them and protect against danger to others.

    b.   **Trespassing adults.** Trespassing adults enter the land of another with no right or privilege; they must take the premises as found and are presumed to assume the risk of looking out for themselves. Thus, the general rule is that a landowner/occupier is not liable for injuries to adult trespassers caused by his failure to exercise due care, to put his land in a safe condition for them, or to carry on his activities in such a manner as not to endanger them.

        1)   **Known trespassers.** In most jurisdictions, the foreseeability of a trespass is deemed to create no duty on the part of the landowner/occupier. However, where the trespassers are known generally (even though the identity or presence of the particular trespasser is not known), the trespass occurs on a particular part of the property (*e.g.*, walking path, etc.) and is tolerated, there is a tendency on the part of the courts to treat the trespasser as a licensee, requiring the landowner/occupier to warn the trespasser of, or make safe, known natural or artificial conditions or

activities involving any risk of harm which he is unlikely to discover. Other courts limit the obligation of the landowner/occupier to a duty to discover and warn the trespasser of, or make safe, known artificial conditions and activities which could cause death or serious bodily injury to the trespasser. Under this position, there is no duty with respect to natural conditions or artificial conditions presenting a risk less than death or serious bodily injury.

c. **Licensees.** A licensee is one who goes on the land of another with the consent of the owner/occupier, through authority of law, or by necessity, and is deemed to take the land as the occupier uses it. However, the landowner/occupier must warn the licensee of, or make safe, known natural or artificial conditions or activities involving any risk of harm which he is unlikely to discover, whether existing at the time of entry or arising thereafter. The licensee has the occupier's consent and nothing more.

1) **Social guest.** "Invitee" is a term of art; it does not include all persons invited onto the premises. [*See* d., below] A social guest, though invited, is only a licensee. The fact that a guest renders some incidental service or that he was invited out of economic motives does not remove him from the status of licensee.

2) **Known danger.** The owner of premises is under a duty to warn a known licensee of known dangerous conditions which the owner cannot reasonably assume that the licensee knows or can detect through a reasonable use of his faculties, or to make such conditions safe.

3) **No duty to inspect.** The duty of a landowner/occupier extends only to known dangerous conditions; there is no duty to inspect in order to discover dangerous conditions.

d. **Invitees.** An invitee is one who goes upon the land of another with the consent of the owner/occupier for some purpose connected with the use of the premises; *e.g.*, a business or a public invitee. The duty owed is coextensive with the invitation. The basis of liability is an implied promise that the premises are, or will be, safe or reasonably safe. This means that the invitor is under a duty to make reasonable inspection of the premises and discover any dangers that may exist. Thereafter, the duty owed the invitee is one of ordinary care. The limitations of responsibility of the invitor in the case of the business invitee are generally determined by specific time, length of stay, part of premises visited, etc. Generally, those entering under public authority during nonbusiness hours (*e.g.*, firefighters) are deemed mere licensees; others entering for a business or public purpose during regular business hours (*e.g.*, postal workers) are considered invitees under the modern view.

1) **Business invitee.** One of the older theories was that to be a business invitee, one must be invited on the premises for potential pecuniary benefit to the owner. Potential gain was not difficult to find, and one who loitered in a store was held to be an invitee because he might buy something.

2) **Limitations on invitation.** A person remains an invitee only while in those areas or parts of the premises held open to him for the purposes for which he came. If an invitee goes outside the area of invitation, but under

the consent of the owner, he becomes a licensee, and if no permission is involved, he may be a trespasser.

3) **Reasonable care required.** The legal obligation of the defendant in all these situations is only to exercise reasonable care. The duty arises only when danger is to be anticipated (*i.e.,* reasonably foreseeable) and the owner/occupier is not required to do anything unreasonable or risk his life.

4) **Protection against third persons.** The owner/occupier must exercise his power of control over the conduct of third persons to prevent injury to an invitee who may be injured by such conduct.

e. **Rejection of common law categories regarding a landowner's visitors-- Rowland v. Christian,** 69 Cal. 2d 108, 443 P.2d 561, 70 Cal. Rptr. 97 (1968).

Rowland v. Christian

1) **Facts.** P, a social guest in D's apartment, was injured when a cracked water faucet handle in D's bathroom broke in P's hand, causing severe injuries. D knew the handle was cracked and had asked the landlord to repair it, but she did not warn P of the condition of the handle. P sued to recover for the injury and appeals the trial judge's granting of D's motion for summary judgment.

2) **Issue.** If the occupier of land is aware of a concealed condition which presents an unreasonable risk of harm to others, is the land occupier's failure to warn or to repair the condition negligence?

3) **Held.** Yes. Judgment for D reversed.

   a) In the past the common law divided a landowner's visitors into three categories: (i) invitees-business guests, (ii) licensees-social guests, and (iii) trespassers.

   b) While the landowner owed a duty of ordinary care to invitees, licensees and trespassers were obliged to take the premises as they found them. This exception to the rule of liability for negligence grew out of the special status that land enjoyed in English and American law and is no longer justifiable.

   c) Applying negligence liability equally regardless of the visitor's status will eliminate complexity and confusion in the law.

   d) A person's life or limb is not less worthy of protection because he has come upon the land of another without a business purpose or without permission.

   e) The basic policy set forth by the legislature is that everyone is responsible for an injury caused to another by his want of ordinary care. We adhere to it.

4) **Dissent.** The judgment should be sustained.

   a) The majority opinion allows for decisions on a case-by-case basis bereft of the guiding principles and precedent of tort law.

b)   This sweeping modification falls within the domain of the legislature.

c)   Social guests ought to take the premises as they find them.

5)   Comment. Most courts retain the traditional common law categories.

f.   Trespassing children. Except with respect to ultrahazardous activities, such as maintaining a turntable, children were treated the same as adults until about the 1920s, when trespassing children began to be recognized as a special class. The rationale for the special classification lies in the fact that (i) children are often incapable of protecting themselves because of their inability to perceive the risk, (ii) out of necessity a parent cannot be expected to follow the child around all day, (iii) maintaining an "attractive nuisance" is deemed undesirable, and (iv) the cost to alleviate the risk of harm is usually slight in comparison with the damages which might be suffered.

1)   Restatement rule. Section 339 of the Restatement (Second) of Torts sets out the duty of a property owner with respect to artificial conditions when infant trespassers are involved. A property owner will be liable for injuries to infant trespassers from dangerous artificial conditions on his land under the following circumstances:

a)   If he knows or should know that children are likely to trespass upon the places where the dangerous condition is maintained;

b)   If he knows or should know that the condition involves an unreasonable risk of injury to them;

c)   If the children, because of their immaturity, do not realize the danger involved;

d)   If the utility of maintaining the condition is slight in relation to the risk of injury to the children; and

e)   If he fails to exercise reasonable care to eliminate the danger or otherwise to protect the children.

g.   Duty owed where defendant charged with care of third persons. Some authorities treat the duty owed by one charged by law with the care of others as simply a duty of due care, with the obligation to care for the third persons being one of the "circumstances." However, many courts treat this duty as imposing a separate, affirmative standard of care, demanding the "highest caution consistent with the undertaking." At any rate, wherever the defendant is legally charged with the safety of a third person (*e.g.,* carrier transporting passengers) or protecting the property of a third person (*e.g.,* bailee in possession of bailor's chattels), a higher *amount* of care, if not a different standard of care, is clearly called for.

1)   Common carriers. Thus, it has been held that a common carrier must always choose the course of action least likely to expose his passengers to harm. Moreover, courts sometimes impose liability on common carriers notwithstanding intervening forces which would be held to excuse other defendants.

2) **Physical custody of third person.** Likewise, one charged with the physical custody of another (*e.g.,* guardian or custodian of a minor or incompetent) owes a duty to exercise reasonable care to protect the ward from foreseeable harm. (A parent also owes such a duty, but is normally immune from any liability to the child.) It sometimes does not take much to find that a defendant was "charged with the care" of a minor. For example, under the "Pied Piper" rule, a hawker who dispenses his wares in the street, having induced a child into the street, owes a duty to maintain a lookout for approaching traffic.

3) **Liability of auto driver to passenger.** The high degree of care owed by a common carrier to his passengers (*see* g.1), above) has never been imposed on the driver of a private automobile with respect to riders therein.

    a) **Common law rule.** The driver of an automobile owes any rider therein a duty to exercise reasonable care to warn of any known dangers or defective conditions which are not reasonably apparent and to exercise reasonable care in operation of the car. This common law duty is basically an analogy to the duty owed by a *land occupier* to his guests or *licensees*.

    b) **"Guest statutes."** A few decades ago, many jurisdictions had statutes that eliminated ordinary negligence liability of the driver of an automobile to a rider therein. Typically, such statutes provided that the driver was liable to a "guest" rider only for "wanton" or "gross" negligence or for accidents that were the result of intoxication or willful misconduct.

    c) **Present status of guest statutes.** Many courts have recently ruled that guest statutes violate the equal protection guarantees of state constitutions—holding that there is no rational basis for the differential treatment accorded to "guests" and "passengers" under the foregoing rules. Today, fewer than 10 states retain guest statutes.

D. LIMITATIONS ON LIABILITY

1. **No Duty to Act.** As a general rule, the law recognizes no duty to come to the aid of another. Although one may see someone else in a position of peril and even have the ability to assist that individual, there is ordinarily no liability for failure to assist. Society may feel that there is a moral or social obligation to aid others, but the law does not enforce this moral obligation. There are, however, exceptional circumstances where the courts have imposed the duty to come to another's aid.

2. **Misfeasance.** Although there is no general duty to come to the aid of another, once assistance is begun, the assisting party has the duty to use reasonable care. This is ordinarily referred to as the difference between nonfeasance and misfeasance. The failure to begin aid (nonfeasance) is not

actionable. Beginning aid and doing it unreasonably (misfeasance) is actionable.

Erie Railroad
Co. v.
Stewart

a. **Application--Erie Railroad Co. v. Stewart**, 40 F.2d 855 (6th Cir. 1930), *cert. denied*, 282 U.S. 843 (1930).

1) **Facts.** Stewart (P) was a passenger in a truck that was struck by a train operated by Erie Railroad Co. (D). The truck was struck as it crossed a heavily traveled railroad crossing. D maintained a watchman at this crossing whose job it was to signal and give warnings when trains were approaching. Although there was no statutory requirement of providing a watchman, use of the watchman had been routine at this crossing for a long time and this practice was well known to the plaintiff. On the day of the accident, the watchman was at the crossing but gave no warning. The trial court instructed the jury that where the watchman had been maintained for a long time with the knowledge of P, the failure of the watchman to warn of approaching trains would be negligent as a matter of law. P recovered a judgment and D appeals.

2) **Issue.** Did D owe a duty to P to use reasonable care to warn of approaching trains?

3) **Held.** Yes. Judgment affirmed.

a) There is no duty required by statute to provide aid, and D would have no other legal duty to aid.

b) Where, however, D assumes a duty to provide a watchman and travelers on the highway grow to rely on that watchman, D must continue to provide such a watchman, and the watchman must exercise reasonable care.

c) Failure to continue to provide the watchman without notice of stopping the service would be creating a trap. The same result will occur if the evidence establishes lack of due care by the watchman.

3. **Instrumentality Under Control of Defendant.** When a plaintiff is injured by an instrumentality under the control of the defendant, whether through the plaintiff's own negligence or that of a third party, the defendant is obligated to take affirmative steps to effectuate rescue, but is liable only for the aggravation of the plaintiff's injury where such duty is not exercised.

Tubbs v.
Argus

a. **Application--Tubbs v. Argus**, 140 Ind. App. 695, 225 N.E.2d 841 (1967).

1) **Facts.** P, a guest passenger in an automobile driven by D, sustained injuries when the automobile struck a tree. Immediately thereafter, D abandoned the vehicle. P brought suit only to recover for alleged additional injuries which P sustained as a result of D's failure to render reasonable assistance to her. The trial court sustained D's demurrer to P's complaint. P appeals.

2)   **Issue.** Where injury results from an instrumentality under a person's control, does that person have a duty to render reasonable aid to the injured party?

3)   **Held.** Yes. Judgment for D reversed.

   a)   The Restatement (Second) of Torts section 322 states: "If the actor knows or has reason to know that by his conduct, whether tortious or innocent, he has caused such bodily harm to another as to make him helpless and in danger of future harm, the actor is under a duty to exercise reasonable care to prevent such future harm."

   b)   Although the common law provided no general duty to assist those in peril, courts have held that under some conditions, moral and humanitarian considerations may require one to render assistance even where the injury does not result from his negligence.

4.   **Duty to Warn--Tarasoff v. Regents of University of California,** 17 Cal. 3d 425, 551 P.2d 334, 131 Cal. Rptr. 14 (1976).

   a.   **Facts.** The Tarasoffs (Ps) are the parents of a girl who was murdered by a psychiatric patient of a psychologist employed by the University of California (D). Ps alleged that the murderer confided his intent to kill their daughter to the psychologist two months before the killing and that, although the killer was briefly detained, no further action was taken to restrain him or to warn Ps. D demurred to the complaint. The trial court and lower appellate court upheld the demurrer and Ps appeal.

   b.   **Issue.** Does a therapist who determines that a patient poses a serious danger of violence to others have a duty to exercise reasonable care to protect the foreseeable victim of that danger?

   c.   **Held.** Yes. Judgment reversed.

      1)   When prevention of a foreseeable harm requires a defendant to control the conduct of another person, or to warn of such conduct, the common law imposes liability only if the defendant bears some special relationship to the dangerous person or to the potential victim. Here the therapist has such a relationship with the murderer.

      2)   D claims that therapists cannot accurately predict violent behavior and in fact are more often wrong than right. We do not require perfection, but once the existence of a serious danger of violence is determined, or should have been determined, the therapist has a duty to exercise reasonable care to protect the foreseeable victim. If such care includes warning the victim, the therapist is liable for his failure to do so.

      3)   D claims that such a warning could damage the professional relationship and the patient. Weighing this uncertain damage against the peril to the victim's life compels the conclusion that inaccuracy in

Tarasoff v. Regents of University of California

predicting violence cannot negate the therapist's duty to protect the threatened victim. The containment of such risks lies in the public interest.

  d. **Concurrence and dissent.** The duty should arise only when the therapist does in fact predict violence. We should not impose a duty where such a determination "should have been" made.

  e. **Dissent.** Imposing this duty will offer a minimum benefit to society but will frustrate psychiatric treatment. People with violent tendencies will be reluctant to seek help, and lack of confidentiality will reduce the effectiveness of whatever help is obtained. The majority rule will thereby increase the danger to society.

  f. **Comment.** The same court refused to hold the state liable for the murder of a child by a released prisoner who had threatened children. [*See* Thompson v. County of Alameda, 614 P.2d 728 (Cal. 1980)]

E. EXTENT OF LIABILITY

 1. **Introduction—Causal Relationship Between Defendant's Conduct and the Harm to Plaintiff (Both Actual and Proximate Cause).** If the defendant did not cause the injury *in fact*, he is not liable, but even if the defendant caused the injury in fact, he is not liable if he was not the *proximate cause* of injury or damage. This may be thought of in terms of the following diagram, with liability accruing to the defendant only if the circumstances are within both circles:

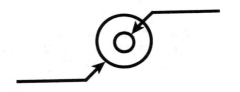

proximate cause

cause in fact

Actual causation is always a question of fact for the jury. The court enters into the decision only in deciding if reasonable persons could find such a fact. Proximate cause is a question of law, not concerning facts; it involves conflicting considerations of policy—it comes into consideration only after causation in fact is established. In order to recover, the plaintiff must sustain the burden of proof as to both.

 2. **Proximate Cause.** Proximate cause is used to determine the extent of the defendant's liability after actual causation (in fact) is established. It is an attempt to deal with the problem of liability for unforeseeable or unusual consequences following the defendant's act. "Proximate cause" is an unfortunate term, since closeness in time and space have nothing to do with the consideration here, which really deals with how far public policy will extend liability to the defendant for the consequences of his act. The Restatement uses the term "legal cause," but this term is not much better.

  a. **Direct results of defendant's act.** When there is no intervening force between a defendant's negligent act and the harm to the plaintiff, such harm is said to be the direct result of the defendant's act. For example, if the defendant negligently reaches for his cigarette lighter while driving his car, and the car hits a telephone pole which falls onto the plaintiff's house, the damage to the plaintiff's house is the direct result of the defendant's negligence. Indirect results (discussed below) occur when there is an intervening force (or forces) between the defendant's act and harm to the plaintiff.

1) **Foreseeability of harm.** The harm caused the plaintiff as a direct result of the defendant's acts may be either foreseeable (*e.g.*, it is foreseeable that pedestrians and other drivers may be injured if a defendant negligently runs a red traffic light) or unforeseeable (*e.g.*, it is unforeseeable in the preceding example that buildings in the neighborhood will have all their windows blown out by an explosion caused by the defendant running into another vehicle, which turns out to be a gasoline tank truck).

2) **Opposing views.** There are two opposing views on foreseeability of consequences of the defendant's act: One view is that the defendant's acts will be considered the proximate cause of the plaintiff's injury only if such consequences, judged at the time and place and under the circumstances when the defendant acted, were reasonably foreseeable. Essentially, this view uses the same criteria for foreseeability to determine whether the defendant's act is negligent: Is the injury reasonably foreseeable as something likely to happen? The other view, where the injury to the plaintiff is the direct result of the defendant's act, is that foreseeability is important only in determining whether there is negligence—if the injury follows in an unbroken sequence of events, the defendant will be liable for the consequences regardless of the remoteness of the injury.

a) **Extent of proximate cause and foreseeability when an intervening act is present--Marshall v. Nugent,** 222 F.2d 604 (1st Cir. 1955). Marshall v. Nugent

(1) **Facts.** Prince, an employee of Socony-Vacuum Oil Co. (D), negligently drove D's truck around a curve on an icy road, forcing* the vehicle in which Marshall (P) was riding off the highway. Prince stopped the truck on the road and offered to help get the vehicle back on the highway. P went up the road to direct traffic around the parked truck. An auto driven by Nugent hit P when it came around the curve and went into a skid in an attempt to avoid the truck. P sued D (Prince's employer) and Nugent as joint tortfeasors. At trial the jury returned a verdict of $25,000 against D and a verdict in favor of Nugent. D appeals, contending that its driver's negligence in cutting the corner was not the proximate cause of P's injuries.

(2) **Issue.** Is a person liable for negligent actions that create a dangerous situation in which a foreseeable intervening act results in injury to another?

(3) **Held.** Yes. Judgment for P affirmed.

(a) Courts have developed the doctrine of proximate causation to confine the liability of a negligent actor to harm that results from a risk, the foreseeability of which rendered the defendant's conduct negligent.

(b) The injury P received was not remote either in time or place from Prince's negligent conduct. It occurred while the traffic mix-up occasioned by D's negligence was still persisting.

(c) Many cases have held a defendant, whose negligence caused a traffic tie-up, liable for subsequent injuries more immediately caused by an oncoming motorist.

(d) It was proper to submit the question of proximate cause to the jury. There was sufficient evidence to justify a finding that the intervening act was foreseeable and the proximate cause of the injury.

Watson v. Kentucky & Indiana Bridge & Railway

b) **Intervening acts as a cause of injury--Watson v. Indiana Bridge & Railway,** 137 Ky. 619, 126 S.W. 146 (1910).

(1) **Facts.** Watson (P) was injured when gasoline which had leaked from a railroad tank car was ignited by a third party who threw a match into it. Evidence conflicted as to the intent or negligence of the third party. P sued the railroad (D), whose negligence caused the tank car to derail and spill the gasoline, for damages resulting from his injuries. The trial court directed a verdict for D. P appeals that verdict, contending that D's negligence proximately caused his injury.

(2) **Issue.** Could a jury find that D's negligence led to or might have been expected to produce P's injuries?

(3) **Held.** Yes. This case must be remanded for decision of this issue by the jury.

(a) A proximate cause is that cause which naturally led to and which might have been expected to produce the result.

(b) A person is responsible if the intervening acts or conditions were set in motion by his negligence or were reasonably to have been anticipated.

(c) It is foreseeable that a third person might negligently discard a match and cause an explosion where a great volume of gasoline is present in the street. In such a circumstance the effective cause of the explosion is not the match but the presence of gas.

(d) If the third party's act in throwing the match was intentional and malicious, that could not have been anticipated by D and would shift liability from D to the third party.

(4) **Comment.** Here, the court used the same criteria for foreseeability that it used to determine whether D's act was negligent.

b. **Violation of a statute.**

1) **Hazard that statute was not designed to prevent--Gorris v. Scott,** 9 L.R. 125 (Ex. 1874).

   a) **Facts.** D contracted to transport P's sheep but failed to place the sheep in pens of certain sizes as required by statute. The purpose of the statute was to prevent the communication of disease among the animals. During a storm the sheep were washed overboard, allegedly because they were not in pens. P bases a negligence action on D's failure to abide by the statute.

   b) **Issue.** Is failure to obey a statute actionable negligence if the statute was not designed to protect against the injury suffered?

   c) **Held.** No. The action is not maintainable.

      (1) The violation of a statute is not negligence per se if the damage complained of is totally different from the object of the legislature in making the law.

   d) **Comment.** This is the minority rule. The majority of courts are not this restrictive in determining whether the issue is in a "class of actions" that the legislature intended to protect.

2) **Hazard that statute was designed to prevent--Ross v. Hartman,** 139 F.2d 14 (D.C. Cir. 1943), *cert. denied*, 321 U.S. 790 (1944).

   a) **Facts.** D's agent violated a traffic law by leaving D's truck unattended in a public alley with the key in the ignition. Two hours later an unknown person drove the truck away and negligently ran over P. P sued for damages resulting from his injuries and appeals the direction by the trial judge of a verdict for D.

   b) **Issue.** If the violation of a statute creates a hazard that the statute was intended to prevent, is the violation such that the violator is responsible for harm caused thereby?

   c) **Held.** Yes. Judgment for D reversed.

      (1) If by creating the hazard that an ordinance was intended to prevent, the violation of that ordinance brings about the harm that the ordinance was intended to avoid, it is a legal cause of harm.

      (2) The purpose of the statute which requires that vehicles be locked was not to prevent theft but to promote the safety of the public streets by preventing children, thieves, and others from meddling with motor vehicles.

      (3) Violating the statute was negligent and the proximate cause of the harm even though the intermeddler was himself a proximate cause and probably criminal.

      (4) This rule puts the burden of the risk on those who create it. Furthermore, it discourages the hazardous conduct that the ordinance forbids.

d) **Comment.** This case is broader than *Gorris v. Scott, supra.* Here, the court states that the statute D violated was intended to prevent the harm P suffered; while in *Gorris* it was not.

3. **Foreseeability of the Plaintiff.** The foreseeability criteria have been further elaborated with respect to the question of to whom the defendant owes a duty.

    a. **Duty owed only to foreseeable plaintiffs--Palsgraf v. Long Island Railroad Co.,** 248 N.Y. 339, 162 N.E. 99 (1928).

        1) **Facts.** Palsgraf (P) purchased a railroad ticket and stood on a platform of the Long Island Railroad Co.'s (D's) railroad when a would-be passenger carrying a package attempted to leap aboard a moving train. A train guard pulled the passenger aboard while another guard pushed him from behind, causing his package to become dislodged and to fall upon the tracks. The package, wrapped in newspaper, contained fireworks, which exploded. The shock of the explosion caused some scales at the other end of the platform to fall and strike P. P was awarded damages resulting from her injuries. An appellate court affirmed. D appeals.

        2) **Issue.** May a defendant's negligence toward a third person be the basis of recovery for injuries to the plaintiff, though no duty toward her was violated?

        3) **Held.** No. Judgment for P reversed.

            a) P must show a wrong to herself; *i.e.,* a violation of her own right, not merely a wrong to someone else or an unsocial act.

            b) The reasonably perceivable risk defines the duty to be obeyed. The risk extends to those within the range of reasonable apprehension.

            c) The purpose of the guard's act was to make the passenger safe. If there was a wrong at all, it was to the safety of the package.

            d) There was nothing in the situation to suggest to the most cautious mind that the parcel would spread wreckage through the station.

            e) Negligence itself is not a tort; it must be negligence in relation to the plaintiff.

        4) **Dissent** (Andrews, J.). Judgment for P should be affirmed.

            a) Where an act unreasonably threatens the safety of others, the doer is liable for all its proximate consequences, whether or not they are unforeseeable or unexpected.

            b) The doctrine of proximate cause is a tool that allows the law to arbitrarily decline to trace a series of events beyond a certain point.

      c)   Due care is a duty imposed on everyone to protect society from unnecessary harm.

      d)   To say that there is no negligence unless there is legal duty owed to the plaintiff himself is too narrow a conception. Where there is an unreasonable act, there is negligence.

   5)   **Comment.** This case illustrates the analysis used to determine who is a proper plaintiff in a tort action. To recover, the plaintiff must show that the defendant owed him a duty that was then breached by the defendant.

b.   **Foreseeable rescuer--Solomon v. Shuell,** 435 Mich. 104, 457 N.W.2d 669 (1990).

Solomon
v. Shuell

   1)   **Facts.** While out-of-uniform police officers (Ds) were arresting robbery suspects, Solomon (P), thinking the suspects needed help, came out of his house carrying a gun that was pointed toward the ground. P was shot and killed by one of the officers. At the trial of P's wrongful death action, the jury was instructed that a victim must be in actual danger for the rescue doctrine to apply. The jury found both P and Ds negligent, and reduced P's recovery under the state's comparative fault regime. P appealed. The court of appeals affirmed, holding that (i) the rescue doctrine applies if the rescuer *reasonably believes* the victim is in actual danger, and (ii) although the jury instructions were erroneous, it was harmless error. P appeals.

   2)   **Issues.**

      a)   Did the trial court erroneously instruct the jury?

      b)   If so, was this harmless error?

   3)   **Held.** a) Yes. b) No. Reversed and remanded.

      a)   Rescuers, as a class, are foreseeable. A tortfeasor whose negligence endangers the victim has a duty of reasonable care to the rescuer, and that duty is independent of the tortfeasor's duty of care to the victim.

      b)   The application of the rescue doctrine requires a two-part analysis; the jury must determine whether (i) a reasonable person would have attempted the rescue under the same or similar circumstances, and (ii) the manner in which the rescue attempt was carried out was reasonable.

      c)   The court of appeals correctly held that the rescue doctrine applies even if the victim was never in actual danger if the rescuer reasonably believes he was.

      d)   The jury instruction was also misleading because it did not clearly charge the jury to apply the reasonable person test when analyzing the rescue attempt; therefore, the jury could not properly analyze P's theory under the rescue doctrine.

c.   **Indirect results of defendant's act.** Indirect results occur when there is an intervening force (or forces) between a defendant's act and the harm caused to a plaintiff. Such forces or causes are of external origin and do not come into operation until after the defendant's negligent act has occurred. Intervening causes generally do not relieve the defendant of liability unless they are both unforeseeable and bring about unforeseeable results. In such cases, the intervening causes are said to be "superseding." However, the test in every case where there is an intervening force or cause is whether the average, reasonable person faced with like or similar circumstances would have foreseen the likelihood that the force or cause would intervene.

Hill v. Lundin & Associates, Inc.

d.   **Duty concept--Hill v. Lundin & Associates, Inc.,** 260 La. 542, 256 So. 2d 620 (1972).

1)   **Facts.** Lundin (D) was performing home repairs after substantial damage had been done to the community by a hurricane. As D moved from job to job, he picked up and delivered equipment as needed. After one particular job, D left a ladder leaning up against a house. An unknown third party took the ladder down and put it on the ground. Later Hill (P), an employee of the property owner, saw a child running toward the ladder. P ran toward the child in an effort to prevent the child from falling on the ladder. P fell on the ladder and was injured. The trial court ruled that P's negligence barred her recovery. The intermediate appellate court reversed, holding that leaving the ladder on the job for several days after finishing the work was negligent in that it was foreseeable that someone would be hurt. D appeals.

2)   **Issue.** Did D owe a duty to prevent all risk of harm?

3)   **Held.** No. Judgment for P reversed and P's claim dismissed.

a)   Leaving the ladder in the yard was the cause in fact of the injury, but that does not necessarily make D liable.

b)   Merely leaving a ladder up against a house does not make D negligent as a matter of law.

c)   Negligence requires a duty, and the court must determine whether D owed P a duty.

d)   A duty is imposed when there is a reasonably foreseeable risk of harm from a particular act. It was not reasonably foreseeable that, by leaving a ladder against a house, someone would place the ladder on the ground and ultimately cause P to fall.

Petition of Kinsman Transit Co.

e.   **Foreseeable injuries with unforeseeable extent of injury--Petition of Kinsman Transit Co.,** 338 F.2d 708 (2d Cir.), *cert. denied,* 380 U.S. 944 (1964).

1)   **Facts.** Kinsman Transit Company (D) owned a ship which was improperly docked at Continental Grain Company's (D's) dock. The dock moorings were negligently constructed and maintained. These elements combined with the current and ice flow to cause the release of the ship, which crashed into and freed another ship. The ships floated down the river, damaging other vessels until they crashed into and collapsed the Michigan Avenue Bridge. The bridge was owned by the City of Buffalo (D) and capable of being raised to allow the ships to pass in two minutes; however, although ample warning was given, the bridge crew failed to raise the bridge. The bridge and ships created a dam and flooding resulted. The trial court found Ds negligent and held in favor of 20 claimants. Ds appeal.

2) **Issue.** Where there exist physical forces that require exercise of greater care than is displayed, does the unforeseeable nature of certain events leading to the injury and the extent of the damage limit liability?

3) **Held.** No. Judgment for Ps affirmed.

a) This case is distinguished from *Palsgraf v. Long Island Railroad Co.*, (*supra*). In *Palsgraf* there was nothing to give notice that dislodgment of the package would cause harm, whereas a ship insecurely moored is a known danger to those downstream. Furthermore, a failure to raise the bridge that results in a collision would almost certainly damage surrounding vessels and cause flooding.

b) Foreseeability of danger is necessary to render conduct negligent. Here, although the danger was foreseeable, the severe consequences were beyond foreseeability. Nevertheless, the damage was caused by the very forces whose existence required the exercise of greater care than was taken. The occurrence of consequences greater than those foreseen does not make the conduct less culpable.

c) Buffalo taxpayers can more equitably bear the loss than the flood victims.

4) **Concurrence and dissent.** Judgment for the flood victims should be reversed.

a) In allowing the flood victims to recover, the majority removes foreseeability from the law of negligence.

b) I can foresee that a negligently moored vessel might break free and strike other ships, piers, and bridges. However, the fortuitous circumstances of the vessels arranging themselves as to create a dam is too tenuous.

5) **Comment.** The key to this court's holding is its finding of a duty of greater care on the part of Ds.

f. **Proximate cause distinguished from foreseeability--Dellwo v. Pearson**, 259 Minn. 452, 107 N.W.2d 859 (1961).

1) **Facts.** Dellwo (P) and her husband were fishing from a boat. As they trolled with 40 or 50 feet of line behind the boat, Pearson (D), a 12-year-old, drove a motorboat across the fishing lines. P felt her line jerk; the reel banged against the boat and disintegrated, and a piece of it injured P's eye. P sued for damages. At trial, the judge, in his instruction on proximate cause, stated that a defendant is not responsible for unforeseen consequences of negligence. P appeals the jury's verdict for D.

2) **Issue.** Is foreseeability a test of proximate cause?

3) Held. No. Judgment for D reversed and a new trial granted.

    a) What a person may foresee may be decisive in determining whether an act is negligent, but it is not at all determinative of the proximate cause of an injury.

    b) Consequences which follow in unbroken sequence from the original negligent act are proximate even though they could not be foreseen.

4. Emotional Distress. A tort action will lie for the negligent infliction of severe mental suffering on the plaintiff. Under the older view, some physical impact or contact was required before the courts would allow recovery by the plaintiff. The rationale was that this gives the defendant reasonable grounds for declaring a defense and acts as a deterrent to fraudulent claims. However, as with the tort of intentional infliction of mental distress (*see* XI.B., *infra*), today there has been a move away from the requirement that there must be physical impact before the tort will be recognized. However, physical injury manifestations from the emotional disturbance caused by the defendant's negligent act generally are still required for the plaintiff to be entitled to any damages.

Waube v.
Warrington

    a. Emotionally distressed third party--Waube v. Warrington, 216 Wis. 603, 258 N.W. 497 (1935).

        1) Facts. P's wife died from the shock of seeing her child negligently killed by D as the child attempted to cross the highway. The wife saw the accident from a window in her home. P sued to recover damages for his wife's death. D appeals the failure of the trial court to sustain his demurrer.

        2) Issue. May a person who, though not put in peril of physical impact, sustains the shock of witnessing negligent physical impact on a third person recover for physical injuries caused by the shock?

        3) Held. No. Lower court ordered to sustain the demurrer.

            a) A person who sustains physical injuries due to shock or fear of injury to another has no cause of action.

            b) The problem must be approached from a duty-risk standpoint and not proximate cause.

            c) Clearly, D had a duty to operate her vehicle so as not to injure or cause fear of injury to any other person. However, the social interests involved do not justify an extension of her duty of care to those who would fear for the safety of others.

            d) Liability imposed by a contrary holding would be out of proportion to the culpability of the tortfeasor and would open the way to fraudulent claims.

            e) While human wrongdoing is seldom limited in its injurious effects to the immediate actors, the law finds it necessary to attach practical limits to the legal consequences of a wrongful act.

    4)   **Comment.** This case represents the majority position in cases involving an emotionally distressed third party (someone who was not within the zone of danger from the defendant's negligent act).

b.   **Bystander recovery--Thing v. La Chusa,** 48 Cal. 3d 644, 771 P.2d 814, 257 Cal. Rptr. 865 (1989).

Thing v. La Chusa

    1)   **Facts.** A child was injured when he was struck by an automobile driven by La Chusa (D). The child's mother (P) was nearby but neither saw nor heard the accident. Upon being told of the accident, P rushed over and saw her bloody, unconscious child, whom P thought was dead, lying in the roadway. P sued for negligent infliction of emotional harm that she suffered as a result of seeing her injured son. The trial court granted D's motion for summary judgment. The court of appeals reversed. D appeals.

    2)   **Issue.** May a mother who did not witness the accident in which an automobile struck and injured her child recover damages for emotional distress she suffered when she arrived at the scene?

    3)   **Held.** No. Judgment reversed.

        a)   A plaintiff may recover damages for emotional distress caused by observing a negligently inflicted injury to a third person only if the plaintiff: (i) is closely related to the victim; (ii) is present at the injury-producing event when it occurs and knows that it is causing injury to the victim; and (iii) as a result, suffers serious emotional distress beyond that which would be anticipated in a disinterested witness and which is not an abnormal response to the situation. Here, P was not present at the scene of the accident in which her son was injured, did not observe Ds' conduct, and was not aware that her son was being injured.

c.   **Direct victim--Burgess v. Superior Court,** 2 Cal. 4th 1064, 831 P.2d 1197, 9 Cal. Rptr. 2d 615 (1992).

Burgess v. Superior Court

    1)   **Facts.** Burgess (P) had a Cesarean section under general anesthesia. As she left the recovery room, she was told that her baby had problems and was given additional sedatives. When P awoke several hours later, she learned her baby had suffered oxygen deprivation and, as a result, permanent brain and nervous system damage. P brought an action for negligent infliction of emotional distress against the physician (D). D was granted summary judgment on the ground that P, who had suffered no injuries herself, was a bystander (not a direct victim) and did not meet the requirements for damages under *Thing v. La Chusa (supra).* P appealed. The intermediate appellate court reversed, ruling that P was a direct victim of D's negligence, not a bystander. D appeals.

    2)   **Issue.** May a mother recover damages for negligently inflicted emotional distress against a physician who entered into a physician-patient relationship with her for care during labor and delivery if her child is injured during the course of delivery?

3) **Held.** Yes. Affirmed.

a) *Molien v. Kaiser Foundation Hospitals*, 27 Cal. 3d 916, 616 P.2d 813, 167 Cal. Rptr. 831 (1980), established two sound principles: (i) damages for negligent infliction of emotional distress may be recovered in the absence of physical injury or impact, and (ii) a cause of action to recover damages for negligently inflicted emotional distress will lie, notwithstanding the criteria imposed upon recovery by bystanders, in cases where a duty arising from a preexisting relationship is negligently breached. This latter principle defines "direct victim." That label signifies nothing more.

b) The source of the duty owed by the D to P determines the distinction between bystander and direct victim cases.

c) Here, the scope of D's duty of care owed to P was not limited to avoiding injury to her; the end purpose of D's medical care may fairly be said to have been to provide treatment consistent with the applicable standard of care in order to maximize that P's baby would be delivered in the condition in which he had been created and nurtured without avoidable injury to the baby or to P.

d) When an obstetrician and pregnant woman enter into a physician-patient relationship, both parties understand that the physician owes a duty to the pregnant woman with respect to the medical treatment provided to her fetus. Any negligence during delivery which causes injury to the fetus and resultant emotional anguish to the mother, therefore, breaches a duty owed directly to the mother.

5. Personal Relationships.

a. **Loss of consortium.** At common law, the husband had a right of action for the loss of consortium (*i.e.,* society, services, and sexual relations) when a third party injured his wife. Either parent had a right of action for the loss of services when a child was injured. The wife had no claim for loss of consortium for an injured husband, and children had no claim for loss of services or society for an injured parent.

b. **Modern law.** Today either spouse may sue for loss of consortium. Parents may still sue for loss of services of minor children. Children still may *not* sue for loss of parental care in most states.

Feliciano v.
Rosemar
Silver Co.

c. **No recovery for loss of consortium if not legally married--Feliciano v. Rosemar Silver Co.,** 401 Mass. 141, 514 N.E.2d 1095 (1987).

1) **Facts.** In 1981, Marcial Feliciano was injured due to Costa's wrongful conduct in the course of his employment at Rosemar Silver Co. Dolores (P) and Marcial had lived together as husband and wife for almost 20 years prior to Marcial's injuries, although they did not legally marry until 1983. Prior to 1981, P used Marcial's surname and the couple owned a home jointly, paid joint taxes, had joint bank

accounts, and thought of and referred to themselves as husband and wife. P brought an action for personal injuries and loss of consortium. D was granted summary judgment on the loss of consortium claim. P appeals.

2) **Issue.** Can a plaintiff recover damages for loss of consortium outside of a legally-sanctioned marriage?

3) **Held.** No. Affirmed.

a) Marriage is more than a contract between the parties; it is the foundation of the family, a social institution of the highest importance. The Commonwealth has a deep interest that its integrity is not jeopardized. The right of recovery for the loss of a spouse's consortium supports that value.

b) That value would be subverted if the court recognized the right to recover for loss of consortium by a person who has not accepted the correlative responsibilities of marriage.

c) Tort liability cannot be extended without limit. Distinguishing between the marriage relationship and the myriad relationships that may exist between mere cohabitants serves the purpose of limiting protection to interests and values that are reasonably ascertainable.

d. **Loss of parental care--Borer v. American Airlines, Inc.,** 19 Cal. 3d 441, 563 P.2d 858, 138 Cal. Rptr. 302 (1977).

Borer v. American Airlines, Inc.

1) **Facts.** The children (Ps) of Borer sought recovery for losses they allegedly suffered due to the injuries caused to their mother by American Airlines (D). Ps alleged loss of companionship, guidance, instruction, and aid. D's motion to dismiss was granted and Ps appeal.

2) **Issue.** Is there a cause of action in the nature of a claim for loss of consortium which accrues to children for injured parents?

3) **Held.** No. Judgment affirmed.

a) The loss is too difficult to figure and not worth the cost to society to force D to pay it. This position is consistent with the continuing development of tort law.

4) **Dissent.** The majority's positions are not well founded. There is no danger of an excessive number of claims. If approved, claims would be limited to minor children. When a parent dies, the children suffer a substantial loss and will need assistance.

6. **Prenatal Harm.** Most jurisdictions allow recovery for some type of prenatal harm. Medical science has advanced to the point where causation of injury to a fetus in the early stages of development can be ascertained.

a. **Wrongful death of child.** Although most jurisdictions will allow recovery for the wrongful death of a child when the fetus is injured, the child is born alive, and then dies, there is a split of authority as to whether recovery should be allowed when the child is born dead. Since actions for wrongful death are statutory, there is a great variance among different jurisdictions on how this issue is treated.

Werling
v. Sandy

1) **Stillborn child--Werling v. Sandy,** 17 Ohio St. 3d 45, 476 N.E.2d 1053 (1985).

   a) **Facts.** Due to the negligence of Ds, P's unborn fetus was injured and born dead. P sued Ds for wrongful death of the child. The trial court held for Ds on the basis that no action would lie when the fetus was born dead. P appeals.

   b) **Issue.** May a wrongful death action be brought for the death of a fetus when the fetus is born dead?

   c) **Held.** Yes. Judgment reversed and remanded.

      (1) An unborn fetus has rights in other areas of the law.

      (2) If the fetus is injured and born alive, an action may be brought for the injuries suffered.

      (3) If the fetus is injured and born alive, and then dies, a wrongful death action is appropriate.

      (4) The court will now recognize a wrongful death action when the fetus is injured and born dead. It is only required that the fetus be a viable fetus at the time of the injury.

   d) **Concurrence.** Viability is too vague a term to allow an action to depend upon it. The court should set a specific time in which the fetus must be injured in order to be allowed to recover.

b. **Wrongful life.** A recent trend in tort law has been the bringing of actions when children have been born with birth defects. These claims usually allege that the child would have been better off having never been born. The basis of the claim is usually that the doctor was negligent in failing to test for or detect the defect, foreclosing the parents' option to seek an abortion. The actions are being brought by both the parents and the children. The action by parents, called a "wrongful birth" action, has met with more favor in the courts than the child's "wrongful life" action.

Fassoulas
v. Ramey

1) **Action by parent--Fassoulas v. Ramey,** 450 So. 2d 822 (Fla. 1984).

   a) **Facts.** Edith and John Fassoulas (Ps) were the parents of two children who had been born with birth defects. In order to avoid having additional such children, John had a vasectomy performed by Dr. Ramey (D). The operation was negligently performed and Ps had another child born with many of the same birth defects as the other children. D performed tests on John, failed to discover the negligent vasectomy, and declared him sterile. Subsequently, a fourth child was born to Ps. This child had minor birth defects which were corrected. Ps sued D for the mental suffering of having two additional children, and the cost of raising the children until age 21. The trial court held for Ps and D appeals.

b) **Issue.** May parents bring an action for the wrongful birth of a child?

c) **Held.** No. Reversed.

   (1) Parents are not damaged by the birth of a normal and healthy child. It is also the obligation of the parents to raise and support the child. The benefits of the child outweigh the cost.

   (2) Some injury has occurred, however, due to the birth of the deformed child. The parents are entitled to recover the special costs and expenses necessary to care for the deformed child, over and above the normal cost of child care.

d) **Dissent.** D was negligent in performing the operation and advising Ps after the birth of the third child. The parents did not want, nor could they afford, more children. The doctor should not be able to avoid liability by saying, "I did you a favor."

2) **Action by child--Turpin v. Sortini,** 31 Cal. 3d 220, 643 P.2d 954, 182 Cal. Rptr. 337 (1982).

   Turpin v. Sortini

a) **Facts.** The Turpin's first child was born deaf due to an inherited trait. Dr. Sortini (D) failed to detect this problem and the Turpins had a second child, Joy (P). P was also born deaf. The Turpins sued D for general damages for emotional distress and special damages for medical bills. They allege that they would not have had a second child if a proper diagnosis had been made. P also seeks general damages for being deprived of the right to be born with hearing, and special damages for costs of medical treatment and teaching. This appeal deals only with P's claims. The trial court dismissed all of P's claims and P appeals.

b) **Issue.** Can a child recover general damages for being born with a birth defect when the alternative was not to be born at all?

c) **Held.** No. Judgment affirmed on issue of general damages but reversed on issue of special damages.

   (1) Courts have begun allowing parents to recover for some of their losses suffered in cases such as this. The extraordinary medical expenses the parents must pay to raise the handicapped child would not have resulted "but for" the negligence of the doctor.

   (2) Courts, routinely, however, deny recovery for general damages. Here, the only alternative was not to be born at all. It is impossible to rationally compare being born with a birth defect to not being born at all. Even if the comparison could be made, the resulting damages would be too speculative.

(3) The special damage claim of P, however, rests on different grounds. Parents are routinely allowed to recover such costs, and children should be treated the same way. These damages will be certain and easy to measure. They are recoverable.

7. **Economic Loss.** Where the negligence of the defendant has caused only an economic loss to the plaintiff, traditional tort decisions have been reluctant to allow recovery. A minority of jurisdictions would still hold that there is no recovery for economic loss alone. A current trend, however, now allows such recovery. Courts adopting this modern trend appear to require that the risk of harm and the plaintiff be clearly foreseeable.

Barber Lines A/S v. M/V Donau Maru

a. **Traditional rule--Barber Lines A/S v. M/V Donau Maru,** 764 F.2d 50 (1st Cir. 1985).

1) **Facts.** The ship *Donau Maru* spilled oil in Boston Harbor, forcing the ship *Tamara* to be diverted to a different location. This diversion to a different pier caused *Tamara's* owners and charters (Ps) to incur additional expenses. Ps sued the owners of the *Donau Maru* (Ds) for these expenses. The trial court denied recovery and Ps appeal.

2) **Issue.** Is an economic loss recoverable in a negligence action in the absence of some physical injury?

3) **Held.** No. Judgment affirmed.

a) Economic losses from a negligent action may be significantly greater than any physical harm. This could occur due to a significant number of possible plaintiffs each suffering different losses.

b) Economic losses are the type that are more easily insured against by the party that would suffer such harm.

c) Due to the possible size of economic losses, those losses would substantially exceed the seriousness of the negligent act.

d) The court will maintain the traditional rule denying recovery for pure economic loss.

J'Aire Corp. v. Gregory

b. **Modern trend--J'Aire Corp. v. Gregory,** 24 Cal. 3d 799, 598 P.2d 60, 157 Cal. Rptr. 407 (1979).

1) **Facts.** J'Aire (P) was a restaurant operator that leased space for a business. Gregory (D) was doing construction work near P's business and caused heating and air conditioning to be shut off for an unreasonable length of time. P sued for the business losses during that time. The trial court dismissed the claim and P appeals.

2) **Issue.** Can P recover in negligence for the anticipated lost profits?

3) **Held.** Yes. Judgment reversed.

a)   The old rule which routinely rejected such claims should be changed. Where the type of harm and the identity of the plaintiff may have been foreseeable by the defendant, the case should be treated the same as other tort actions. The plaintiff must be given an opportunity to try to prove that foreseeability.

c.   **Identifiable plaintiffs--People Express Airlines, Inc. v. Consolidated Rail Corp.,** 100 N.J. 246, 495 A.2d 107 (1985).

1)   **Facts.** Consolidated Rail (D) allowed a dangerous chemical to escape from a tank car. Due to the risk of harm, the area had to be evacuated. People Express (P) suffered an interruption in its business and suffered an economic loss as a result. P sued D for that loss. The trial court entered judgment for D and P appeals.

2)   **Issue.** Can P recover for a purely economic loss caused by the negligence of D?

3)   **Held.** Yes. Reversed and remanded.

a)   The traditional rule which prohibited recovery for economic losses was created because of fears of fraudulent claims, mass litigation, and limitless liability. A better rule would be to allow valid claims.

b)   Two common concepts have existed in exceptions to the old no liability rule. Courts have allowed recovery where the risk of harm was foreseeable and the plaintiff was identifiable.

c)   In order to recover for economic loss, the plaintiff must be more than merely reasonably foreseeable. The plaintiff must be a part of a clearly identifiable class of persons whose presence and numbers were predictable.

d)   Where the risk of harm is foreseeable and the plaintiff is a member of this clearly identifiable class, recovery for purely economic harm is allowed.

F.   DEFENSES

1.   **Contributory Negligence.** Contributory negligence is conduct on the part of the plaintiff which contributes, as a legal cause, to the harm he has suffered, which conduct falls below the standard to which he must conform. Contributory negligence is much like negligence itself—the criteria are the same—but it involves a person's duty to exercise reasonable care for his own safety rather than the safety of others. While the formula for determining negligence and contributory negligence is the same, the results are not necessarily the same. The same act may be negligent when done by the defendant yet not so when done by the plaintiff. The standard of care, as in negligence, is determined by what the reasonable person would have done under the same or similar circumstances.

a. **General common law rule.** In applying contributory negligence rules, the prevailing approach is that the plaintiff's own negligent conduct will be considered by the court if such conduct is a substantial factor in bringing about his injury. Its effect at common law was to give the defendant a complete defense—*i.e.*, no liability to the defendant.

    1) **Ordinary care--Butterfield v. Forrester,** 103 Eng. Rep. 926 (K.B. 1809).

        a) **Facts.** In order to fix his house, D obstructed the public road with a pole. At about 8 p.m., while there was still enough light to see the obstruction from 100 yards, P rode his horse violently down the road. He did not see the pole, rode into it, fell from his horse, and was badly injured. P filed an action on the case against D for obstructing the road, by means of which P was injured. The judge instructed the jury that if a person riding with reasonable and ordinary care could have seen and avoided the obstruction, and if the jury was satisfied that P was riding along the street extremely hard, and without ordinary care, they should find a verdict for D. They did. P appeals.

        b) **Issue.** If P failed to use ordinary care in avoiding the accident, may he still recover damages from D?

        c) **Held.** No. Rule refused.

            (1) For P to prevail, two things would have had to concur: (i) D's fault in placing the obstruction, and (ii) P's use of ordinary care to avoid it. One person being in fault will not dispense with another's using ordinary care for himself.

b. **Minority rule.** The minority rule was that minute contribution was sufficient to prevent a defendant's liability.

c. **Burden of pleading.** The burden of pleading and proving contributory negligence is on the defendant.

d. **Avoidable consequences distinguished.** Contributory negligence should be distinguished from "avoidable consequences." If the plaintiff fails to act as a reasonable person in order to mitigate his damages, he will be barred from recovering for the damages which could have been avoided. Note that this doctrine is a rule as to damages and not as to liability.

e. **Limitations on defendant's use of contributory negligence as a defense.** Although contributory negligence will normally act as a complete defense at common law, there are several circumstances or situations in which a defendant will not be allowed to use it.

    1) **Limitation to the particular risk.** The defense of contributory negligence is not available to the defendant if the plaintiff's injury did not result from a hazard with respect to which the plaintiff failed to exercise reasonable care. In *Smithwick v. Hall & Upson Co.*, 59 Conn. 261, 21 A. 924 (1890), the plaintiff negligently failed to heed a warning about an icy platform but was injured when a wall fell on him. Since the plaintiff's actions were reasonable in regard to the danger that actually caused his injury (the falling wall), the defendant was held liable.

2) Injuries intentionally or recklessly caused. Contributory negligence is not a defense to intentional or willful and wanton torts, or reckless misconduct.

3) Violation of statute. Generally, contributory negligence is as much a defense to negligence resulting from violation of a statute as any other type of negligence.

 a) With certain types of statutes, however, contributory negligence is not allowed as a defense. The purpose of such statutes is to place the entire responsibility upon the defendant to protect a limited class of people (*e.g.,* child labor laws). If contributory negligence were recognized, such purposes would be defeated. These special statutes usually have three characteristics:

  (i) They are strict liability statutes;

  (ii) Contributory negligence is not a defense; and

  (iii) Assumption of risk is no defense.

 b) On the other hand, if the legislative purpose behind the statute is to establish a standard of ordinary care toward the plaintiff, contributory negligence is a bar to recovery, for this would not subvert the statute's purpose.

f. Last clear chance. The doctrine of last clear chance was promulgated to ameliorate the harsh effects of contributory negligence as a complete defense. It applies where the defendant was negligent and the plaintiff, through his contributory negligence, placed himself in a position of either "helpless" or "inattentive" peril. The defendant must be aware of the plaintiff's presence or peril; or, in helpless peril situations, the defendant must owe a duty to discover the plaintiff and, by the exercise of due care, have been able to the recognize the plaintiff's peril and avoid injury to the plaintiff.

1) Origin of the doctrine. In *Davies v. Mann,* 152 Eng. Rep. 588 (1842), a man fettered his donkey and turned it onto a highway where the defendant drove into it. The court held that if the defendant could have avoided the animal, the plaintiff could recover notwithstanding the obvious contributory negligence on his part. This case is the origin of the doctrine of last clear chance and reflects the reluctance courts have for denying recovery on the basis of contributory negligence. Because of the current trend modifying the "all or nothing" effect of contributory negligence (*see* 4., *infra*), many states have abandoned the last clear chance doctrine.

2) Classification. Last clear chance situations may be classified into four categories, in each of which both the plaintiff and the defendant are negligent.

 a) **Where plaintiff is helpless.**

  (1) If the defendant discovers the plaintiff and his peril and fails to use reasonable care to avoid injuring the plaintiff, the defendant is liable to the plaintiff.

(2) If the defendant fails to discover the plaintiff or his peril and is negligent in not doing so, the defendant is liable to the plaintiff.

b) **Where plaintiff is inattentive**—*i.e.,* the plaintiff could have recognized the peril, if he had been looking, and protected himself.

(1) If the defendant discovers the plaintiff and his peril, and the plaintiff's inattentiveness, yet fails to exercise reasonable care, the defendant is liable to the plaintiff.

(2) If the defendant does not discover the plaintiff or his peril, or his inattentiveness, but could have discovered the situation by conducting himself as a reasonable person under the circumstances, the general rule is that the defendant is not liable.

3) **Antecedent negligence.** Where the defendant, because of his negligence at some time prior to the time he discovers the helpless or inattentive plaintiff, is unable to exercise his "last clear chance," he will generally not be held liable. The defendant must be negligent in failing to exercise an actual last clear chance to avoid injury to the plaintiff for the doctrine to apply; *i.e.,* it is the defendant's negligence after he discovers, or in the exercise of reasonable care should have discovered, the plaintiff's danger that is critical.

2. **Imputed Contributory Negligence.** Under the theory of imputed negligence, if X is negligent and if there exists a special relationship between X and Y, the negligence of X may be "imputed" or charged to Y, even though Y has had nothing to do with X's conduct and may even have tried to prevent it (*see* III., *supra*). The effect of "imputed negligence" may be either to make Y liable to Z (who has an action against X for negligence, which negligence may be imputed to Y—*e.g.,* in master (Y)-servant (X) situation) or to bar recovery by Y against Z where X has been contributorily negligent and such contributory negligence is imputed to Y (*e.g.,* driver (X)-passenger (Y) versus other driver (Z) where both drivers are negligent and Y seeks recovery from Z, who defends on basis of imputed contributory negligence).

3. **Assumption of Risk.** The defense of assumption of risk arises when the plaintiff voluntarily encounters a known danger and by his conduct expressly or impliedly consents to take the risk of the danger. In such a case, the defendant will be relieved of responsibility for his negligence.

a. **Not negligence.** The plaintiff's voluntary assumption of risk need not be a negligent act on his part—*e.g.,* a spectator at a baseball game may be held to assume the risks of flying balls, but it is not negligence to go to a baseball game.

b. **Unreasonable assumption.** On the other hand, the plaintiff's action may constitute contributory negligence where the plaintiff is unreasonable in assuming the risks of the defendant's conduct.

c. **Knowledge required.** The plaintiff may be contributorily negligent for failing to discover danger of which a reasonable person should be aware.

Yet there can be no assumption of risk where the plaintiff had no knowledge or awareness of the particular danger involved.

d. **Must be voluntary.** The plaintiff's assumption of risk must be voluntary, and if the defendant's acts leave the plaintiff with no reasonable alternative to encountering the danger, then there is no assumption of risk.

e. **Rejection of theory.** Courts have consistently attacked assumption of risk. Some courts have rejected assumption of risk completely by stating that one must find either (i) contributory negligence, or (ii) the plaintiff's consent to negligence, which simply means that the defendant owed him no duty. Many courts that have adopted comparative negligence have taken this approach.

f. **Duty analysis of assumption of risk--Meistrich v. Casino Arena Attractions, Inc.,** 31 N.J. 44, 155 A.2d 90 (1959).

Meistrich v. Casino Arena Attractions, Inc.

1) **Facts.** Casino (D), an ice skating rink proprietor, prepared the ice so that it became too hard and too slippery for the patron of average ability. Meistrich (P), a patron, noticed that his skates slipped on turns but continued to skate until he fell and was injured. At trial of the suit brought by P for damages based on D's negligence, the trial court charged that P may be found to have assumed the risk if he reasonably should have known of it, notwithstanding that a reasonably prudent person would have continued to skate in the face of the risk. The jury found for D but the Appellate Division reversed, charging the assumption of risk instruction as error. D appeals.

2) **Issue.** Is the standard by which assumption of risk is determined that of the conduct of a reasonably prudent person?

3) **Held.** Yes. Judgment of the Appellate Division affirmed.

a) Assumption of risk has two basic meanings: (i) it expresses the proposition that the defendant was not negligent; *i.e.,* that no duty was owed, and (ii) it is an affirmative defense to an established breach of duty.

b) In this second sense, assumption of risk is merely a phase of contributory negligence. The test is whether a reasonably prudent person would have encountered the risk, and if so, whether he would have conducted himself as P did.

c) There is no reason to charge assumption of the risk in its secondary sense as something distinct from contributory negligence; to do so was error.

4. Comparative Negligence.

a. **Introduction.** Comparative negligence is a civil law doctrine. The countries that have adopted the 1909 Brussels agreement follow admiralty law and, therefore, accept comparative negligence. (Interestingly enough, the admiralty law in the United States initially rejected comparative negligence and adopted a practice of dividing the loss equally until 1975.) Most jurisdictions in the United States have now adopted some form of comparative negligence, which does not completely bar a plaintiff's recovery when the plaintiff is partially at fault, but merely reduces the plaintiff's recovery based upon the plaintiff's percentage of fault.

    b.   **"Pure" vs. "partial" comparative negligence.** Two major types of comparative negligence that have developed in the United States.

        1)   **"Pure."** The Uniform Comparative Fault Act recommends the pure form of comparative negligence. This form allows the plaintiff to recover damages, regardless of the amount of the plaintiff's fault, while reducing that award by the plaintiff's percentage of fault. If, for example, the plaintiff was 90% at fault, the plaintiff would still receive 10% of his damages.

        2)   **"Partial."** The form of comparative negligence which is referred to as partial or modified allows the plaintiff to recover only when the plaintiff's negligence is less than (or, in some of these states, no greater than) the defendant's negligence. Where the plaintiff's negligence is greater than the defendant's negligence, recovery is barred. Where, for example, the plaintiff's negligence is 60%, the plaintiff receives nothing.

Knight
v. Jewett

    c.   **Assumption of risk--Knight v. Jewett,** 3 Cal. 4th 296, 834 P.2d 696, 11 Cal. Rptr. 2d 2 (1992).

        1)   **Facts.** Knight (P) was injured by Jewett (D) in a touch football game. According to P, she caught a pass and D ran into her from behind, knocked her down, and stepped on her hand. According to D, he and P collided in an unsuccessful attempt to intercept the pass. P sued D for personal injuries. D moved for summary judgment, arguing that P assumed the risk of injury by participating in the game. D's motion was granted by the trial court and affirmed by the court of appeals. P appeals.

        2)   **Issue.** Is a plaintiff's action for damages for injuries incurred while playing football barred under the primary assumption of risk doctrine?

        3)   **Held.** Yes. Affirmed.

            a)   In 1975, the Supreme Court of California adopted comparative fault in *Li v. Yellow Cab*, 13 Cal. 3d 804, 532 P.2d 1226, 119 Cal. Rptr. 858 (1975). However, subsequent appellate decisions have misinterpreted *Li* and have made erroneous distinctions.

            b)   The distinction should be between those instances in which the assumption of risk doctrine embodies a legal conclusion that the defendant has no duty to protect the plaintiff from a particular risk ("primary assumption of risk"), and (ii) those instances in which the defendant owes a duty of care but the plaintiff knowingly encounters a risk of injury caused by the defendant's breach of duty ("secondary assumption of risk").

c) *Li* provides that primary assumption of risk cases are not merged into the comparative negligence system; the plaintiff's recovery continues to be completely barred where the defendant's conduct did not breach a legal duty of care to the plaintiff. Only secondary assumption of risk cases are properly merged into the comprehensive fault system adopted in *Li*.

d) This case turns on whether, given the nature of the activity in which D and P were engaged, D breached any legal duty of care to P.

e) A participant in an active sport breaches a legal duty of care to other participants only if that participant (i) intentionally injures another player, or (ii) engages in conduct so reckless as to be totally outside the range of ordinary activity involved in the sport.

f) D did not breach any legal duty of care owed to the plaintiff; thus, this case falls within the primary assumption of risk doctrine.

5. **Immunities.** An immunity is an exemption from all tort liability because of a defendant's status or relation to the plaintiff or injured party. The defendant's conduct may still be tortious but it cannot result in his liability.

   a. **Governmental immunity.**

      1) **Federal government.** The state has historically enjoyed tort immunity under the common law doctrine "the King can do no wrong." The rationale in the United States was that whatever the state does must be lawful. Thus, the federal government and its agencies have a tort liability immunity.

         a) **Federal Tort Claims Act.** However, under the Federal Tort Claims Act [28 U.S.C. §§1346, 2671, *et seq.*] the federal government, by its consent, is stripped of all immunities with regard to negligent or wrongful acts or omissions by government employees. Still, one cannot maintain an action for intentional torts, strict liability, or discretionary acts by government agents. ("Discretionary" acts have been defined by case law to mean administrative decisions at the "planning" level as opposed to those at the "operational" level.)

      2) **State and local governments.**

         a) **State governments.** State government immunity has the same common law basis as federal immunity.

            (1) The Eleventh Amendment to the United States Constitution provides that a state cannot be sued in the federal courts by a private citizen without the state's permission.

            (2) State constitutions have similar provisions with regard to such actions in state courts.

(a) However, statutes in most states grant such consent to limited types of actions.

(b) Even in the limited actions, courts have held that this consent to suit does not bring with it consent to tort liability—basing this immunity upon public policy.

b) **Municipal corporations.** Traditionally, municipal corporations were extended immunity as arms of the state. In response to considerable criticism, municipal corporation immunity has given way to many recognized exceptions. Further, a substantial minority of jurisdictions, including California, have abrogated this immunity entirely.

b. **Family and charitable immunities.**

1) **Interfamily immunities.**

a) **Husband and wife.** At common law, husband and wife were considered a single legal entity; therefore, one spouse could not sue the other for tort. Today, most states have rejected the doctrine of interspousal immunity entirely. The rationale for abolition of the doctrine is twofold:

(1) The common law fiction of single identity is abolished.

(2) Losses are probably covered by insurance, so allowing suit should not threaten the marriage institution.

b) **Parent and child.** At common law an action could not be maintained between parent and child for personal torts. There was no immunity with regard to torts to property. In a growing minority of the states, a child may now recover for the willful misconduct of its parents or where insurance coverage protects the parents. Some jurisdictions have abolished the doctrine of parent-child immunity altogether.

2) **Charities.** At common law, tort immunity was granted on behalf of all charitable organizations under the theory that the charity is working for the public good. This immunity has now been rejected entirely in almost all states; where it does remain, exceptions have arisen which, practically speaking, "swallow up" the rule.

V. TRESPASS TO LAND AND NUISANCE

A. SUMMARY OF SUBSTANTIVE LAW

1. **Trespass to Land.** Every unauthorized entry of a person or thing on land in the possession of another is a trespass. The basis of the tort is the right of another to the exclusive possession of land.

   a. **Prima facie case.** The plaintiff's prima facie case consists of the following elements: (i) an act by the defendant; (ii) the invasion of land in possession of the plaintiff; (iii) intent of the defendant; and (iv) causal relationship.

   b. **Possession.** For purposes of trespass to land, possession means occupancy of the land with intent to control it and to exclude others. The possession which is sufficient to entitle the plaintiff to bring an action for trespass may be actual or constructive (land in the custody of a person responsible to the plaintiff, *e.g.*, employee or agent). It has been argued that one who has immediate right to possession, though never having made actual entry on the land, has a right to maintain an action for trespass if the act of trespass occurs after creation of the right to possession. Note that an owner of land may commit a trespass on his own land if the right to exclusive possession has been transferred to another (as under a lease).

   c. **Intent and damages.**

      1) **Common law.** At common law, the important factor in determining liability was an unauthorized entry on the land of another. The plaintiff did not need to prove damages. However, the intent of the defendant to commit the trespass was determined only on the basis of whether the act forming the basis of liability was voluntary. For example, if, without his consent, the defendant is pushed by a third party into the plaintiff's store and causes damage, he will not be held liable for a trespass since he did no voluntary act. As with other intentional torts, there was no requirement that the defendant's "intent" be malicious or intentionally harmful.

      2) **Present authority.** Under the majority rule, if the defendant intends to be on the land of the plaintiff (whether the defendant's presence is based upon mistake, ignorance as to the ownership or boundary, claim of right, or some other matter), he is liable for trespass. The common law rule that the plaintiff need prove no damages or actual harm to the land continues to apply. Since the gist of the tort is interference with the right to possession, it is considered immaterial that the defendant's acts were intended but did benefit the land (*i.e.*, the defendant entered and constructed fences and made other improvements). In addition to the liability for intentional trespass, present authority recognizes liability for harm done to the land of another which results from negligence of an ultra-hazardous activity, such as blasting, even though unintentional. However, such actions are prosecuted on the basis of negligence or strict liabili-

ty and not under the guise of an intentional tort, and, unlike intentional trespass, require proof of some actual damages.

2. **Nuisance.** Nuisance refers to interference by the defendant with a right of the plaintiff to the use or enjoyment of property. Nuisances are types of damage or harm. It is best considered as a field of liability rather than as a particular tort. Utility of the defendant's activity versus harm to the plaintiff's interests is the key to nuisance. Each possessor of land is privileged to use his own property or to conduct his own affairs at the expense of some harm to his neighbors—if "unreasonable," then it will constitute a nuisance.

    a. **Kinds of nuisances.** There are two kinds of nuisances.

        1) **Public nuisance.** Public nuisance refers to an act or omission which obstructs or causes inconvenience or damage to the public in the exercise of rights common to all citizens.

        2) **Private nuisance.** Private nuisance on the other hand, refers to an unreasonable and substantial interference with the use or enjoyment of an individual's property interest in land. It is distinguished from trespass in that it does not require a physical entry upon the plaintiff's premises. It follows from the principle that everyone should use his property so as not to injure the property of another.

    b. **Bases of liability.**

        1) **Three bases.** Liability can rest on any of three bases: (i) intentional conduct; (ii) negligence; or (iii) strict liability.

        2) **Substantial interference.** There must be a substantial interference with the use and enjoyment of land which would be offensive to a reasonable person of ordinary sensibilities.

    c. **Reasonable use doctrine.** An activity which has great social value will be permitted even if it seriously interferes with the environment.

        1) **Utility vs. harm.** Courts are often forced to strike a balance between what they determine to be a reasonable use and an unreasonable interference.

        2) **Locality.** The nature of the locality becomes an important factor here. The courts must determine what is a reasonable use within the context of the custom of the community.

3. **Defenses.** Consent of the plaintiff or the existence of a privilege in the defendant will exonerate the defendant from liability for an act which, on its face, would otherwise give rise to tort liability. Of course, the burden is on the defendant to plead and prove the existence of a privilege or consent.

    a. **Consent.** Under the general rule, consent by the plaintiff to an act which would otherwise give rise to tort liability will act as a bar to an action based on such act. However, the consent must be effective to act as a bar. Problems often arise as to whether the plaintiff has in fact given consent and whether the plaintiff has the capacity to give consent. [*See* I.C., *supra*]

b. Privilege.

    1) Introduction. [*See* I.D., *supra*]

    2) Removing trespassing chattels. The person in possession of land or chattels is privileged to use reasonable force to remove chattels belonging to another, in order to protect his interest in his own land or chattels.

        a) Amount of force used. The "reasonableness" of the force applied to the trespassing chattels is in part determined by the relative value of the actor's property as opposed to the value of the trespassing chattels (*i.e.*, the actor is not privileged to totally destroy a valuable trespassing chattel in order to effect immediate removal when the damage caused to his property by a more time-consuming but orderly removal would be nominal).

    3) Necessity.

        a) Public necessity. One is privileged to enter land or interfere with chattels of another if it is reasonably necessary or if it reasonably appears necessary to avert a public disaster. To invoke the privilege, the following is required: (i) an immediate and imperative necessity and not just one that is expedient or utilitarian; (ii) an act that is in good faith, for the public good. The privilege is conditional, and it disappears when the act becomes unreasonable under the existing circumstances. The rationale behind this privilege is that when peril threatens the whole community, or so many people that there is public interest involved, one has a complete defense or privilege to act to protect the public interest.

        b) Private necessity. Where there is no public interest involved and the defendant acts to protect his own interest, he is not liable for the technical tort and the landowner has no privilege to expel him.

B. JUDICIAL APPLICATION OF SUBSTANTIVE LAW

1. Interference with Enjoyment of Property as a Trespass--Atkinson v. Bernard, Inc., 223 Or. 624, 355 P.2d 229 (1960).

    Atkinson v. Bernard, Inc.

    a. Facts. In 1918, an airport owned by Bernard, Inc. (D) commenced operation. The airport has one runway and serves mainly single-engine, noncommercial aircraft. After 1948, a residential area was created beginning about 1,000 feet north of the airport's runway. Generally, weather conditions require that planes take off to the north. Nearby residents (Ps) brought suit to enjoin takeoffs over their land.

They alleged that the planes flew at altitudes of 50 to 300 feet and created noise which substantially interfered with the enjoyment of their land. At trial, the judge enjoined all flights taking off over Ps' property which make appreciably more noise than a 1954 Piper Tri-Pacer. D appeals the decree as too vague and Ps cross-appeal, demanding an end to all northerly takeoffs.

b.   **Issue.** Is interference with the enjoyment of property caused by low-flying aircraft an action for trespass?

c.   **Held.** No. Cause remanded for further evidence.

1)   Intrusion by low-flying aircraft is subject to the law of nuisance.

2)   The key to these aircraft cases is the reasonableness of one interest yielding to another. This balancing requires the employment of nuisance concepts.

3)   The protection of private property must be weighed against the protection of the freedom of air travel.

4)   The trial judge attempted to define a subjective standard for use in weighing these interests. The case is remanded for further acoustical studies and the development of an objective standard for testing unreasonable interference with the landowner's enjoyment.

Davis v.
Georgia-
Pacific Corp.

2.   **Justification for Intrusion--Davis v. Georgia-Pacific Corp.**, 251 Or. 239, 445 P.2d 481 (1968).

a.   **Facts.** After Davis (P) began occupation of her residence in Toledo, Georgia-Pacific (D) commenced operation of a pulp and paper mill nearby which emanated vibrations, odors, fumes, smoke, and particles that allegedly made P's residence uninhabitable. P sued and secured a judgment against D for compensatory and punitive damages for trespass. D appeals, contending that trespass requires a direct intrusion by a tangible and visible object and that the trial court should have allowed the jury to weigh the utility of D's conduct against the seriousness of the harm to P.

b.   **Issue.** In a trespass action, is the trier of fact allowed to consider the social value of the defendant's conduct and its efforts to prevent harm as justification for the intrusion?

c.   **Held.** No. Judgment for P affirmed.

1)   In a trespass action the jury is not allowed to consider the utility of the use to which D is putting his land or his efforts to prevent harm. If the jury finds an unprivileged intrusion, strict liability results.

2)   Such a weighing process is allowed in a nuisance action and is also performed by the court in determining whether a certain intrusion should be classified trespass or nuisance.

3)   The traditional concept that a trespass must be a direct intrusion by a visible and tangible object has been abandoned in this state.

3. **Balancing of Interests--Waschak v. Moffat,** 379 Pa. 441, 109 A.2d 310 (1954).

   a. **Facts.** P brought suit against the operators of a coal breaker (D) for the escape of hydrogen sulfide from D's coal operation, which turned the white paint on P's home black. P alleged that D maintained a nuisance and was absolutely liable therefor. The trial court awarded judgment for P. D appeals.

   b. **Issue.** If a person unintentionally invades another's property rights, may an action for nuisance be maintained against him where the utility of his conduct outweighs the gravity of the harm caused thereby?

   c. **Held.** No. Judgment for P reversed.

      1) No liability for nuisance may be imposed for non-negligent, unintentional invasion of another's property rights if the actor's conduct is more important than the property right invaded.

      2) Coal is a vital industry in this area; in choosing to live near this industry, P must accept his fate.

   d. **Dissent.** The judgment of the trial court should be affirmed.

      1) The evidence is overwhelming that D maintained a nuisance. Not only does the escaping gas damage property, but it imperils the health of the residents.

      2) There is no showing that coal mining refuse dumps from which the gas emanates were of necessity located near residential areas.

      3) D's knowledge of the consequences of its discarding operations makes its invasion an intentional one.

4. **Balancing Test—Gravity of Plaintiff's Injury Compared with Defendant's Due Care--Jost v. Dairyland Power Cooperative,** 45 Wis. 2d 164, 172 N.W.2d 647 (1969).

   a. **Facts.** A group of farmers (Ps) sued for crop losses and diminished value of their farmland as a result of Dairyland's (D's) coal burning electric generating plant, which discharged 90 tons of sulfur dioxide gas into the atmosphere each day. The gas settled on alfalfa leaves, causing them to whiten and drop off. The gas caused other damage as well. The trial court entered a verdict for Ps based on D's maintenance of a nuisance. D appeals.

   b. **Issues.**

      1) Will proof of the exercise of due care defeat an action for nuisance?

      2) May the social utility of the defendant's conduct be balanced against the gravity of the injury inflicted by it?

c.   **Held.** 1) No. 2) No. Judgment for P affirmed.

   1)   Even though D exercised due care in the construction and operation of its plant, an action for nuisance may be maintained. In any event, continued knowing invasion of the farmer's interests is intentional, and the fact that the injury was inflicted non-negligently is not a defense.

   2)   Those who are engaged in important and desirable enterprises may not injure with impunity those who are engaged in activities of lesser economic significance. Even the government, which is endowed with the power of eminent domain, may not take or damage private property for the public good without paying fair market value for what is taken.

d.   **Comment.** Most courts allow a balancing between the defendant's and the plaintiff's interest.

5.   **Injunctive Relief--Crushed Stone Co. v. Moore,** 369 P.2d 811 (Okla. 1962).

   a.   **Facts.** The Moores (Ps) bought property near Crushed Stone's (D's) quarry during a period when it was not operating, and Ps were ignorant of its existence. When activities at the quarry resumed, Ps brought suit against D for maintenance of nuisance, alleging that the dust, noise, concussions, and flying debris from the quarry prevented the use and enjoyment of their land. The trial judge visited the quarry site and ruled that it was a nuisance but gave D two months to correct it. Three months later the trial judge ruled that D's efforts had not abated the nuisance and granted Ps' requests for cessation of the quarry activities. D appeals, contending that the quarry is worth more than $300,000 and provides an annual payroll of $140,000 and that cessation places on D a hardship disproportionate to the nuisance Ps suffer.

   b.   **Issues.**

      1)   Where damages for substantial injuries will not give an adequate remedy, may a nuisance be enjoined notwithstanding the comparative injury which will result to the enjoined party?

      2)   Is an injured party entitled to an injunction if he moved near the preexisting objectionable business operation without knowledge of its existence?

   c.   **Held.** 1) Yes. 2) Yes. Judgment for Ps affirmed.

      1)   While the matter of comparative injury should be given prominent consideration, in cases where legal damages will not give an adequate remedy against a business which creates a nuisance and causes substantial and irreparable injury, the injured party is entitled to the abatement of the nuisance by injunction regardless of harm caused to the business or the comparative benefit which it supplies.

      2)   Some courts hold that persons who move near a business must necessarily submit to the noise annoyance that is incident to the ordinary

operation of the business. This is the doctrine of "coming to a nuisance." However, before the doctrine may be applied, it must be shown that Ps had knowledge of the nuisance when they moved near it. Here, Ps had no knowledge of the nuisance and may therefore seek its abatement.

6. **Permanent Damages in Lieu of an Injunction--Boomer v. Atlantic Cement Co.**, 26 N.Y.2d 219, 257 N.E.2d 870, 309 N.Y.S.2d 312 (1970).

    a. Facts. The residences of Boomer and others (Ps) suffered damages from dirt, smoke, and vibrations emanating from Atlantic's (D's) large cement plant. Although the trial court found that D maintained a nuisance which substantially damages Ps' properties, the court failed to issue the injunction which Ps sought because of the relatively small damage suffered in comparison with the value of D's operation. The trial court did award damages for injuries up to the time of trial and also found the amount of permanent damages for the guidance of the parties in a settlement. An appellate court affirmed. Ps appeal.

    b. Issue. Where a business is so operated as to be a nuisance which substantially injures nearby residents, and where the value of the business operation is far more than the relatively small damages suffered, may permanent damages be awarded in lieu of an injunction?

    c. Held. Yes. Lower court ordered to grant an injunction which shall be vacated upon payment of permanent damages.

        1) Permanent damages may be awarded in lieu of an injunction where the value of the activities sought to be enjoined is disproportionate to the relatively small damage caused thereby.

        2) Permanent damages are fair because they fully recompense the damaged property owner while at the same time providing an incentive to the business to abate the nuisance and avoid suits by others.

        3) The granting of a short-term grace period in which to solve the problem prior to issuance of an injunction is impractical and will lead to requests for extensions. Furthermore, it puts the burden for correction of an industry-wide problem on one private enterprise.

    d. Dissent. An injunction should be granted to take effect 18 months hence unless the nuisance is abated.

        1) In permitting the injunction to become inoperative upon the payment of permanent damages, the majority is licensing a continuing wrong.

        2) The incentive to eliminate the wrong is alleviated by the majority's holding.

        3) The holding of the majority imposes a servitude upon Ps' lands without their consent and is unconstitutional.

Spur Industries, Inc. v. Del E. Webb Development Co.

7. **Coming to the Nuisance--Spur Industries, Inc. v. Del E. Webb Development Co., 108 Ariz. 178, 494 P.2d 700 (1972).**

   a. **Facts.** Spur Industries, Inc. (D) operated a large cattle feedlot several miles from the city of Phoenix. Del E. Webb Development Co. (P) purchased a large ranch near D and began developing a new community (Sun City). The odors and flies from D's feedlot constituted a nuisance to the new residents of Sun City, and P sought an injunction against continued operation of D's feedlot. A permanent injunction was granted, and D appeals.

   b. **Issue.** May one who "comes to the nuisance" obtain an injunction against continued operation of the nuisance?

   c. **Held.** Yes. Judgment affirmed.

      1) D's feedlot is clearly both a public and a private nuisance as to Sun City residents. Therefore, an injunction against its continued operation is appropriate.

      2) However, D did not locate the feedlot in the path of residential development. D must move not because of any wrongdoing but because of the rights and interests of the public. Since P brought people to the nuisance to the foreseeable detriment of D, P must indemnify D for the cost of moving or shutting down.

      3) The relief granted to D is limited to situations where a developer brings the public into a previously agricultural or industrial area, foreseeably justifying an injunction against a lawful business.

VI. STRICT LIABILITY

A. INTRODUCTION

Strict liability is liability without fault. It is based on a policy of the law that the particular injured plaintiff must be given a right of recovery, notwithstanding that there is no fault in the conduct of the defendant. However, strict liability does not mean absolute liability. There still remain problems of causation, and there are some defenses.

B. ANIMALS

1. **Trespassing.** The general rule is that the owner of animals which are likely to stray and do stray onto the land of another is strictly liable for any damage caused by such animals. An exception to this rule was made for domestic pets.

2. **Wild Animals.** The possessor of wild animals is strictly liable for harm done by the animal if such harm results from its normally dangerous propensities. However, where animals are kept under a public duty (as in a zoo), strict liability does not apply—negligence must be shown, although a high degree of care will be required.

3. **Known Dangerous Domestic Animals.** If the defendant has knowledge of the dangerous propensities of his animal (*i.e.*, that the animal threatened serious bodily harm or property damage to others), he will be strictly liable for all injuries resulting from that dangerous propensity.

4. **"Dog Bite" Statutes.** Many jurisdictions have now enacted "dog bite" statutes. Basically, these statutes reverse the common law rule that every dog was entitled to one bite before he became known to be an animal with dangerous propensities, and make his keeper liable for all damage or harm caused by the animal, unless the plaintiff was a trespasser or was committing a tort.

C. ABNORMAL OR ULTRAHAZARDOUS ACTIVITIES

Certain activities are so dangerous that they involve serious risk of harm to others despite the use of utmost care to prevent harm. Strict liability is imposed upon those who engage in such activities. Ultrahazardous activities are those abnormal to the area, which necessarily involve a risk to persons, land, or chattels and which cannot be eliminated by the use of utmost care. [Restatement (Second) of Torts, §520]

1. **Unnatural Conditions on Land.**

   a. **Construction of reservoir--Fletcher v. Rylands,** 1 Exch. 265 (1866).

   Fletcher v. Rylands

      1) **Facts.** Rylands (D) constructed a reservoir on his land which, when filled with water, burst, causing water to flow into coal mines on Fletcher's (P's) property. Unknown to D, there were old coal mine shafts under his property which were discovered by his employees during construction of the reservoir and which

weakened the reservoir and permitted the flow of water onto P's property. P sued for damages and the trial court awarded a verdict in his favor. The Exchequer reversed and P appeals to the Exchequer Chamber.

2) **Issue.** Does a person who brings onto his land something which will cause harm to another if it escapes have an absolute duty to prevent its escape?

3) **Held.** Yes. Judgment of trial court for P affirmed.

   a) One who brings onto his land anything likely to do mischief if it escapes keeps it at his peril and is prima facie answerable for all damage that is the natural consequence of its escape.

   b) He can only excuse himself by showing that the escape was the plaintiff's fault.

   c) But for D's act no mischief could have occurred.

   d) This case is distinguishable from traffic and other cases which require proof of a defendant's negligence for recovery. They involve situations where people have subjected themselves to some inevitable risk. Here, there is no ground for contending that P took upon himself any risk arising from the use to which D chose to put his land.

Rylands v. Fletcher

b. **On appeal--Rylands v. Fletcher,** 3 H.L. 330 (1868).

   1) **Facts.** *See* preceding case. The Exchequer Chamber affirmed the trial court. D appeals.

   2) **Issue.** Is a person who makes a non-natural use of his land strictly liable for any damages which result to another's property?

   3) **Held.** Yes. Judgment of the Court of Exchequer affirmed.

   a) An owner of land may use it for any purpose for which it might, in the ordinary course of enjoyment, be used. Thus, if the water had accumulated naturally and run off onto adjoining land, there could be no complaint.

   b) Nevertheless, a landowner who introduces onto the land that which in its natural condition was not upon it does so at the peril of absolute liability for consequences arising therefrom.

c. **The *Rylands* Rule.** The rule of *Rylands* is that one is liable to adjacent landowners when he brings an artificial device, which is unnatural, onto his land, where the unnatural device causes something to escape from the land and harm another's land or other property. However, *Turner v. Big Lake Oil Co.*, below, rejected strict liability in favor of a negligence standard on facts similar to *Rylands*. Reservoirs of the type built were common in that part of Texas.

Turner v. Big Lake Oil Co.

1) ***Rylands* rejected--Turner v. Big Lake Oil Co.,** 128 Tex. 155, 96 S.W.2d 221 (1936).

   a) **Facts.** Big Lake Oil Co. (D) constructed ponds to store salt water produced by the operation of D's oil wells. Water from the ponds escaped, injuring Turner's (P's) water holes and pastureland. A jury in P's damages trial found that D did permit the polluted water to flow onto P's land but acquitted D of negligence. P appeals.

b) **Issue.** Is a person who allows polluted water to flow from containers constructed on his land to another's land strictly liable for damages which result?

c) **Held.** No. Judgment for D affirmed.

(1) Negligence is the necessary basis for actions of this nature.

(2) *Rylands v. Fletcher* (*supra*) was, in fact, a case of negligence and should have been decided based on the negligence of D's employees in ignoring the abandoned shafts.

(3) In Texas, unlike England, the arid climate requires that storage of water on one's land is a natural use. Furthermore, one of the byproducts of oil productions, a prevalent Texas industry, is salt water.

(4) The key in determining a natural use of land is what the parties contemplated at the time of the grant. In Texas, salt water storage is a natural and necessary use. Therefore, actions for damages which result therefrom must be based on negligence.

d) **Comment.** The jurisdictions are split as to applying the doctrine to personal injury as well as to property damage.

d. **Ultrahazardous transportation--Siegler v. Kuhlman,** 81 Wash. 2d 448, 502 P.2d 1181 (1972).

Siegler v. Kuhlman

1) **Facts.** Kuhlman (D's employee) was pulling a loaded gasoline trailer when it came loose and catapulted upside down onto Capital Lake Drive. Siegler's (P's) decedent, a 17-year-old girl, drove her car into the spilled gasoline and it exploded, killing her. The causes of the trailer coming loose and the gas exploding are unknown. P sought recovery on the basis of negligence and strict liability. The jury found for D. An intermediate court affirmed. P appeals.

2) **Issue.** Is the transportation of gasoline as cargo sufficiently dangerous to justify the imposition of strict liability on those who engage in it?

3) **Held.** Yes. Judgment for D reversed and a new trial is granted.

a) The explosive quality of gasoline coupled with the sheer bulk of a truck load creates an extraordinary danger.

b) This danger is amplified when it is transported at high speed and spilled across the highway.

c) Furthermore, an explosion is likely to destroy all evidence of its cause.

d)   Gasoline transportation involves a high degree of risk of great harm and creates dangers which cannot be eliminated by the exercise of reasonable care. It therefore meets the Restatement test of an abnormally dangerous activity to which strict liability applies.

4)   Concurrence.

a)   The commercial transporter can best spread the loss among his customers who benefit from the ultrahazardous activity.

b)   However, where an outside force beyond the control of the manufacturer or operator causes the gasoline to escape, strict liability should not apply.

Foster v.
Preston
Mill Co.

e.   Ultrahazardous activities—remoteness of risk of harm--Foster v. Preston Mill Co., 44 Wash. 2d 440, 268 P.2d 645 (1954).

1)   Facts. Preston Mill Co. (D) used blasting to clear a road necessary to its logging operation. The vibrations from the blasting frightened mother mink at Foster's (P's) mink ranch over two miles away, causing them to kill their young. D was informed of the effect of the blasting on the mink but continued, using smaller charges. P sued and the trial court awarded damages based on D's absolute liability for the loss of mink after notice was given to him of the effect of his blasting. D appeals.

2)   Issue. Where injuries which result from an ultrahazardous activity are not the consequence of the extraordinary risk, may strict liability be used as a basis of recovery?

3)   Held. No. Judgment for P reversed.

a)   One who carries on an ultrahazardous activity is liable to another, who the actor should recognize will suffer damage by the unpreventable miscarriage of the activity, for harm resulting from that which makes the activity ultrahazardous.

b)   Blasting is ultrahazardous because of the risk that property or persons may be damaged by flying debris or concussions of the air.

c)   The risk that an unusual vibration may cause a wild animal to kill its young is not the risk that made D's activity ultrahazardous.

d)   The nervous disposition of the mink, not the hazard of blasting, is responsible for the loss.

4)   Comment. This is the majority position.

f.   Limitations on strict liability. For strict liability to be imposed, the injury must have been within the group of risks that made the activity ultrahazardous.

1)   Different risk. [*See* Foster v. Preston Mill Co., *supra*]

2) Unforeseeable intervening cause. Even where the damage is within the foreseeable risk, the majority holds that there is no strict liability if it was brought about by an unforeseeable intervening cause; *e.g.*, an act of God or the negligence of third persons.

3) Contributory negligence. Contributory negligence is no defense to strict liability unless the plaintiff's negligence was the cause of the ultrahazardous activity.

4) Assumption of risk. This defense may be asserted against a plaintiff who voluntarily encounters a known danger and by his conduct expressly or impliedly consents to the risk of danger.

VII. PRODUCTS LIABILITY

A. INTRODUCTION

At early English common law, liability for defective products was grounded in either contract or tort.

1. **Tort Actions.** Originally, the action in tort was in the nature of deceit—an action on the case by the purchaser for breach of an assumed duty.

2. **Contract Actions.** By the beginning of the nineteenth century, the plaintiff's action gained substantial recognition in contract, but only those injured plaintiffs in "privity of contract" with the manufacturer or supplier of the defective product were permitted a cause of action against them. The cause of action sounding in contract was in assumpsit, either express, implied-in-fact, or implied-in-law, and the recoverable damages were determined by application of the *Hadley v. Baxendale* rules. In 1842, Lord Abinger, in *Winterbottom v. Wright,* 10 M. & W. 109 (Exch. 1842), rejected the claim against a coach repairman by a passenger injured when the coach collapsed (the repairman had agreed with the owner to keep it in repair), stating that the most absurd and outrageous consequences would result if those not in privity of contract were allowed to sue in contract. Thus, early cases sounding in contract developed the "privity of contract" theory as a shield to the manufacturer and supplier of a defective product not in privity with the injured plaintiff.

3. **Privity Requirement.** Unless the injured plaintiff was the buyer, no recovery could be had, either in tort or in contract, no matter how negligent the seller's conduct. On the tort side, the early cases generally involved defects known to the seller but undisclosed to the buyer.

4. **Foreseeable Plaintiff.** Gradually, the courts began to make cracks in the privity wall, moving from contracts to torts, and accepting a theory that manufacturers and suppliers of products owe duty of due care with respect to the condition of the product. Breach of this duty (*i.e.,* supplying the plaintiff with a defective product) was held to be negligence. As the crack opened wider, the courts began to extend this duty to nonpurchasers. At first, special relationships were required between the purchaser and the injured nonpurchaser (*e.g.,* husband-wife, family member, employee). Later, the rule was relaxed so that in some instances unrelated bystanders could be recognized as plaintiffs and the concept of the foreseeable plaintiff came into play.

5. **Strict Liability.** The next step in the development of products liability law, which proceeded to some extent in parallel with the development of negligence theory, was a move away from negligence and into the area of strict liability, and in some jurisdictions toward absolute liability (*i.e.,* manufacturers and suppliers are absolutely liable for injuries sustained through use of defective products). The strict liability theory, which at first was applied in cases involving inherently dangerous products (such as firearms, poisons, and explosives) was extended into the area of products foreseeably dangerous by reason of the defendant's failure to exercise due care. Today, both the strict liability and negligence theories have become

alternative theories upon which injured plaintiffs often rely in stating their cause of action in tort. While this dual theory approach is common, there is also an increased emphasis being placed on the contract theory of warranty, both express and implied, especially with respect to commercial loss. Part of this trend toward use of warranty as a basis for recovery lies in the fact that the Uniform Commercial Code ("UCC") has now been adopted in the District of Columbia and in 49 of the 50 states and specifically places substantial burdens in the warranty area on manufacturers and suppliers of goods. [*See* UCC §§2-312, 2-314, 2-315]

6. **Breakdown of the Privity Requirement.** The real breakthrough in providing the plaintiff recourse against manufacturers and suppliers of defective products on a negligence theory came in the next case.

   a. **Landmark case--MacPherson v. Buick Motor Co.,** 217 N.Y. 382, 111 N.E. 1050 (1916).

   MacPherson v. Buick Motor Co.

      1) **Facts.** MacPherson (P) purchased a Buick from a dealer, who had purchased the car from Buick Motor Co., the manufacturer (D). While P was driving the car, a wheel with defective wooden spokes collapsed and P was thrown out of the car and injured. The wheel was not made by D, but was purchased from a subcontractor. P brought a negligence action against D. Evidence indicated that D could have discovered the defect by reasonable inspection, which was omitted. On a judgment for P, D appeals.

      2) **Issue.** Is privity between the manufacturer and P necessary for P to be allowed to recover against D?

      3) **Held.** No. Judgment affirmed.

         a) If the nature of a product is such that it is reasonably certain to place life and limb in peril when negligently made, then it is a thing of danger. If the manufacturer knows or can reasonably foresee that it will be used by persons other than the immediate purchaser (supplier) without new tests, then, irrespective of contract, the manufacturer is under a duty to make it carefully. This holding can be drawn from prior cases involving poisons, explosives, and deadly weapons that had placed a duty on the manufacturer thereof, based on the fact that such products were "implements of destruction" in their normal operation.

         b) The negligence of the wheel manufacturer, such as to constitute an actionable wrong with respect to users of the finished product incorporating the wheel, was a question of proximate cause and remoteness. However, in order for the wheel manufacturer's original negligence to become a cause of the danger, it was necessary for an independent cause to intervene; *i.e.,* the omission of the car manufacturer to fulfill his duty of inspection.

      4) **Dissent.** D relied on the seller of the wheels to inspect them. The wheel that failed here was the only bad one in more than 80,000 supplied to D. Also, there should be liability only where there is

privity of contract between the parties. The manufacturer should not be liable for the negligence of one of his subvendees.

   5)   Comment. The rule as originally propounded by the court in *MacPherson* was as follows: If a reasonable person would have foreseen that the product would create a risk of harm to human life or limb if not carefully made or supplied, then the manufacturer and supplier are under a duty to all foreseeable users to exercise reasonable care in the manufacture and supply of the product.

b.   Extensions of the *MacPherson* rule. The *MacPherson* rule has been further developed in the cases to cover the following situations:

   1) Damage to the product sold resulting from its own defects.

   2) Damage to reasonably foreseeable nonusers in the vicinity of the expected use of the product.

   3) Damage caused by defects in design as opposed to defects in manufacture.

   4) Damage to property in the vicinity of the expected use, where the product itself is dangerous to life and limb because it is negligently made.

   5) Liability for products negligently manufactured but posing a foreseeable risk to property only.

   6) Liability of a processor of a product at an intermediate stage.

   7) Liability of one who sells another's products as his own (including dealers, distributors, and any other party in the chain of sale).

c.   Restatement provisions.

   1) Section 401 of the Restatement (Second) of Torts places a duty on dealers and distributors to make a reasonable inspection of their products that are inherently dangerous in normal use and to remedy, or warn buyers against, such defects or dangers. The failure of the dealer to inspect, however, does not relieve the manufacturer of his obligations, since the dealer's omissions are considered foreseeable.

   2) However, section 402 of the Restatement does not place such a duty on the dealer where the products are manufactured by others and are not inherently dangerous in normal use. In such cases, the manufacturer is still liable under the *MacPherson* rule, and the dealer may be liable only under the theory of warranty or the theory of strict liability. But if the dealer discovers the defect, the common law rule will make him liable to any injured person who was not warned of the defect prior to the sale. This failure to warn of known defects will operate as an unforeseeable intervening force with respect to the manufacturer's negligence and will relieve him of liability under a negligence theory.

d.   Defenses. The defenses available to a defendant under a typical negligence action (*e.g.,* contributory negligence, assumption of risk) may be raised by the defendant in a products liability action grounded in negligence.

B. INTENTIONAL ACTS AS A BASIS OF LIABILITY

If a manufacturer or supplier of a chattel sells it with knowledge, or with reason to know, that it is dangerous or defective, and fails to warn of the danger or defect, he may be held liable for a battery to *any person* injured through use or consumption of the product. The requisite intent is established by showing that the injuries suffered were substantially certain to result from use of the chattel in the condition as sold by the manufacturer or supplier.

C. WARRANTY AS A BASIS OF LIABILITY

As stated previously, products liability actions can be based in contract upon breach of warranty. The "warranty" upon which the plaintiff will rely generally will be a statement or representation, either express or implied, made by the seller (or attributed to him) with respect to the character, quality, function, performance, reliability, or other matter of the item sold.

1. **Cause of Action.** Where the plaintiff brings his cause of action on a warranty theory, he must show:

    (i)   The existence of the warranty;

    (ii) Breach of that warranty (sale of the product in a condition which does not comply with the warranty); and

    (iii) Injury proximately caused by reason of the warranty defect in the product.

    With respect to this last element, if, for example, a warranty states that a widget has five coats of waterproof paint and in fact it has only one coat, the fact that this warranty is breached will not give the plaintiff a cause of action for physical injuries suffered as a result of some mechanism unrelated to the warranty (though the plaintiff would have a breach of contract action for contract damages based on the failure of the widget to comply with the express warranty).

2. **Privity.** In the past, courts considered an action for breach of warranty a contract action and required privity of contract between the plaintiff and the defendant as a precondition to a finding of liability. However, this requirement has been either modified or discarded by the courts or by statute in many jurisdictions.

3. **Express Warranties.** An express warranty is an affirmation of fact or a promise made by the seller about the product sold which acts as an inducement to the purchaser to buy the product. UCC section 2-313 states that an express warranty can be created by such an affirmation of fact or promise, by any description of the product which is made part of the basis of the sale transaction, or by furnishing a sample or model where the product is represented to conform to such sample or model. This section further states that the words "guarantee" or "warranty" need not appear anywhere in the transaction for such a warranty to arise. The affirmation of fact or promise may be expressly included in the contract by written representations or oral statements made by the supplier, or by a salesperson, or through advertising, or otherwise. The courts, however, have made an

exception for statements of opinion or "puffing language"; on the other hand, the risk that such a statement may be construed by the courts as an express warranty is on the seller, and the tendency has been to find that such statements were warranties where such a construction was reasonable.

4. **Implied Warranties.** Implied warranties are creatures of the law and become part of a sales transaction by operation of law rather than by the acts or agreements of the parties.

Henningsen v.
Bloomfield
Motors, Inc.

a. **Abandonment of privity--Henningsen v. Bloomfield Motors, Inc.,** 32 N.J. 358, 161 A.2d 69 (1960).

1) **Facts.** Henningsen (P) purchased a Plymouth auto from Bloomfield Motors (D), a dealer, with the intention of making it a Mother's Day gift to his wife, and he communicated that intention to the dealer. P signed a sales contract that disclaimed all warranties and other agreements except a 90-day warranty limited to replacement of defective parts. P did not read this provision, which was on the back of the contract. Ten days after delivery, while P's wife was driving the car, something seemed to go wrong with the steering and the car suddenly veered off the road and into a wall. The vehicle was a total loss, and was so destroyed that it was impossible to determine the existence of a defect. P sued the dealer and manufacturer for injuries to his wife and damage to his car based on negligence and breach of implied and express warranties. The trial court dismissed the negligence claim and submitted only the implied warranty issue to the jury. The jury found for P and D appeals. P cross-appeals dismissal of the negligence claim.

2) **Issues.**

a) Is an implied warranty of merchantability of an automobile limited only to the parties to the transaction?

b) May the implied warranty of merchantability of an auto be disclaimed in the sales contract?

c) Is the dealer subject to an implied warranty along with the manufacturer?

3) **Held.** a) No. b) No. c) Yes. Judgment of the trial court affirmed.

a) An implied warranty extends to the reasonably expected ultimate consumer. The requirement that one seeking to enforce a warranty be in privity of contract with the other party is no longer justifiable. With the advent of mass marketing, it became the reasonable contemplation of manufacturers and dealers that the consumer would be the ultimate user of the product. Eliminating privity places the burden of loss on those who can best control the danger and spread the loss.

b) The implied warranty of merchantability may not be disclaimed. A uniform sales contract is used by all of the major auto producers. A buyer must accept the disclaimer in order to purchase a car. This inequality of bargaining power, together with the dangerous nature of a defective automobile, requires that D's attempt to disclaim an implied warranty be deemed counter to the public good and invalid.

    c)   The dealers' association joined with the automobile manufacturers in creating the warranty disclaimer. They assisted in placing the purchaser in an unequal bargaining position and are subject to the implied warranty. The implied warranty extends to the purchaser's family and others who use the auto with his consent.

  4)   **Comment.** *Henningsen* disposed of the requirement of privity on the basis that social policy requires that a manufacturer be held liable for defects in its products and that warranty disclaimers and limitations on liability in consumer situations are "unconscionable" because of the relative inequality of bargaining positions.

    a)   Thus, even an express disclaimer of liability in a contract will not necessarily bar a products liability action. Note also that this decision extended the concept of manufacturer's liability beyond consumer products intended for bodily use.

    b)   Difficulties remained, however, because actions based on "warranty" were still subject to limiting commercial rules unsuited to the protection of consumers.

5. **Statutes.** Until adoption of the Uniform Commercial Code ("UCC"), which was accomplished principally during the 1960s, the principal statute giving buyers implied warranties was the Uniform Sales Act ("USA"), originally drafted in 1905. The USA provisions, however, were designed to apply only between the seller and his immediate buyer. The UCC, while specifically applicable only to the sale of "goods," followed, in general, the USA's "privity" format in sections 2-314 and 2-315, but attempted in one version of section 2-318 to create rights in remote purchasers and any "natural person who may reasonably be expected to use, consume or be affected by the goods and who is injured in person by breach of the warranty." This version of section 2-318 has not been widely adopted, though some states have adopted similar, even more encompassing consumer legislation. [*See, e.g.,* Cal. Civ. Code §§1790 *et seq.*] Also, in 1972, the federal government adopted the Consumer Products Safety Act (discussed below).

  a. **Merchantability: UCC section 2-314.** Where goods are supplied by a merchant who deals in goods of that description, the law implies a warranty in the sale transaction that the goods are of fair average quality and reasonably fit for the general purposes for which they are sold.

  b. **Fitness for particular purpose: UCC section 2-315.** Where goods are supplied by a seller who knows or has reason to know that the buyer is purchasing the goods for a particular purpose and is relying on the seller's skill or judgment in the selection of the goods, the law implies a warranty in the sales transaction that the goods are suitable or fit for the special purpose of the buyer. Fitness of the goods for general purposes will not satisfy this warranty.

c.   Special consumer legislation.

1)   Some states have expanded the UCC warranties in cases where the transaction involves consumer goods. Typical of such expanded protection is the California consumer protection legislation, which includes within the implied warranty of merchantability attached to the consumer goods the warranty that the goods are free from defects in workmanship and materials, are adequately contained, packaged, and labeled, and conform to the representations on the label. [Cal. Civil Code §1791]

2)   The Consumer Products Safety Act provides that the designer, manufacturer, and/or seller of a defective consumer product may be sued in federal court by an injured consumer for recovery of damages. The Act also establishes a Consumer Product Safety Commission charged with protection of the public from "unreasonable risks of injury" by adoption of consumer product safety standards. The Act, while applicable to consumer products, specifically exempts consumer goods such as tobacco, automobiles, guns, planes, boats, drugs, cosmetics, and food.

3)   The Magnuson-Moss Consumer Warranty Act of 1975 does not pertain to commercial transactions (*i.e.,* those between merchants), which are still governed by the provisions of the UCC. However, it significantly alters the law of warranty as applied to the sale of consumer products. Generally, the Act applies only to the sale of consumer products (tangible personal property distributed in commerce and normally used for personal, household, or family use). While the implied warranties of merchantability and fitness for particular purpose found in the UCC are left intact, the Act prohibits a disclaimer of an implied warranty whenever an express warranty is given. The Act provides for limited written warranties and permits the supplier of goods under limited warranty to limit the duration of implied warranties to the duration of the limited warranty. The Act also provides a wide range of public and private remedies for the consumer.

6.   Defenses.

a.   **Disclaimers.** Liability based on warranty is generally subject to disclaimer by the seller. Since it arises out of contract conditions (either express or implied-in-law), the seller may limit or exclude such warranties by use of an appropriate statement in the contract of sale, but only in strict accordance with, and to the extent allowed, by law. UCC section 2-316 permits the seller to disclaim warranties in the sales contract by use of words indicating that the goods are sold on an "AS IS, WHERE IS" basis "WITHOUT WARRANTIES, EXPRESS OR IMPLIED, AS TO MERCHANTABILITY, FITNESS FOR PARTICULAR PURPOSE, OR ANY OTHER MATTER." The UCC requires that the word "merchantability" appear in any disclaimer of that warranty and that disclaimers be conspicuous (typically accomplished by setting out the disclaimer language in all capitals, bold face, different type font, different color ink, or such similar distinguishing device). UCC section 2-719 declares that otherwise valid disclaimers are unenforceable if unconscionable (a disclaimer which attempts to limit the seller's liability for personal injuries arising out of use of consumer goods is prima facie unconscionable). Note also that warranty disclaimers, since they apply in a contract, are effective only between the parties to the contract, and have no binding effect on injured third parties who are not purchasers of the goods. The UCC also requires the buyer to timely (promptly) notify the seller of his claims or else they will be barred.

    b.   **Contributory negligence.** Contributory negligence is not a defense to a warranty action, but assumption of risk may eliminate the "proximate cause" element if the plaintiff knowingly uses a product after discovering a defect and is then injured by reason of such defect.

D.   STRICT LIABILITY

As stated previously, strict liability is liability without fault. The seller is held liable for injuries caused to the plaintiff irrespective of the seller's negligence or even his exercise of all possible care. The rationale of this theory of liability is that the defendant is considered better able to assume the risk of loss through insurance or otherwise than is the innocent consumer.

1.   **Proof.** The plaintiff has the burden of proving that the product was defective when sold by the defendant and that the defect was causally related to his injury. In some cases, however, the mere fact that something went wrong may create an inference that the product was defective when sold; this is similar to giving the plaintiff the benefit of res ipsa loquitur in negligence cases. However, problems often arise in trying to connect the defect with a particular defendant and in trying to eliminate other intervening causes.

2.   **Unsafe Products.** The first area of strict products liability is for unsafe products. Generally, a product can be considered unsafe if it is defective in manufacture (either workmanship or materials) or design, which defect or danger renders it potentially harmful to normal individuals in the foreseeable use of the product.

3.   **Concealed Danger.** The second area of strict liability is for products which may have no manufacturing or design defects but have a concealed danger. The manufacturer and seller may be liable for injuries suffered by users of the product if use of the product involves a risk of harm which is not apparent and the manufacturer or seller fails to give adequate warning of the concealed danger.

4.   **Effect of Delegated Final Preparation of the Product--Vandermark v. Ford Motor Co.,** 61 Cal. 2d 256, 391 P.2d 168, 37 Cal. Rptr. 896 (1964).

    Vandermark v. Ford Motor Co.

    a.   **Facts.** Vandermark (P) bought a new Ford from D, a retailer. Six weeks later while P was driving on a freeway the car went out of control and crashed into a light post, injuring P and a passenger. P alleges that failure in a master brake cylinder caused the brakes to apply themselves and the car to veer sharply to the right despite P's efforts to correct it. P brought suit for negligence and breach of implied warranty against the auto's retailer and its manufacturer, Ford

(D). The trial court granted Ford's motion for nonsuit on both causes of action and directed a verdict for the retailer on the warranty issue. P appeals these rulings. The jury found for the retailer on the negligence cause of action.

    b.   **Issues.**

        1)   Is a manufacturer who delegates final preparation of the product to an authorized dealer liable for damages which result from defective preparation?

        2)   Is a retailer strictly liable for injuries caused by a defective product which he sells?

    c.   **Held.** 1) Yes. 2) Yes. Judgment of nonsuit in favor of Ford reversed, and judgment for retailer reversed on the warranty cause of action.

        1)   In *Greenman v. Yuba Power Products, Inc.,* this court held that "a manufacturer is strictly liable in tort when an article he places on the market proves to have a defect which causes injury." This rule focuses responsibility for defects on the manufacturer and applies regardless of what part of the manufacturing process is delegated to a third party. D cannot delegate its duty to deliver cars to the ultimate purchasers free from dangerous defects.

        2)   Strict liability of the manufacturer and retailer alike affords maximum protection to the injured plaintiff and works no injustice. The retailer is an integral part of the overall marketing enterprise. In some cases he may be the only member of the enterprise available to the plaintiff.

    d.   **Comment.** Most courts follow the approach of this decision in holding all commercial entities in the vertical chain of distribution strictly liable.

E.   CAUSATION

    1.   **Proof Required.** As with all tort actions, the plaintiff must prove a causal relation between a breach of duty by the defendant and the injury suffered by the plaintiff. In a products liability action, this ordinarily means that the plaintiff must prove that a defect in the product actually caused the injury. In addition, the plaintiff must show that the manufacturer named as defendant was actually the manufacturer of the product that was defective.

    2.   **Identifying the Defendant.** One of the more difficult issues is proving which of several possible defendants was the cause of the ultimate injury. This difficulty may arise in at least two types of situations: (i) where the injury may have been caused by a defective product or by negligent use of the product; and (ii) where the product may have been made by one of a number of different manufacturers.

        a.   **Multiple manufacturers.** Where the manufacturer of the particular product that injured the plaintiff is unknown, ordinarily the plaintiff loses. [*See* Sindell v. Abbott Laboratories, *supra*—apportionment of loss among all manufacturers of the type of product that injured the plaintiff]

F. AFFIRMATIVE DEFENSE BASED ON PLAINTIFF'S CONDUCT

1. **Contributory Negligence.** The Restatement (Second) of Torts, section 402A comment n, explains how the contributory fault of the plaintiff should be considered when the basis of the claim is strict liability. Where the contributory negligence is an unreasonable failure to investigate and find the defect in the product, that should ***not*** be considered a defense to strict liability. Where, however, the plaintiff knows of the defect and unreasonably continues to use the product, that should be considered a defense.

2. **Comparative Fault--Murray v. Fairbanks Morse,** 610 F.2d 149 (3d Cir. 1979).

   Murray v. Fairbanks Morse

   a. **Facts.** Beloit (D) manufactured an electrical control panel that had to be installed at a refinery. The panel weighed one and a half tons. The bottom of the panel was left open to allow conduits to be run into the panel. In order to stabilize the panel during shipping, two metal rods were welded across the bottom of the panel. A temporary method of welding was used since the bars were not to remain. When the panel was lifted into place, it did not line up with the mounting holes. Murray (P) tried to rock the panel using an iron bar. In order to do this, P stood on one of the iron rods. The weld on the rod broke loose and P fell. P brought a strict liability action. The trial court instructed the jury on comparative negligence. The jury returned a verdict of $2 million, which was reduced by 5%—the amount of negligence for which the jury found P responsible. Both parties appeal.

   b. **Issue.** Can comparative fault be used in a strict liability case?

   c. **Held.** Yes. Judgment affirmed.

      1) Applying a negligence defense to a strict liability action is difficult. It must be noted, however, that strict liability is not a no-fault concept. The manufacturer is at fault in the fact that the product is defective.

      2) Comparing P's negligent act to D's defective product, however, is not an appropriate method of applying the defense.

      3) The real basis of comparison should be causation. The jury should compare the extent that the defect caused the injury with the extent that the negligent conduct of P caused the injury.

   d. **Comment.** About half of the comparative negligence jurisdictions permit any type of fault on the plaintiff's part to reduce his recovery. The others hold that unreasonable failure to investigate and discover the defect is not a defense, while other unreasonable use of the product is a defense.

G. FAILURE TO INSTRUCT AND WARN

1. **Adequate Warning.** Where a product creates a risk of harm for users, the manufacturer must warn of the known risks associated with the use of that product.

Sheckells v.
AGV Corp.

a. **Failure to warn--Sheckells v. AGV Corp.,** 987 F.2d 1532 (11th Cir. 1993).

1) **Facts.** John Sheckells was injured in a motorcycle accident while wearing a motorcycle helmet manufactured by AGV Corp. (D). Sheckells's father (P), brought an action on John's behalf, alleging (i) the helmet was defectively designed and manufactured, and (ii) D failed to warn that the helmet would not afford any significant protection under certain foreseeable circumstances. The district court entered summary judgment for D on a failure to warn theory on the ground that it was open and obvious that the helmet would not offer significant protection between 30 and 45 m.p.h. P appeals.

2) **Issue.** Did the trial court err in granting summary judgment for D on the failure to warn claim?

3) **Held.** Yes. Reversed on the failure to warn claim. (Affirmed on the defective design claim.)

a) Georgia's failure to warn law states that a manufacturer is liable for damages if it "knows or has reason to know that the chattel is or is likely to be dangerous for the use for which it is supplied." Georgia law imposes no duty on a manufacturer to warn of a danger that is open or obvious.

b) A consumer information sheet in the packaging of the helmet stated, "[y]our helmet is the single most important piece of safety equipment you own." P's expert witness, a medical doctor, testified that no available helmet provides any significant protection from facial or brain injury at speeds between 30 and 45 m.p.h., and opined that the average consumer would not know this. This testimony suggests that the limited degree of protection afforded by a helmet is not common knowledge. Conceivably, a purchaser might expect more from "the single most important piece of safety equipment" that he owns.

c) The evidence presented by P was sufficient to raise an issue of fact regarding the open or obvious nature of this hazard. The district court erred by resolving a material and genuinely disputed issue of fact against P.

d) D also claimed its warnings were adequate as a matter of law: a label stated "some reasonably foreseeable impacts may exceed this helmet's capability to protect against severe injury or death." A notice packaged with the helmet stated that no helmet "can protect the wearer against all foreseeable impacts." However, this warning does not inform the purchaser that the helmet will not provide any significant degree of protection at speeds of 30 to 45 m.p.h. D has not, at this stage of litigation, proffered sufficient facts to show that this warning was sufficient as a matter of law.

b.   Drug warnings--MacDonald v. Ortho Pharmaceutical Corp., 394 Mass. 131, 475 N.E.2d 65, *cert. denied*, 794 U.S. 920 (1985).

MacDonald v. Ortho Phar- maceutical Corp.

    1)   Facts. Ortho (D) was the manufacturer of birth control pills. D supplied warnings to physicians who prescribed the pills and warnings in the packages of the pills. The warnings in the packages met FDA guidelines but did not use the word "stroke." A stroke is a risk associated with using birth control pills. MacDonald (P) took birth control pills for three years and had a stroke. P sued D, claiming a failure to adequately warn. The jury returned a verdict for P, but the trial court entered a judgment n.o.v. The basis of the trial court's decision was that a drug manufacturer fulfills its duty to warn about prescription drugs by providing a warning to physicians. P appeals.

    2)   Issue. Is there a duty to warn the actual consumer of prescription drugs?

    3)   Held. Yes. Judgment reversed and jury verdict ordered reinstated.

        a)   Ordinarily, the duty to warn for prescription drugs is met by warning the physician. Birth control pills, however, are different. They create a high risk of injury due to stroke, and the patient might only visit the doctor once a year for consultation. The manufacturer, therefore, must also warn the user.

        b)   This warning was inadequate. Although the warning met the FDA guidelines, that is not conclusive. The lack of reference to "stroke" resulted in the warning failing to adequately alert the user of a clear risk of harm from the pill.

    4)   Dissent. Manufacturers of prescription drugs should only have a duty to warn physicians.

2.   Unavoidably Unsafe Products. Some products are so dangerous that they cannot be made safe. Where the utility of that product, however, outweighs the risk, the product may still be marketed. Clearly, such a product requires a warning which informs the user of the risk.

3.   Warnings Defect--Anderson v. Owens-Corning Fiberglas Corp., 53 Cal. 3d 987, 810 P.2d 549, 281 Cal. Rptr. 528 (1991).

Anderson v. Owens-Corn- ing Fiberglas Corp.

    a.   Facts. Anderson (P) alleged that he contracted asbestosis and other lung ailments through exposure to asbestos and asbestos products while working at the Long Beach Naval Shipyard from 1941 to 1976. After a verdict for Owens-Corning (D), the manufacturer of the asbestos products, the trial court granted a new trial, and the parties argued whether state of the art evidence was admissible in a failure to warn case. P contended that D was strictly liable for P's injuries in that D failed to warn P of the risk of harm that ultimately caused P's injuries. D, on the other hand, argued that in a strict liability action for failure to warn, it should only be held liable if it had knowledge, actual or constructive, of a potential risk or danger. D also argued that evidence of the state of the art is relevant and, subject to the normal rules of evidence, admissible. The court of appeals agreed with D and the California Supreme Court granted review.

    b.   **Issue.** May a defendant in a strict liability action based upon an alleged failure to warn of a risk of harm present evidence of the state of the art?

    c.   **Held.** Yes. Judgment affirmed.

        1)   Knowledge, actual or constructive, of a potential risk or danger is required before a defendant may be held strictly liable for injuries based upon an alleged failure to warn. Evidence of the state of the art, *i.e.*, evidence that the particular risk was neither known nor knowable by application of scientific knowledge available at the time of manufacture and/or distribution of the product, is both relevant and, subject to the normal rules of evidence, admissible.

        2)   To hold otherwise (*i.e.*, that knowledge or knowability is irrelevant in a failure to warn case) would render the manufacturer the virtual insurer of the product's safe use, which was never the intention of the strict liability doctrine. In strict liability for failure to warn, as opposed to such an action based on negligence, the reasonableness of the defendant's failure to warn is immaterial; the plaintiff need only show that the defendant did not adequately warn of a particular risk that was known or knowable in light of the generally recognized and prevailing best scientific and medical knowledge available at the time of manufacture and distribution.

    d.   **Comments.**

        1)   Note that a product defect cannot be overcome by a warning. Also, the determination of whether the warning given was adequate is usually left for the jury to decide, normally in reliance on expert testimony.

        2)   The "learned intermediary rule" has been applied with regard to warnings associated with harm from pharmaceuticals. Under the rule, the duty to warn of risks associated with a prescription drug is fulfilled by adequate warning to those authorized to prescribe the drug (*i.e.*, by informing the physician who prescribes the drug).

H. DEFECTIVE DESIGN

    1.   **Unreasonable Design.** The manufacturer has a duty to produce a product that has neither manufacturing defects nor design defects. A design defect may be based on negligence of the manufacturer or strict liability. Ordinarily, the key element of proof in a design defect case is evidence that a feasible alternative was available in the design of the product.

a. Design duty--McCormack v. Hankscraft Co., 278 Minn. 322, 154 N.W.2d 488 (1967).

1) **Facts.** Hankscraft (D) manufactured a vaporizer that it represented to be tip-proof, safe, and practically foolproof. Although the vaporizer's reservoir held nearly a gallon of water which reached 211° F, the vaporizer was designed so that the lid which covered the water only rested on the reservoir and was not fastened to it. This was to allow a release of pressure. McCormack's (P's) mother bought the vaporizer because she had used one before satisfactorily and because of D's representations that it was safe. A few months later while the vaporizer was in use in P's bedroom, P, a three-year-old, awoke and somehow tipped the vaporizer over, causing severe burns on 30% of her body, disfigurement, and permanent disability. P brought suit for negligent design of the product, of which there was ample expert testimony, and for failure to warn of the scalding temperature of the water in the reservoir while the vaporizer is in use. A jury returned a verdict for P but the trial judge granted judgment n.o.v. for D and a new trial. P appeals.

2) **Issues.**

   a) Does a manufacturer who knows that use of his product will involve certain dangers which are not readily apparent to the purchaser have a duty to warn of these dangers?

   b) Does a manufacturer have a duty to use reasonable care in designing a product so that those it should expect will use it, and who use it properly, are protected from unreasonable risk of harm?

3) **Held.** a) Yes. b) Yes. Judgment reversed with directions to enter judgment upon the verdict.

   a) A manufacturer has a duty of due care to inform purchasers of dangers inherent in the use of its product which are not obvious to potential users. A failure to warn will support a jury verdict of negligence.

   b) In this case, D, knowing that its product was primarily for the treatment of children, had a duty to design the vaporizer to be reasonably safe for use around children. The jury was justified in concluding that failure to secure the lid which covered the scalding water was a defect. This is especially true where experts testified that pressure might have been released by two or three small holes in the cap rather than by failing to fasten it down.

b. Risk/benefit analysis--Troja v. Black & Decker Manufacturing Co., 62 Md. App. 101, 488 A.2d 516 (1985).

1) **Facts.** Troja (P) borrowed a radial saw which had been manufactured by Black & Decker (D). In order to move the saw to the location where it would be used, several parts were removed. One of the parts removed was

the guide fence. While using the saw at the new location, P guided the wood into the saw with his hand. While using the saw in this manner, P cut his finger off with the saw. P sued D for defective design, claiming that the saw should have been made in such a way that it would not operate with the guide fence removed. The trial court granted D's motion for directed verdict, and P appeals.

2) Issue. Was the saw defectively designed?

3) Held. No. Judgment affirmed.

    a) In determining defective design, the court must do a risk/benefit analysis. This requires that the court balance the risk, available alternatives, and dangers against the utility of the product.

    b) Although a witness suggested that the product could be made such that it would not operate without the original guide fence, there was no evidence that this could actually be done or that any manufacturer had done it. That evidence, therefore, was properly excluded.

    c) There was no evidence of design defect in this case.

Heaton v.
Ford Motor
Co.

c. Consumer expectation--Heaton v. Ford Motor Co., 248 Or. 467, 435 P.2d 806 (1967).

1) Facts. Heaton (P) purchased a four-wheel drive pickup truck, and drove it for 7,000 miles without a problem. While driving at highway speed on a blacktop surface road, he hit a rock about five or six inches in diameter. Thirty-five miles later, his truck left the road and tipped over. His wheel had become detached from the "spider" (that part of the wheel attached to the vehicle by the lug nuts.) P sued Ford (D) and was nonsuited. P appeals.

2) Issue. Was there sufficient evidence of design defect to overcome a nonsuit?

3) Held. No. Judgment for D is affirmed.

    a) P must prove that a product is dangerously defective; the manufacturer will be held liable only for harm caused if the product is "unreasonably dangerous."

    b) The prior rule of strict liability only for "ultrahazardous" defects is replaced by the lower threshold of "unreasonably dangerous."

    c) Unreasonably dangerous is defined as dangerous beyond the extent that would be contemplated by the ordinary consumer.

    d) An inference of the existence of the defect is possible if the product fails to meet reasonable expectations, but here there is insufficient evidence to support P's claim that it is reasonable to expect a truck not to be damaged after hitting a big rock at highway speed.

4)   Dissent. The jury should be allowed to consider whether hitting a five- to six-inch rock is a foreseeable event. If it is foreseeable, the manufacturer must design with that event in mind.

d.   Defective design and failure to warn--Tobin v. Astra Pharmaceutical Products, Inc., 993 F.2d 528 (6th Cir. 1993).

1)   **Facts.** Tobin (P) was a 19-year-old woman who, other than a heart murmur, was healthy. In January 1987, P, who was pregnant with twins, went into early labor. She was given ritodrine, a drug purported to prolong pregnancy. P experienced side effects, including a rapid heart rate, which she was told were normal. In March, when P was admitted to the hospital with congestive heart failure, the ritodrine was discontinued; she gave birth to healthy twins. About one month later, following three hospital admissions, P's heart failed and she underwent a heart transplant. P sued Astra Pharmaceutical Products, Inc. (D), the distributor of ritodrine. At trial, the jury was instructed as to (i) defective condition unreasonably dangerous of the drug, and (ii) failure to warn for the conditions that led to P's heart transplant. Separate verdict forms were used for each theory of liability. The design defect instruction included the statement: "In determining whether the ritodrine was in a defective condition unreasonably dangerous to the user, you may consider the adequacy of the warnings and instructions . . . . A warning is adequate if it affords fair and adequate notice of the possible consequences of use of the product." The jury found for P on both theories. The district court denied D's motion for judgment notwithstanding the verdict or, in the alternative, for a new trial. D appeals.

2)   **Issue.** Did the court err in submitting a separate instruction on failure to warn when the nature of the warning is one of several factors to be considered on the issue of product defect?

3)   **Held.** No. Affirmed.

a)   Under state law, when a plaintiff has claimed negligence in addition to product defect, a separate negligence instruction is warranted. Here, the duty to warn instruction was a negligence instruction using the standard of ordinary care. Thus, the separate instruction was appropriate.

b)   The test for defective condition unreasonably dangerous is whether an ordinarily prudent manufacturer, being fully aware of the risks, would have placed the product on the market. We agree with P that this risk/benefit analysis is appropriate.

c)   The strict liability standard includes a consideration of whether a product creates "such a risk" of an accident of the general nature of the one in question "that an ordinarily prudent company engaged in the manufacture" of such a product "would not have put it on the market." The instruction was consistent with state law.

d)   There was sufficient evidence before the jury to conclude that a prudent manufacturer knowing all the risks would not market ritodrine.

e)   D may not be shielded from liability under Comment k of the Restatement (Second) of Torts, section 402A, because the useful or effective nature of ritodrine was attacked by P and supported by the evidence.

e.   Product misuse--Jurado v. Western Gear Works, 131 N.J. 375, 619 A.2d 1312 (1993).

1)   **Facts.** Jurado (P) was injured while operating a collating machine manufactured by Western Gear Works (D). While attempting to clear the vacuum tube that was blocked with paper, P's hand was caught in a "nip point." At trial, expert testimony conflicted in several areas, including whether there should have been a guard on the nip point and whether P should have stopped the machine before trying to clear it. The jury was instructed to answer four special interrogatories and responded as follows: D's product (i) was not defective as designed, manufactured, or sold; (ii) was not defective when it left D's hands; (iii) was being used for an intended and reasonably foreseeable purpose, *i.e., not being misused or had not been substantially altered in any way that was not reasonably foreseeable*; and (iv) was not a proximate cause of the accident. The jury returned verdict for D, and, in response to the court's instruction to reach a verdict on damages even if the jury found for D on liability, awarded hypothetical damages of $65,000. The court granted P's motion for judgment notwithstanding the verdict. The appellate division affirmed the judgment on liability and remanded for a trial on damages only, finding that an affirmative answer to the third interrogatory constituted a rejection of D's expert testimony and therefore left the testimony of P's expert uncontradicted. The court grants certification.

2)   **Issue.** Was the jury properly instructed about the meaning of "misuse" in a design defect products liability case?

3)   **Held.** No. Judgment reversed on liability and remanded for a new trial on both liability and damages.

a)   The third interrogatory confuses the ***purpose*** for which a product is used with the ***manner*** in which it is used, and could be understood to define "misuse" solely in terms of purpose. However, a product may be misused if it is used for an improper purpose or in an improper manner.

b)   Risk-utility analysis is used to determine if a product is defective because it is not suitable for its intended purposes, *i.e.,* whether its risk of harm outweighs its usefulness. A defendant may still be liable under this analysis if the misuse was foreseeable; thus, the plaintiff has the burden of showing the absence of misuse as part of his case. Misuse could relate to (i) an actual defect; (ii) the issue of causation; or (iii) the issue of comparative fault.

c)   When misuse is an issue in a design-defect case, the jury should first determine whether the plaintiff used the product for an objectively foreseeable ***purpose***. If the jury finds that the plaintiff's purpose was not foreseeable, the defendant did not breach any duty owed to the plaintiff. If, however, the jury finds that the plaintiff's purpose was foreseeable, it must then decide whether the product was defective. Under the risk-utility analysis, the jury must then determine whether the plaintiff used the product in an objectively foreseeable *manner*. If the jury finds that the plaintiff used the product in an objectively foreseeable manner, it should then evaluate the product's utility, *i.e.,* whether the defendant feasibly could have modified the product's design to prevent the injury or whether that modification would have either unreasonably impaired the utility of the product or excessively increased its cost. If the jury finds that the product is defective, it must decide whether the misuse proximately caused the injury.

d) The appellate division interpreted the jury's response to the third interrogatory to mean that P's use of the machine was reasonably foreseeable, and it was not being misused at the time. The court erred in assuming the jury had decided the issue of misuse on the manner in which P used the machine. The third interrogatory does not mention manner; it focuses on the purpose for which the product was being used at the time of the accident.

e) The inconsistencies in the jury's findings and its implications for proximate cause merit a retrial. If on retrial the jury determines that P's misuse was objectively foreseeable, that will predetermine that the defect was the proximate cause of the accident. The trial court should so inform the jury.

4) **Dissent.** There was no need for the jury to reach the third interrogatory because it found D's product was not defective.

I. STATUTORY REFORM

1. **State.** Although there has been some attempt at reform at the state level, there has been little comprehensive statutory change.

2. **Federal.** Several comprehensive bills have been proposed at the federal level, but none have passed.

VIII. DAMAGES

A. COMPENSATORY DAMAGES

The measure of damages in a tort case is that amount that will make the plaintiff whole (as he was before the injury). This will include a number of different factors, depending on the case at hand.

1. **Personal Injury.** In the recovery for personal injury, several different factors must be taken into consideration.

   a. **Medical expenses.** In order to seek recovery for medical expenses, the expenses must be reasonably related to the injury caused by the defendant and must be reasonable in amount.

Coyne v.
Campbell

   1) **Limited to actual pecuniary loss--Coyne v. Campbell,** 11 N.Y.2d 372, 183 N.E.2d 891 (1962).

      a) **Facts.** Coyne (P), a physician, sustained a whiplash injury when his auto was struck from the rear by an auto driven by Campbell (D). Although P received gratuitous treatment from his nurse and fellow physicians, he claimed special damages of $2,235 for medical treatment. The trial court ruled that the gratuitous services were not a proper item of special damages. P appeals the trial court ruling.

      b) **Issue.** May a plaintiff recover for medical treatment which he received gratuitously?

      c) **Held.** No. The judgment of the lower court is affirmed.

         (1) New York does not adhere to the majority rule that payments from collateral sources do not reduce the amount recoverable in a personal injury action.

         (2) The legislature has failed to adopt a proposed amendment which would follow the majority rule.

         (3) Tort damages must be compensatory only.

         (4) Gratuitous service, although it gives rise to a moral obligation on the part of the recipient to give service in return, is not compensable.

      d) **Concurrence.** Because P paid nothing for the medical treatment, to allow him to receive payment therefor would unjustly enrich him.

      e) **Dissent.** P should recover for the value of the medical service gratuitously rendered.

         (1) The "collateral source doctrine" is an established exception to the doctrine that damages are awarded only to compensate.

(2)   A tortfeasor should not be allowed to deduct benefits which the plaintiff receives from another source.

f)   **Comment.** A number of states have recently modified their collateral source rule in certain actions, permitting the defendant to offer evidence of payments to the plaintiff from collateral sources such as insurance.

b.   **Lost earnings and impairment of earning capacity.** Along with bodily injury, the potential loss of earning power is generally the plaintiff's largest loss.

1)   **Measure of recovery.** There are two elements of the basic measure of recovery. First, there is the out-of-pocket losses from the time of the accident until the time of trial; second, there is the diminution in the victim's capacity to earn in the future.

a)   **Loss of earning capacity is an issue for the jury--Holton v. Gibson,** 402 Pa. 37, 166 A.2d 4 (1960).

Holton v. Gibson

(1)   **Facts.** Holton (P) sustained injuries to his head and legs in an automobile collision with Gibson (D), which resulted in reduced mobility and removal of skull structure. Thereafter, P was not able to resume his job as a guard but was employed taking phone messages. P sued to recover damages for personal injuries. Although P did not show at trial that his wages had been decreased, the court submitted the issue of loss of earning capacity to the jury. D appeals a verdict of $24,416.75 in favor of P.

(2)   **Issue.** Must a person show that his wages have been diminished in order to recover damages for loss of earning capacity?

(3)   **Held.** No. Judgment for P is affirmed.

(a)   A tortfeasor is not entitled to a reduction of his financial responsibility because, through fortuitous circumstances, the wages of the injured person equal those he received before the accident.

(b)   Where permanent injury is involved, the whole span of life must be considered.

(c)   The test is: Has the economic horizon of the disabled person been shortened?

b)   **Unquantified enhanced risk--Mauro v. Raymark Industries, Inc.,** 116 N.J. 126, 561 A.2d 257 (1989).

Mauro v. Raymark Industries, Inc.

(1)   **Facts.** Mauro (P) was employed at a state hospital where, from 1964 until the mid-to-late 1970s, he was exposed to asbestos-containing materials manufactured by Ds. In 1981, P was tested and informed that his test results were normal but that he had bilateral thickening of both chest walls and calcification of the diaphragm. P was informed in writing that he had significant

exposure to asbestos and there was evidence that such exposure may increase the risk of development of lung cancer. Fearing contracting the disease, P has been examined every six months since 1982. In 1986, P's primary physician examined P and testified that P had "plural asbestosis," which can cause cancer. He said he could not predict that P would get cancer but that there was a high probability that P was at increased risk for developing cancer. P's effort to have an expert quantify the enhanced risk at 20 to 43% was rejected by the trial judge, who also barred the jury from awarding damages for the enhanced risk of developing cancer. The jury considered damages for emotional distress, for continued medical surveillance, and for damages attributable to P's current condition, and awarded $7,500, denying recovery to P's wife for loss of consortium. The appellate division affirmed. P appeals.

(2) **Issue.** Is a claim for enhanced risk of disease cognizable in a case involving a personal injury claim by a plaintiff with present injuries attributed to asbestos exposure?

(3) **Held.** No. Judgment affirmed.

   (a) The general rule limits recovery for future injury claims to those that can be proven likely to occur to a reasonable medical probability. P's expert was unable to testify that it was probable that P would contract cancer, and evidence of statistical studies offered to show a correlation between asbestos-related disease and cancer was excluded.

   (b) By removing the statute of limitations and single controversy doctrines as a bar to bringing an action when the injury ultimately occurs, we have ameliorated the potential unfairness of applying the reasonable-probability standard to this type of litigation. If the disease never occurs, there will be no claim and no recovery. If the disease does occur, the jury will be better able to award damages in an amount that fairly reflects the nature and severity of the plaintiff's injury.

   (c) Ps may presently recover damages for any provable diminution of bodily health, accommodating all damage claims attributable to present injury and deferring compensation for disease not yet incurred and not reasonably probable to occur. Ps may also recover for medical surveillance and emotional distress.

(4) **Dissent.** In light of current knowledge and experience, there is no valid reason why P's enhanced risk of cancer should not be considered an element of a present injury caused by D and to be compensated now.

Grayson v. Irvmar Realty Corp.

c) **Unproven talents can be a basis for loss of future earnings--Grayson v. Irvmar Realty Corp.,** 7 A.D.2d 436, 184 N.Y.S.2d 33 (1959).

   (1) **Facts.** Grayson (P), 21 years of age, slipped and fell on an inadequately-lighted sidewalk, fracturing her leg and suffering a loss of hearing. Although P had studied music and voice since childhood and was hopeful of a successful operatic career, she had never performed for pay. She had, however, participated in opera workshops and benefit performances. P's teachers testified that she had a bright future. P sought damages for

personal injuries and loss of earning capacity and was awarded $50,000. D appeals the judgment.

    (2) Issue. May damages for loss of earning capacity be awarded where the probability of future earnings is not based upon any prior actual engagement in the vocational earning of income?

    (3) Held. Yes. But judgment is reversed unless P will remit $30,000 of the verdict.

        (a) Damages for loss of future earning capacity may be awarded where there is no evidence of any prior vocational income.

        (b) This situation is similar to a wrongful death action where the earning potential of a child which has not yet been developed must be estimated.

        (c) There is a distinction between professional careers requiring a great deal of training and those also requiring rare talents. Musicians, actors, and athletes who exploit special talents are far less probable of success than students of professions which require no unusual gifts.

        (d) The jury must weigh the talents, training, and opportunities of the plaintiff against the improbabilities of success.

        (e) Any verdict in excess of $20,000 in this case would be excessive.

2) Adjustment to recovery. In the calculation of the recovery for the plaintiff, some states require that the recovery for future earnings be reduced to "present value." Some states also allow the plaintiff to introduce evidence of the need to increase the judgment due to expected future inflation.

c. Pain, suffering, and other intangible elements.

1) Past and future pain. In addition to recovery for medical expenses associated with personal injury, most states allow recovery for the pain and suffering arising out of that injury. Various methods are used to calculate the award for pain and suffering, but most courts allow recovery for past and future mental and physical pain and suffering.

2) Appellate review of award--Walters v. Hitchcock, 237 Kan. 31, 697 P.2d 847 (1985).

    a) Facts. Walters (P) consulted a physician because of a lump in her throat. Dr. Hitchcock (D) surgically removed a diseased portion of P's thyroid gland in what should have been minor surgery. After the surgery, P suffered swelling and infection in her neck. Subsequent surgery revealed that a portion of her esophagus tube had been cut away by mistake. After several operations, a portion of her colon was used to make an esophagus. No further remedy can be per-

Walters v.
Hitchcock

formed. P continues to suffer due to the fact that she cannot swallow normally, food clogs in her throat and must be manually forced down, and she cannot lie down flat since food will come back up the throat. P sued D for medical bills and pain and suffering for the medical malpractice. P recovered a judgment of $2 million, of which approximately $59,000 covered the actual medical bills. This leaves approximately $1.94 million for the pain and suffering. D appeals.

b) **Issue.** Was the jury award excessive?

c) **Held.** No. Judgment for P affirmed.

(1) During the closing arguments by the plaintiff's counsel, he asked the jury, "Who would sell their esophagus . . . ? I wouldn't." This question was not error by requiring the jury to decide what they personally would do. In addition, although the attorney stated his own opinion, this was not reversible error.

(2) The injury suffered by P is embarrassing, distasteful to persons around her, and a major obstacle to leading a normal life.

(3) The award is not so high as to "shock the conscience" of the judges.

d) **Dissent.** The pain and suffering award is out of proportion to the actual medical injury suffered. Such outrageous pain and suffering awards are a threat to the continued existence of the right to a jury trial in civil actions.

3) **Back injury.** Back injury cases, especially those associated with a herniated disc, are difficult cases to determine damages for. They may range from cases where there is some doubt as to whether any real injury occurred, to serious, disabling injuries. Substantial medical testimony may be necessary in such a case to prove the actual existence of the injury. In addition, proof that a particular accident was the actual cause of the claimed injury may be difficult.

McDougald v. Garber

a) **Nonpecuniary damages--McDougald v. Garber,** 73 N.Y.2d 246, 536 N.E.2d 372 (1989).

(1) **Facts.** When McDougald (P) was 31 years old, she underwent a Caesarean section and a tubal ligation. During the surgery, she was deprived of oxygen and suffered severe brain damage and was left in a permanent coma. P and her husband, suing derivatively, brought malpractice actions against the physician and the anesthesiologists (Ds). The jury found for P and awarded nonpecuniary damages of more than $9 million—of which $1 million was for conscious pain and suffering; $3.5 million for loss of the pleasures and pursuits of life; and the remainder for pecuniary damages, lost earnings, and custodial and nursing care. P's husband was awarded $1.5 million for loss of his wife's services. On Ds' post-trial motions, the judge reduced the total award to P to about $4.7 million, striking the award for future nursing care and reducing the separate awards for conscious pain and suffering and loss of the pleasures and pursuits of life to a single award of $2 million. Both parties appealed. The Appellate Division affirmed. Ds appeal.

(2) Issues.

    (a)   Is some degree of cognitive awareness a prerequisite to recovery for loss of enjoyment of life?

    (b)   Should a jury be instructed to consider and award damages for loss of enjoyment of life separately from damages for pain and suffering?

(3) Held. (a) Yes. (b) No. Order affirmed as modified; remanded for new trial on nonpecuniary damages.

    (a)   Damages for another's negligence are to compensate the victim, not punish the wrongdoer. Nonpecuniary losses are among those that can be compensated. If the injured party is unaware of the loss of enjoyment of life, the award of money damages serves no compensatory purpose.

    (b)   Although distinctions can be found between the concepts of pain and suffering and loss of enjoyment of life, we disagree that they must be treated separately to fully compensate P. Nonpecuniary damages cannot be calculated with analytical precision. To divide nonpecuniary injuries into component parts will amplify the distortion that already exists when human suffering is translated into dollars and cents.

(4) Dissent. Loss of enjoyment is an objective damage item, distinct from pain and suffering. The injured plaintiff's awareness should not be a necessary precondition to recovery. Pain and suffering compensate for physical and mental discomfort; loss of enjoyment compensates for limitations on the person's life.

b) Cause of back injury--Delaney v. The Empire Insurance Co., 469 So. 2d 1173 (La. App. 1985).

    Delaney v.
The Empire
Insurance Co.

(1) Facts. Delaney (P) and others were riding in an automobile when they were struck in the rear by a vehicle driven by Pickens (D). P had suffered a back injury at work during 1976, some four years prior to the accident. As a result of that back injury, he had back surgery performed and was permanently disabled. After the auto accident in 1980, problems still lingering from the original back injury were aggravated and serious pain resulted. P had additional surgery to correct this condition. P sued Pickens (D), Kimbel Trucking (D), and Empire Insurance Company (D) claiming, among other things, damages for his current back injury. Ds claim that P's back injury is the result of the previous work accident and should receive, at best, minimal recovery. The jury returned a verdict for P in the amount of $54,900, and Ds appeal.

(2) Issue. Was the jury award for the back injury excessive?

(3) Held. No. Judgment for plaintiff affirmed.

    (a)   Although some of P's condition was caused by the earlier accident, a substantial portion of the pain and disability was caused by the auto accident. P's condition may have existed prior to the accident, but the accident caused it to be a severe injury. The jury award for the back injury is, therefore, not excessive.

(4) **Comment.** It should be noted that this case reflects a well established principle. The defendant takes the plaintiff as he finds him. The defendant is liable for the aggravation of preexisting problems.

4) **Out-of-court determinations of damages; settlement.** In reality, most tort disputes are resolved by out-of-court settlements. Such settlements are binding on both the plaintiff and the defendant; *i.e.,* the plaintiff forfeits his legal claim against the defendant, and the defendant must pay the settlement amount. The advantage of settling is avoiding the costs and delays of litigation. The disadvantage is that the claim is compromised, so that the plaintiff gets less than he would have if he had won the litigation and the defendant pays more than he would have if he had won. The process of negotiating has been widely discussed in legal literature and some law schools offer special courses in negotiation.

2. **Wrongful Death.** At common law one could not sue for wrongful death recovery. Any action for damages caused by the wrongful act terminated upon the death of the plaintiff. The death itself was not actionable, but became a matter for the crown to handle. This common law tradition has been changed by statute in almost all of the modern jurisdictions. Two types of statutes exist which preserve actions against the defendant for his tortious actions. The first is a survival statute which prevents the abatement of existing causes of action due to the death of the injured party. Second, wrongful death statutes protect the loss to the estate of the deceased (*i.e.,* the recovery is for the benefit of the beneficiaries).

a. **Recovery measure of the loss to the beneficiaries.** The loss to the beneficiaries is covered by the wrongful death statutes, and the measure of damages is the amount of harm caused to the decedent's family.

b. **Recovery to the estate.** This recovery is based upon the pecuniary loss to the estate of the deceased rather than the loss to any particular individual beneficiary, and is usually based on a state survival statute. Thus, this recovery excludes recovery for loss of companionship or grief and mental suffering of the surviving family members. The loss that the estate of the decedent incurred is measured in three ways:

1) **Net earnings.** Net earnings entail the present value of the deceased's future earnings reduced to present value and then reduced by the normal expenditures that he would make for his own upkeep.

2) **Gross earnings.** Gross earnings is simply the present value of the future earnings of the decedent.

3) **Net accumulations.** The net accumulations approach is far more conservative than the prior two approaches, and entails the amount that the decedent might be expected to save from his earnings and thus would be left as part of the estate.

3. **Damage to Personal Property.**

   a. **Irreparable damage.** When the article of personal property is completely destroyed, the measure of damages is the difference between the fair market value before the injury and the market value after the injury, which would usually only be the salvage value.

   b. **Repairable damage.** Where the damage is repairable there are three approaches that the courts have used to determine the recovery:

      1) The first method basically follows the decrease in market value approach, and the cost of repairs is usually the determining factor.

      2) The second method holds that, although the cost of repairs is a main factor, also taken into consideration is any decrease in market value that is suffered even though the repairs are made.

      3) A third method of recovery is allowed when the loss suffered is a loss of use. Courts may allow damages equal to the rental value of the property or lost profits resulting from the loss of use.

B. PUNITIVE DAMAGES

Punitive damages are those that are received beyond compensatory damages and are used to punish the tortfeasor for his antisocial behavior. The courts and society also use punitive damages in those instances where the tortfeasor's actions are of an aggravated nature (*e.g.,* intentional, reckless, willful, or wanton) in order to make an example of the defendant so as to deter others from the same conduct.

1. **Elements.** In order to recover punitive damages, most courts require something more than mere negligence. Ordinarily, the plaintiff must prove willful or wanton conduct.

2. **Clear and Convincing Evidence Standard--Owens-Illinois, Inc. v. Zenobia,** 325 Md. 420, 601 A.2d 633 (1992).

   a. **Facts.** Zenobia (P) sued for damages alleged to have been caused by asbestos manufactured by various defendants, including Owens-Illinois (D). The jury awarded punitive damages D. The intermediate appellate court affirmed the award. D appealed. The Maryland Supreme Court issued a writ of certiorari.

   b. **Issue.** Is clear and convincing evidence the correct standard under Maryland law for awarding punitive damages in negligence and products liability cases?

   c. **Held.** Yes.

Owens-
Illinois, Inc.
v. Zenobia

1) Criticism of the concept of punitive damages in tort actions, where compensation for injured parties is the primary goal, is fueled because juries are provided with imprecise and uncertain characterizations of the type of conduct that will expose a defendant to a potential award of punitive damages.

2) In a nonintentional tort action, the trier of facts may not award punitive damages unless the plaintiff has established that the defendant's conduct was characterized by evil motive, intent to injure, ill will, or fraud, *i.e.*, "actual malice." In 1972, we allowed an award of punitive damages based upon implied malice. The court allowed the plaintiff to recover punitive damages based on a showing that the defendant was guilty of "gross negligence," *i.e.*, wanton or reckless disregard for human life. The gross negligence standard led to inconsistency and frustration of the purposes of punitive damages in nonintentional tort cases.

3) We adopt the standard that many states have established, *i.e.*, that a plaintiff must prove a defendant's malicious conduct by clear and convincing evidence before punitive damages can be considered.

d. **Concurrence and dissent.** I am opposed to excising from the standard adopted by the majority the concept of gross negligence. By changing both the burden of proof and the standard, the majority affects a greater percentage of deserving cases, heretofore eligible for punitive damage awards.

IX. LIABILITY INSURANCE

A. INTRODUCTION

Liability insurance started in 1880 to protect employers from actions by injured employees. Today, liability insurance is available to protect from almost any action within the range of tort law.

B. INSURANCE AS "REAL" DEFENDANT

The basic insurance policy consists of a contract between the insured and the insurer that, on the occurrence of certain events, the insurer will indemnify the insured for any loss that she might sustain. With this type of arrangement it is not difficult to see that when the insured is the defendant in a tort case which is covered by the terms of the insurance contract, the "real" defendant is not the insured but the insurer.

1. **Insurance Role in Settlement Negotiations--Crisci v. Security Insurance Co.,** 66 Cal. 2d 425, 426 P.2d 173, 58 Cal. Rptr. 13 (1967).

   Crisci v. Security Insurance Co.

   a. **Facts.** Mrs. Crisci (P) carried a $10,000 liability policy on an apartment building she owned. P's negligent maintenance resulted in injury to a tenant, who brought suit for $400,000 but prior to trial made a settlement offer of $9,000. P was willing to pay $2,500 of the demand but P's insurer, Security (D), refused to contribute more than $3,000, although D's attorney and claims manager believed a jury verdict of more than $100,000 was likely if the jury accepted the strong evidence that the tenant's injury resulted in psychosis. At trial a jury awarded the tenant $101,000 damages. D paid $10,000 and P, in trying to satisfy the remainder, was left indigent and physically and mentally ill. P sued D for failure to settle and was awarded $91,000 plus $25,000 for mental suffering. D appeals the judgment, claiming that any recovery could be based only on actual dishonesty.

   b. **Issue.** Must an insurer in considering a settlement offer do so as if its potential liability is the same as the insured's?

   c. **Held.** Yes. Judgment for P is affirmed.

      1) Insurance contracts contain an implied covenant of good faith that neither party will injure the right of the other to receive the benefits of the agreement.

      2) In determining whether to settle a claim where there is a risk of recovery beyond policy limits, the insurer must give the interests of the insured as much consideration as its own.

      3) The test in determining whether the insurer has considered the insured's interests is whether a prudent insurer without policy limits would have accepted the settlement offer.

      4) The insurer's belief that the tenant had no chance of prevailing on the psychosis issue was unreasonable.

5) An action such as this one sounds in both tort and contract and P may elect her remedy.

6) Where tortious conduct results in loss of property, the injured party may recover for mental suffering occasioned by the loss.

d. **Comment.** The traditional test for liability to the insurer for failure to settle or insisting on litigation is actual bad faith. This traditional test has slowly given way to the holding in the instant case, with some states even adopting a strict liability standard imposed on the insurer for any excess judgments that exceed a settlement offer that was within the scope of the policy.

Commercial Union Assurance Companies v. Safeway Stores, Inc.

2. **Insurer's Protection Not Object of the Bargain--Commercial Union Assurance Companies v. Safeway Stores, Inc.,** 164 Cal. Rptr. 709, 610 P.2d 1038 (1980).

a. **Facts.** Safeway (D) had liability insurance coverage as follows: (i) Travelers insured D for the first $50,000 of liability; (ii) D was self-insured for liability between $50,000 and $100,000; (iii) Commercial Union Assurance Companies (P) provided coverage to D in excess of $100,000 to $20 million. A judgment was recovered from D for $125,000. P was required to pay $25,000 of said judgment in order to discharge its liability under the excess insurance policy. P brought an action against D and Travelers to recover the $25,000, alleging D had an opportunity to settle for $50,000 or $60,000 and D had a duty to do so. D demurred on grounds of failure to state a claim. The court sustained. P failed to amend its complaint, which was dismissed. P appeals.

b. **Issue.** Does an insured owe a duty to its excess liability insurance carrier that requires it to accept a settlement offer below the threshold figure of the excess carrier's exposure where there is a substantial probability of liability in excess of that figure?

c. **Held.** No. Affirmed.

1) Any duty between the parties to an insurance contract arises from the nature of the bargain struck and the legitimate expectations of the parties that arise from the contract.

2) The object of an excess insurance policy is to provide additional resources should the insured's liability surpass a specified sum. The protection of the insurer's pecuniary interests is not the object of the bargain.

American Home Assurance Co. v. Hermann's Warehouse Corp.

3. **Voluntary Settlement Not Barred--American Home Assurance Co. v. Hermann's Warehouse Corp.,** 215 N.J. Super. 260, 521 A.2d 903 (1987).

a. **Facts.** American Home (P) issued a liability insurance policy to Hermann's Warehouse Corp. (D) with a $2 million limit and a $20,000 deductible for losses other than inventory shortages or unexplained disappearances, in which case the deductible was $40,000, to protect D's warehouse business. All Freight Trucking Company contacted D to deliver to D for storage cargo freight belonging to Adler. D advised All Freight it could not unload and take possession of the trailers that day. All Freight dropped off three trailers in D's yard and asked that D unload the next day. D permitted the trailers to remain in its yard, but did not unload or formally acknowledge their receipt. The next morning two trailers were missing. Adler instituted an action against D for the lost merchandise. P claims and D does not deny that Adler's potential recovery was $100,000. D turned the case over to P for defense. Pursuant to a policy provision, P settled the claim for $67,500 without D's consent and requested D to reimburse P for the deductible. D refused. P filed suit and summary judgment was granted for D. P appeals.

b. **Issue.** Is an insurer who settles an action against its insured for an amount within the policy limits entitled to recover the deductible from the insured?

c. **Held.** Yes. Reversed and remanded to determine applicable deductible amount.

1) The policy provision that provides P cannot be liable until D's liability is established by judgment or agreement does not bar voluntary settlements.

2) An insurance company may not be held liable or be held to lose its rights to recover a deductible on a claim of bad faith to its insured when it settles a case within the policy limits.

3) D could have had the jury trial it sought by defending Adler's action itself. However, since D sought the protection of its insurance, D had to accept the burdens that accompanied it.

X. COMPENSATION SYSTEMS

A. POLICIES OF TORT LIABILITY

Judicial opinions resolve controversies between two parties. Thus, the premises underlying tort law are seldom discussed in depth. There are several, sometimes conflicting, values involved:

(i)   Compensating individuals who have been injured; preserving individual choice.

(ii) Determining the social cost-benefit of a given policy.

(iii) The emphasis on value choice.

(iv) The emphasis on reason to elucidate the premises underlying choices.

For example, should the legal system force all persons to be vaccinated for polio? Even if there is some chance that a few will die from the vaccination? Should individual choice be allowed if the benefit to society is greater than the cost of loss of some individuals?

B. OBJECTIVES OF THE TORT SYSTEM

There are many possible compensation systems: negligence; negligence plus liability insurance; strict liability; strict liability plus insurance, etc. Whatever system is employed, it should fulfill the following objectives:

(i)   Be equitable (between those who receive benefits and those who bear the burden; among beneficiaries; and among the cost-bearers).

(ii)   Contribute to the wise allocation of human and economic resources.

(iii) Compensate promptly.

(iv)   Be reliable.

(v)   Distribute losses rather than leave them on single individuals.

(vi)   Be efficient.

(vii) Deter risky conduct.

(viii) Minimize fraud.

Each compensation system meets these objectives to some extent or other. For example, negligence law is founded on the notion of compensation based on fault. But fault is objective. Thus, the moral basis of liability is eroded. Objectification may be defended in that it reduces cost and the error in administering the system. Also, fault is supported by commonly shared values of people. Possibly the system deters risky conduct.

C. COMPENSATION FOR INJURED EMPLOYEES

Employer liability for employees injured at work was the field in which liability insurance first developed. Shortly thereafter, legislation was passed (now every state has such a system) to provide employer contributions to a state fund to compensate injured employees, regardless of fault (known as "worker's compensation"). Benefits are limited in amount and duration. In most states employers can alternatively insure against these risks, or employees may choose to be governed by traditional fault principles.

1. **Worker's Compensation.** Worker's compensation covers accidents "arising out of and in the course of employment." Typically worker's compensation is the *sole* remedy an employee has against his employer. Further, accidents occurring in commuting to and from work are not covered.

   a. **Application--Shaw's Case,** 247 Mass. 157, 141 N.E. 858 (1923).   Shaw's Case

   1) **Facts.** In 1920 Shaw (P) was injured while working for a hotel for $24 per week. The hotel's insurer agreed to pay him $16 for the period of his total incapacity. The insurer decreased the payments to $4 on January 21, 1922, when P went back to work and performed some but not all of his prior duties, because the hotel resumed paying P his salary. Furthermore, before P's return to work, the hotel had made weekly payments to P of $8 to provide him with his full income prior to the accident. Nevertheless, a member of the Industrial Accident Board ruled that P was still incapacitated and entitled to the $16 per week worker's compensation. The insurer appeals.

   2) **Issues.**

      a) Is a worker's compensation award enforceable so long as the worker remains incapacitated, even though he returns to work and receives his previous salary?

      b) Is a worker's compensation award enforceable even though the employer contributes gratuitously to the employee's income to bring it up to what it was prior to the accident?

   3) **Held.** a) No. b) Yes. Order of the Board reversed.

      a) The industrial compensation statute awards compensation for loss of earning capacity caused by injury, but the insurer cannot be held for the full amount awarded after the employee returns to work and earns his prior wages.

      b) On the other hand, the finding of the Board that P is entitled to the statutory award despite the employer's gratuitous contribution is sustained. As long as P was incapacitated and did not work, he was entitled to receive the statutory award of $16 per week even though his employer paid him an extra $8 per week as a gratuity.

D. COMPENSATION OF AUTOMOBILE ACCIDENT VICTIMS

1. **Present "Third Party" Liability Insurance System.** At present, most car owners carry insurance against whatever liability they may incur to third parties in connection with the operation of their vehicles (hence, known as "third party" insurance). Such insurance is also carried for homeowners' liability, products liability and malpractice; and the same principles apply.

2. **"No Fault" Auto Insurance.** A number of states have adopted substantial reforms in the handling of auto accident claims through so-called "no fault" insurance plans.

   a. **Advantages of adopting "no fault" plans.** Eliminating "fault" as the basis for liability in auto accident cases alleviates the following objectionable features of negligence actions:

      1) **"All or nothing" recoveries.** The plaintiff gets nothing unless she can convince the jury that the defendant was "at fault"; likewise, where the defendant can convince the jury that the plaintiff was contributorily negligent or had assumed the risk (assuming no comparative negligence standard).

      2) **Delays and expenses of litigation.** Proving "fault" requires litigation with attendant expenses and attorney's fees for both parties. Until a judgment is returned (or settlement made), an injured plaintiff gets nothing (although it is in the interim that he needs help the most), and the increasing burden of such litigation has congested court calendars to the extent that plaintiffs frequently have to wait years for a trial.

      3) **Inaccurate compensation.** There has also been concern that the settlement process has led to the overcompensation of small cases and the undercompensation of large cases.

      4) **Cost of insurance.** Insurance premiums have soared due to the costs of litigation and high verdicts.

   b. **Operation of proposed "no fault" plans.** Although the plans enacted vary considerably, the following are the essential provisions:

      1) **Mandatory insurance.** All car owners are required to obtain (and keep in effect) insurance covering claims arising out of the operation of their cars; failure to do so usually results in forfeiture of auto registration and/or drivers' licenses. This policy would cover both liability and no-fault claims.

      2) **Scope of coverage.** The insurance extends to all claims arising out of operation of any motor vehicle, without regard to fault.

         a) Generally, this includes claims allowed under traditional tort concepts, as well as certain claims not presently allowed—*e.g.*, claims by an injured "guest" in an auto and by the driver who hurts himself by his own fault.

b) But the insurance does *not* apply to claims arising out of defects in the vehicle itself (*i.e.*, products liability claims).

3) **Claims handled on "first party" basis.** Any driver or rider injured in an auto accident would make a claim against his or her own insurer (*i.e.*, the policy covering the car the injured party was riding in), so that in the typical two-car crash, the occupants of each car would claim against the insurance covering that car.

   a) In comparison, under the present "third party" insurance system, the injured party usually makes a claim against the insurer of the other car.

   b) The "third party" procedure would be retained only where the accident is not covered by first party insurance; *e.g.*, a pedestrian injured by an auto would still make claim against the insurer covering the car that struck her. (Under a few plans, however, if the pedestrian owned a car, she would claim against her own insurer.)

   c) Since "fault" would be immaterial, the claims procedure is relatively simple; any disagreement between the policyholder and his insurance company as to the amount recoverable (below) is subject to arbitration.

4) **Damages recoverable.** None of the major plans provide insurance coverage for pain and suffering or disfigurement. Coverage is limited to economic losses (lost wages, medical bills, etc.). However, the plans vary considerably as to the amount of such coverage:

   a) Under the Massachusetts statute, the limit is $2,000.

   b) Under the New York statute, the limit is $50,000, which might include recovery of *all* medical losses without limit and up to $800 per month in lost earnings for up to 36 months.

c. **Impact of "no fault" plans.**

1) **Curtailment of tort litigation.** The plans vary concerning the extent to which traditional negligence actions (with traditional "fault" principles) would still be permitted:

   a) **"Pure" no fault.** A few proposals would abolish tort actions altogether (*e.g.*, the American Insurance Association proposal). However, no state has adopted such a plan.

   b) **"Partial" no fault.** All existing plans currently allow at least certain actions.

      (1) Under some plans, tort actions can still be maintained for all but relatively minor cases; *e.g.*, under the Massachusetts statute, the plaintiff can sue for pain and suffering whenever the medical expenses exceed $500, or where any permanent or disabling injury (*e.g.*, bone fracture) is involved.

(2) Under other plans, however, only severe cases could ever be pursued in court. Thus, under one plan, a tort action could be maintained for economic losses not covered by the injured party's own insurance, and for general damages in excess of $5,000, but *only if* the accident caused death, permanent injury or disfigurement, or inability to work for more than six consecutive months.

E. COMPENSATION FOR VICTIMS OF MEDICAL ACCIDENTS

1. **The Crisis.** Throughout the 1970s and 1980s, the medical profession and liability insurers for the medical profession have claimed that there is a major crisis in medical malpractice. There have been threats and fears that certain doctors or specialists would refuse to practice medicine. Due to the inability to obtain clear facts and statistics, it is impossible to determine the true nature of the crisis.

2. **Reaction to the Crisis.** Although most states have passed some type of legislation in reaction to the crisis, there has been no uniform or systematic approach to dealing with it. Some common features of such legislation have included absolute caps on the amount of recovery, abolition of the collateral source rule, and attempts to set up administrative review of claims.

F. UNIVERSAL NO FAULT

In 1972, New Zealand began a program of universal no fault coverage. The program is designed to provide coverage of accident cost, including lost wages and medical expenses, for most citizens of the country. In addition, traditional tort actions have been abolished.

XI. DIGNITARY WRONGS

A. INTRODUCTION

The intentional torts include the traditional causes of action of (i) assault; (ii) battery; and (iii) false imprisonment, along with some relatively newer torts like (iv) interference with peace of mind, and (v) violation of civil rights. This section will also consider some variations on nonconsensual privileges, which include defense of the person and protection of property.

B. PRIMA FACIE CASE

1. **Assault.** The basic elements of an assault case are as follows:

    a. **Act by the defendant.** This element of the tort is satisfied by some volitional, external movement of the defendant. This would preclude an unconscious act or a movement made by a person under the influence of drugs. This requirement also eliminates any purely reflex action by the defendant.

        1) **Words alone are usually not sufficient.** There must be an apprehension of immediate, offensive touching by the plaintiff before there can be an assault. Words alone usually will not be sufficient to create the apprehension of the imminent touching; *i.e.,* unless there is some act or action which indicates the present ability and intention to do personal violence, there is no assault.

    b. **Intent.** The defendant must have intended to inflict a harm on the plaintiff or put him in fear of an immediate harmful or offensive touching. This can be established under "transfer of intent theory" (*i.e.,* A intends the act which he does, also intending to injure B, but C is injured instead; the intent to injure B is transferred to C).

    c. **Apprehension.** The actions of the defendant must actually put the plaintiff in apprehension of an imminent harmful or offensive touching. The standard laid down for this test is not subjective (was the plaintiff apprehensive?) but is based on what a reasonable person in the plaintiff's shoes might have thought (*i.e.,* would a reasonable person have been apprehensive?).

    d. **Causation.** The plaintiff's apprehension must have been caused by the actions of the defendant.

    e. **Damages.** The plaintiff must be able to establish some form of damages. (*See* 2., below).

    f. **Proving elements--Read v. Coker,** 13 C.B. 850, 138 Eng. Rep. 1437 (1853).

        1) **Facts.** Read (P) worked in Coker's (D's) shop. D fired P, but several days later P returned and refused to leave. D got several of his employees, who gathered around P and said they would

"break his neck" if he did not leave. P sued D for damages and received a judgment in the lower court. D appeals.

2) **Issue.** Has P proved a cause of action for assault?

3) **Held.** Yes. Judgment affirmed.

   a) There was an assault since the facts showed a threat of violence, the intent to assault, and the present ability to carry out the violence.

4) **Comment.** Counsel for D argued that there was no assault since words alone cannot constitute that tort. In this case, counsel argued, there was no attempt to carry out the words and, therefore, no action would lie.

Beach v.
Hancock

g. **Necessity for present ability to harm--Beach v. Hancock,** 27 N.H. 223 (1853).

1) **Facts.** P and D had been arguing when D stepped into his office and brought out a gun, which he aimed at P in a threatening manner, and pulled the trigger twice. The gun was not loaded but P did not know whether it was or not. P sued D for assault. The trial court held that pointing a gun (in an angry manner) at a person who did not know if it was loaded is an assault. The court also held that the jury could consider the effect which an award of trivial damages would have in encouraging breaches of the peace. D appeals.

2) **Issue.** Can there be an assault where there is no present ability to harm?

3) **Held.** Yes. Judgment for P affirmed.

   a) An assault may be committed where there is no present ability to harm.

   b) People have a right to live in society without being put in fear of personal harm.

   c) It is reasonable for a person to fear personal injury when a pistol which he does not know to be unloaded is pointed at him in an angry manner.

   d) A finding of trivial damages would lead the ill-disposed to consider an assault as a thing to be committed with impunity. This was a proper consideration for the jury in awarding damages.

4) **Comment.** There need not be actual present ability to harm as long as there is an *apparent* present ability to harm.

2. **Battery.** The elements necessary to establish the tort of battery are as follows:

a. **Act by the defendant.** Like an action for assault, there must be a volitional act by the defendant which causes the plaintiff's injury.

b. **Intent.** The act done by the defendant must have been done with the requisite intent to commit the harmful or offensive touching.

  1) **Test.** The general test used to determine intent is whether the defendant acted with the desire to cause, or substantially knew that his actions would cause, harm or offense. Since this test is founded on the defendant's desire or what he believed would be the consequences of his actions, the test is entirely subjective.

c. **Harmful or offensive touching.** The action of the defendant must result in the infliction of a harmful or offensive touching to the plaintiff or to something that is so closely associated with the plaintiff as to be tantamount to touching of the plaintiff. A harmful touching is one that inflicts any pain or injury, while an offensive touching is one that offends a reasonable person's sense of personal dignity.

d. **Causation.** The action of the defendant must be the legal cause of or be the force that puts in motion the force that results in the plaintiff's injury.

e. **Damages.** An award of damages is based on the commission of a harmful or offensive touching. The plaintiff can receive compensatory damages for all damages directly caused by the touching as well as for all consequential damages. Punitive damages are also recoverable when it appears that the defendant was motivated to intentionally harm the plaintiff.

f. **Offensive touching--Fisher v. Carrousel Motor Hotel,** 424 S.W.2d 627 (Tex. 1967).

  1) **Facts.** Fisher (P), a black, attended a meeting and buffet luncheon at D's hotel. At the luncheon, as P was about to be served, D's employee grabbed the plate out of P's hand and shouted that he could not be served. Although the employee never touched P, P brought suit for battery. At trial P did not testify that he feared injury but only that he was highly embarrassed. The trial court awarded P $400 actual damages and $500 exemplary damages based on the maliciousness of the employee's conduct. The trial judge entered judgment n.o.v. for D and an appellate court affirmed. P appeals.

  2) **Issues.**

   a) Can there be a battery when there is no physical contact and no fear thereof?

   b) May an employer be held responsible for the malicious act of a manager employed by him?

  3) **Held.** a) Yes. b) Yes. Judgment for D as to both awards reversed.

   a) The fear of physical contact necessary for an assault is not necessary for a battery. An action for battery may be maintained where there is no assault.

b) Actual physical contact is not necessary to constitute a battery as long as there is contact with clothing or an object closely identified with the body.

c) Damages for mental suffering are recoverable without a showing of physical injury in the case of a willful touching because the basis of the action is the intentional invasion of the person, not the harm.

d) D is liable for exemplary damages because the employee was a manager and his actions were in the scope of his employment.

4) Comment. The court here found the requisite physical contact as being the grabbing of the plate. The majority of courts do not require a touching of the plaintiff's body for there to be an assault.

McCracken v. Sloan

g. No battery from second-hand smoke--McCracken v. Sloan, 252 S.E.2d 250 (N.C. 1979).

1) Facts. A postal worker (P), who had a documented history of being allergic to tobacco smoke, had complained of and distributed literature in the post office regarding the dangers of smoking. On two occasions, when P was in his employer's (D's) office discussing his application for sick leave for his allergic condition, D smoked a cigar in P's presence. P filed suit, claiming D twice committed a battery on him. After a pretrial conference where the parties stipulated what the evidence most favorable to P would be, the trial court dismissed the case. P appeals.

2) Issue. Where an employer smokes in the presence of an employee who has made known his allergy to tobacco smoke, is there sufficient evidence to support a claim by the employee for assault and battery?

3) Held. No. Affirmed.

a) An action for assault protects the interest in freedom from apprehension of a harmful or offensive contact with the person.

b) An action for battery protects the interest in freedom from intentional and unpermitted contacts with the plaintiff's person.

c) The absence of the plaintiff's consent to the contact, not the hostile intent of the defendant, is the basis of an action for battery.

d) Smelling smoke from a cigar smoked by a person in his own office would usually be considered an innocuous and generally permitted contact of the nature of those contacts customary and reasonably necessary to the common intercourse of life. Here, however, P had made his allergy known.

e) There is no evidence P suffered any physical illness from inhaling D's smoke, although he did experience some mental distress. However, we find this is not enough evidence to support a claim for assault or battery. Apprehension of smelling or inhaling smoke is an apprehension of a touching that must be endured in a crowded world.

3. **False Imprisonment.** False imprisonment is the total obstruction and detention of the plaintiff, of which he is aware, within boundaries, for any length of time, with intent by the defendant to obstruct or detain the plaintiff or another, and without privilege or consent. The plaintiff's prima facie case includes the following elements: (i) act by the defendant; (ii) obstruction or detention of the plaintiff; (iii) intent; and (iv) causal relationship. For liability to attach, there must be an absence of consent and privilege.

   a. **Obstruction or detention of plaintiff.**

      1) **No escape.** It is not necessary that the plaintiff be totally imprisoned to support an action for false imprisonment. False imprisonment will arise if there is no "reasonable avenue of exit" available to the plaintiff. An exit is not "reasonable" if it: (i) is unknown to the plaintiff, or (ii) requires the plaintiff to take risks to escape, is dangerous, or is simply uncomfortable.

      2) **Exclusion.** Generally, it is not sufficient that the plaintiff is not allowed to go where he wishes if he can go somewhere else. Under certain circumstances an exclusion (as from one's home) may be sufficient. Further, it is sufficient for a finding of false imprisonment that the plaintiff, allowed to move freely about several rooms in a house, is restrained from leaving the house, without consent or privilege.

      3) **Knowledge of the obstruction or detention.**

         a) **Submission of will.** Obstruction or detention for purposes of false imprisonment must be against the will of the one restrained. Therefore, the majority holds that if there is no knowledge on the part of the plaintiff at the time of his detention, there can be no submission of his will and hence no false imprisonment. The fact that the plaintiff makes no resistance does not necessarily negate the element of submission against his will.

         b) **Restatement exception.** The Restatement (Second) of Torts, section 42, allows recovery for false imprisonment where there is (i) knowledge of imprisonment, or (ii) damage resulting from the imprisonment, even though no knowledge.

      4) **Means of obstruction or detention.** The means of obstructing or detaining the plaintiff may be by conduct, words, force, threats, or refusal to permit egress.

         a) **Apparent physical barriers.** Locking the plaintiff in a room where there is another concealed and unlocked door will still constitute confinement of the plaintiff. As indicated previously, the plaintiff must know of the available exit.

         b) **Submission where plaintiff has the power to break confinement.** If the plaintiff, who is bigger and stronger than the defendant and has the power to break the physical force or restraint placed upon him by the defendant, instead physically submits to the unlawful detention, the defendant nonetheless is chargeable with false imprisonment.

    c)   **Great inconvenience.** Great inconvenience is sufficient "total restraint" of freedom of movement. False imprisonment may also arise from duress of person or property, but threats of duress in the future are not sufficient.

    d)   **Moral pressure.** A plaintiff's self-imposed moral pressure only to clear herself, or threats to have the plaintiff arrested if she leaves, are not sufficient for false imprisonment.

    e)   **Absence of physical force--Whittaker v. Sanford,** 110 Me. 77, 85 A. 399 (1912).

        (1)   **Facts.** D, the leader of a religious sect with colonies in Maine and Syria, agreed to transport P, who wanted to quit the sect, from Syria to Maine in the sect's yacht. D further agreed that P and her children would be free to leave at any time. Upon arriving in Maine, D refused to allow P to be taken ashore in the ship's rowboat; nevertheless, P was allowed all of the liberties of the yacht and was taken ashore to visit neighboring islands. P was eventually released under a writ of habeas corpus. P sued for false imprisonment and was awarded a verdict of $1,100. D appeals.

        (2)   **Issue.** In an action for false imprisonment, is it required that the plaintiff be restrained by the exertion of physical force?

        (3)   **Held.** No. Judgment for P affirmed but P required to remit all but $500 damages.

            (a)   To constitute false imprisonment, there must be actual physical restraint but not necessarily involving physical force.

            (b)   If one should turn a key in a door and thereby prevent someone from leaving, that would be false imprisonment.

            (c)   When one who is in control of a vessel within rowing distance of shore, who had agreed that his guest would be free to leave, refuses the use of the rowboat, he turns the key.

            (d)   Inasmuch as P was not kept in close confinement but was allowed the freedom of the yacht, and suffered none of the humiliation generally associated with false imprisonment, the damages are excessive.

5)   **Total restraint required--Rougeau v. Firestone Tire & Rubber Co.,** 274 So. 2d 454 (La. App. 1973).

    a)   **Facts.** Rougeau (P) was a guard at Firestone's (D's) plant. During P's shift two lawn mowers were stolen. D's corporate security manager and two others went to P's home to search it but P refused to allow it on advice from his attorney. P and D's agent then returned to the plant, where P was asked to wait in the guardhouse. Two guards were instructed not to allow P to leave; however, they testified that they did not consider P to be a prisoner. P was allowed to leave the guardhouse (within 30 minutes of being placed there) when he fell ill. P sued for false imprisonment but was denied recovery. P appeals.

- b) **Issue.** Was P falsely imprisoned?

- c) **Held.** No. Judgment for D affirmed.

  - (1) Although false imprisonment is the intentional confinement of another, P was not imprisoned because he was not totally restrained. Furthermore, P never told anyone that he did not want to stay in the guardhouse, thus showing implied consent.

6) **Words as a restraint.** Words can restrain a person if he fears disregarding them, even if there is no physical restraint.

7) **Escape.** It is generally held that false imprisonment invites escape and that the plaintiff may recover for any injuries sustained in an escape attempt.

b. **Intent.** Intent of the defendant to obstruct or detain the plaintiff or another is a required element of false imprisonment. However, as noted, omission to carry out one's duty, thereby causing confinement, will give rise to false imprisonment. Hostile or malicious intent is not required.

1) **Transferred intent.** Also, the doctrine of transferred intent applies; *e.g.,* if the defendant intends to detain butcher A in a frozen locker, and thinking A is inside, shuts the door on B, the defendant is subject to an action by B for false imprisonment.

c. **Causal relationship.** There must be a causal relationship between the act or omission of the defendant and the obstruction or detention of the plaintiff.

d. **Consent or privilege.** A defendant's act which was the legal cause of the false imprisonment of the plaintiff must have been without consent or privilege in order for liability to attach.

1) **Privilege--Sindle v. New York City Transit Authority,** 33 N.Y.2d 293, 307 N.E.2d 245 (1973).

   Sindle v. New York City Transit Authority

   - a) **Facts.** Sindle (P) was a passenger on a school bus driven by Transit's (D's) employee. It was the last day of school and some of the students defaced the bus during their ride home. The driver, learning of the damage, departed from the normal route and announced that he was taking the children to the police station. Although there was not evidence that he participated in the vandalism, P jumped from one of the rear windows as the bus turned a corner and received severe injuries when he fell under the rear wheels of the bus. P brought suit for false imprisonment and was awarded more than $80,000 for mental anguish, physical injuries, and medical expenses. D appeals based on the trial court's refusal to allow D to amend its answer to plead the defense of justification and the court's exclusion of all evidence of justification.

**b)	Issues.**

(1)	Is justification a legal defense to false imprisonment?

(2)	Does one wrongfully imprisoned have a duty of reasonable care for his own safety in his attempts to extricate himself?

**c)	Held.** (1) Yes. (2) Yes. Judgment for P reversed and remanded for new trial.

(1)	A person may reasonably restrain another in order to protect property in his custody. Additionally, a bus driver, who is entrusted with the care of his passengers and the custody of public property, has a duty to the care and safety of both. The bus driver's actions, if reasonable, would justify the imprisonment.

(2)	If one falsely imprisoned places himself in a perilous situation in attempting to extricate himself, recovery for subsequent injuries is barred. Upon retrial, if the trier finds false imprisonment, it must further determine whether P acted unreasonably in jumping from the window.

Coblyn v.
Kennedy's,
Inc.

**2)	Lack of reasonable grounds--Coblyn v. Kennedy's, Inc.,** 359 Mass. 319, 268 N.E.2d 860 (1971).

**a)	Facts.** Coblyn (P), 70 years old and 5 feet, 4 inches tall, went to the second floor of Kennedy's (D's) store to buy a sport coat. In having it fitted he removed an ascot which he had worn and placed it in his pocket. After the fitting P walked down to the first floor and to one of the store exits, where he paused to replace the ascot around his neck. As he did so, two of D's employees approached him and asked where he had obtained the scarf. One of them grabbed P by the arm and said that he had better see the manager. P complied. The sport coat sales clerk confirmed that the scarf was P's, but then P suffered a myocardial infarction. P sued for false imprisonment and was awarded $12,500 damages. D appeals, contending that there had been no imprisonment and that the detention was justified by a shoplifting statute which allows detentions of reasonable length where there are reasonable grounds to believe that larceny is being committed.

**b)	Issues.**

(1)	Does the demonstration of physical power which apparently can only be avoided by submission constitute imprisonment?

(2)	May a merchant detain a person without reasonable grounds for belief that the person had shoplifted?

**c)	Held.** (1) Yes. (2) No. Judgment for P affirmed.

(1)	Any genuine restraint is sufficient to constitute an imprisonment. Here, the 70-year-old plaintiff could do nothing other than comply with the "request" of D's employees.

(2) The Massachusetts statute provides that a merchant may detain a person if there are reasonable grounds to believe that the person was attempting to shoplift and if the detention is effected in a reasonable manner and for a reasonable time.

(3) "Reasonable grounds" is an objective standard and means the same thing as "probable cause."

(4) While D's employees may have had an honest suspicion, there was nothing in P's conduct to justify a reasonably prudent person in believing that P was a shoplifter.

e. **Damages.** When liability is established, a plaintiff may recover damages from the defendant even though no special damages (*e.g.,* injuries, loss of earnings) are proved. If special damages are proved, they are of course recoverable. Also note that any injuries sustained in an escape attempt are recoverable.

C. INTENTIONAL INFLICTION OF MENTAL DISTRESS

1. **Introduction.** The cause of action for mental distress is characterized by (i) physical injury or severe mental suffering by the plaintiff resulting from emotional disturbance (without physical impact), (ii) caused by highly aggravated words or acts of the defendant, (iii) done with intent to cause mental suffering or with knowledge or belief on the part of the defendant that such suffering is substantially certain to result from such words or acts (or, in most jurisdictions, with recklessness as to this result).

   a. The words or acts must be severe, exceeding all socially acceptable standards, and must cause injury of a serious kind to the plaintiff.

   b. Today, however, there seems to be a move away from the requirement that there must be some physical injury manifestations from the emotional disturbance caused by the defendant. On the other hand, the law recognizes that humans must occasionally "blow off steam," and ordinarily defendants are not liable for mere insults that cause emotional disturbance to hypersensitive persons.

   c. Intentional infliction of mental distress differs from negligent infliction of mental disturbance in that it is done with a more culpable state of mind.

2. **Traditional Objections to Mental Distress as a Basis of Tort Liability.** Mental distress was recognized as an element of damages in early assault cases. However, it was not until relatively recent times (about the turn of the century) that the intentional infliction of mental distress, without any other accompanying tort (such as assault), gained recognition as a separate basis for finding tort liability. The relatively slow development of the law to recognize the plaintiff's peace of mind as a legally protected interest has been due to the following objections:

(i)   The character of the injury suffered in mental distress is difficult to determine; you cannot see mental anguish whereas it is easy to see a broken arm, an unlawful restraint, etc.

(ii)   The damages resulting from mental distress are of a subtle and speculative nature (peculiar, variable, hard to assess, etc.).

(iii)   Mental distress lends itself to fictitious claims.

(iv)   Recognition of the basis of liability will open up a flood of litigation.

(v)   Permitting recovery for mental distress will encourage perjury, through either overstating the facts or fabrication.

Notwithstanding the objections cited above, the law seems to be moving toward an expansion of the circumstances under which liability for the infliction of mental distress will be found.

State Rubbish
Collectors
Association v.
Siliznoff

3. **Physical Injury Requirement--State Rubbish Collectors Association v. Siliznoff,** 38 Cal. 2d 330, 240 P.2d 282 (1952).

a. **Facts.** Siliznoff (D), through his father-in-law, contracted to collect rubbish from the Acme Brewing Co. Because D was not a member of the Rubbish Collectors Association (P), members of the association threatened to beat him up and burn his truck unless he joined and paid the prior collector of Acme's rubbish a fee for taking over the account. The threats caused D to suffer physical illness and emotional distress. He signed promissory notes to pay the prior collector, through the association, but did not honor them. The association brought suit to collect on the notes. D countersued for intentional infliction of emotional distress and for exemplary damages. The jury awarded D $1,250 general and special damages and $7,500 exemplary damages. The trial court denied a motion for new trial subject to reduction of the exemplary damages to $5,000. P appeals, contending that the threats did not constitute an assault because they related to future action that might take place.

b. **Issue.** Is a cause of action established when one, in the absence of any privilege, intentionally subjects another to the mental suffering incident to serious threats to his physical well-being, whether or not the threats constitute a technical assault?

c. **Held.** Yes. Judgment for D affirmed.

1) In the past the law has denied recovery for intentionally inflicted emotional distress unless it manifested itself in a physical injury.

2) In many cases mental suffering constitutes the major element of damages. It is anomalous to deny recovery because the intentional misconduct did not produce physical injury.

3) While it may be contended that allowing recovery in the absence of physical injury will open the door to unfounded claims, this is not so. The proof that suffering occurred is in the extent of the defendant's misconduct.

4) Actions for intentional infliction of emotional distress are allowed even in the absence of physical injuries.

d. **Comment.** This case illustrates the modern view that physical injury is no longer required. Note, however, that outrageous conduct is required.

4. **Solicitation to Sexual Intercourse with Aggravated Circumstances--Samms v. Eccles,** 11 Utah 2d 289, 358 P.2d 344 (1961).

Samms v. Eccles

a. **Facts.** Samms (P) sought to recover actual and punitive damages from Eccles (D) for injury P claims to have suffered because D persistently telephoned her for several months at various hours, soliciting P to have illicit sexual relations with him. P claims D came to her home on one occasion and indecently exposed his person. P claimed she suffered great anxiety, fear for her personal safety, and severe emotional distress. After a pretrial hearing, the trial court dismissed P's action. P appeals.

b. **Issue.** May a plaintiff recover against a defendant for emotional distress resulting from the defendant's conduct even if such conduct is not the result of a recognized tort?

c. **Held.** Yes. Reversed.

1) Courts have historically been reluctant to allow recovery for emotional distress unless such distress was suffered as a result of some other overt tort.

2) We feel an action for severe emotional distress should be recognized, though not accompanied by physical injury, where the defendant intentionally engaged in some conduct toward the plaintiff: (i) with the purpose of inflicting emotional distress, or (ii) where any reasonable person would have known that such would result; and his actions are of such a nature as to be considered outrageous and intolerable in that they offend against the generally accepted standards of decency and morality.

5. **Racial Slur--Alcorn v. Anbro Engineering, Inc.,** 2 Cal. 3d 493, 468 P.2d 216, 86 Cal. Rptr. 88 (1970).

Alcorn v. Anbro Engineering, Inc.

a. **Facts.** Alcorn (P) was employed as a truck driver by Anbro Engineering (D). P, in his capacity as shop steward for the Teamsters' Union, informed his field superintendent that P had advised another employee he should not drive a truck to the job site since he was not a Teamster. P was allegedly not rude or otherwise violative of his duties as an employee. The superintendent shouted at P in a violent and insolent manner, calling P a "nigger" and firing P. D's secretary ratified the firing on behalf of D. P was reinstated through grievance and arbitration procedures and received back pay. P filed suit, alleging intentional infliction of emotional distress, alleging African-Americans are particularly susceptible to conduct such as D's. P's complaint was dismissed after D's demurrer was sustained without leave to amend. P appeals.

b. **Issue.** Has P stated a cause of action upon which relief may be granted?

c. **Held.** Yes. Reversed.

    1)   The courts of this state have acknowledged the right to recover for emotional distress unaccompanied by physical injury where there has been extreme and outrageous intentional invasion of one's mental and emotional tranquility.

    2)   Here, P has alleged the following circumstances: D was (i) in a position of authority; (ii) aware of P's particular susceptibility; and (iii) intentionally humiliated P, insulted P's race, ignored P's union status, and terminated P—all without just cause or provocation. These facts could reasonably lead a jury to conclude that D's conduct was sufficiently extreme and outrageous to result in injury.

Logan v. Sears, Roebuck & Co.

6. **Trivial Insult--Logan v. Sears, Roebuck & Co.,** 466 So. 2d 121 (Ala. 1985).

    a. **Facts.** When Sears's (D's) employee telephoned P to inquire about P's charge account payment, while P was looking for his checkbook, he heard the employee tell someone on her end of the line "this guy is as queer as a three dollar bill." No one on P's end of the line, other than P, heard the statement. P brought suit based on outrage and invasion of privacy. D moved for and was granted summary judgment. P appeals.

    b. **Issue.** Was the statement sufficient to support a claim of outrage or invasion of privacy?

    c. **Held.** No. Affirmed.

        1)   While there is a recognized cause of action in Alabama based on tort of outrage, it does not recognize recovery for "mere insults, indignities, threats, annoyances, petty oppressions, or other trivialities." The principle applies only to unprivileged, intentional, or reckless conduct of an extreme and outrageous nature that causes severe emotional distress.

        2)   Extreme and outrageous conduct is that which goes beyond all possible bounds of decency and is atrocious and utterly intolerable in a civilized society.

        3)   The term "queer" has been used to describe homosexuals for a long time. Since P is admittedly a homosexual, we do not think that being described as "queer" should cause him shame or humiliation. It is a relatively trivial insult for which the law grants no relief.

Ford v. Revlon, Inc.

7. **Sexual Harassment--Ford v. Revlon, Inc.,** 153 Ariz. 38, 734 P.2d 580 (1987).

    a. **Facts.** Ford (P) worked as a buyer for Revlon (D). She had worked for D for approximately six years when a new supervisor was assigned to her. The new supervisor began a systematic program of sexual harassment. P notified D of the harassment, but D did nothing for over a year. D ultimately fired the supervisor. P sued D for, among other things, intentional infliction of emotional distress. The trial court found for P, but the court of appeals reversed. P appeals.

    b.   **Issue.** Can an employer be liable for the emotional distress caused by an agent?

    c.   **Held.** Yes. Judgment for P reinstated.

        1)   The employer was liable for the intentional infliction of emotional distress. D acted recklessly, in an extreme and outrageous manner, and this caused the emotional distress.

        2)   Knowing of the events, D should have acted much quicker.

        3)   The action is not covered by worker's compensation provisions. It was not an accident under the statute. Hence, recovery in tort is permitted.

D. CIVIL RIGHTS

    1.   **Background.** Many actions based on dignitary harms may overlap between basic tort claims and claims of civil rights violations. Most modern civil rights actions are based upon statutes passed immediately following the Civil War. These statutes remained unused until fairly recently. They are now being used to seek damages when the violation of constitutional rights leads to injury.

    2.   **Basic Elements.** The modern claim for violation of constitutional rights is ordinarily based on 42 U.S.C. section 1983. This statute requires the plaintiff to show that:

    a.   Any person,

    b.   Under the color of state law,

    c.   Deprived the plaintiff of rights guaranteed under the Constitution.

    3.   **State of Mind--Daniels v. Williams,** 474 U.S. 327 (1986).   Daniels v. Williams

    a.   **Facts.** P was an inmate in a jail in Richmond, Virginia. A jailer (D) negligently left a pillow on a staircase. P tripped on the pillow, was injured, and sued D. P alleged that his constitutional right to life, liberty, and property was denied without due process of law by the negligent act of D. The trial court granted D's motion for directed verdict and the court of appeals affirmed. P appeals.

    b.   **Issue.** Can a claim for constitutional deprivation of rights be based on negligent conduct?

    c.   **Held.** No. Judgment affirmed.

        1)   P's claim was based on 42 U.S.C. section 1983, which requires the deprivation of constitutional rights under the color of state law.

2) D was acting under state law since he was an employee of the state.

3) The language and history of the Fourteenth Amendment and the federal statute make it appear that something more than negligence is required. The legislation was intended to prevent arbitrary action, not negligence.

4) Due process of law is adequately served by P's state court tort action.

Memphis
Community
School
District
v. Stachura

4. **Damages--Memphis Community School District v. Stachura,** 477 U.S. 299 (1986).

a. **Facts.** Stachura (P) was a tenured teacher in the Memphis Community School District (D). Some parents became upset when P taught a unit on human sexuality. P had used approved materials in teaching the unit. To deal with complaints, D held a meeting at which it was suggested that P not attend. After the meeting, P was suspended and told there would be an evaluation of him. P was reinstated after filing this action for violation of his constitutional rights. In addition to instructing the jury on compensatory and punitive damages, the court invited the jury to award damages based upon the value of the rights that had been deprived. The jury returned a verdict for P and D appealed. The court of appeals affirmed. D appeals.

b. **Issue.** May damages be awarded based on the "value" of the constitutional rights?

c. **Held.** No. Judgment reversed and remanded.

1) Although federal statutes define the right of action, damages are determined as in the ordinary common law tort action.

2) No damages can be awarded in the absence of actual injury.

3) Compensatory damages and punitive damages may be awarded. The jury, however, may not be allowed to award damages on some speculative determination of the value of some constitutional rights.

d. **Concurrence** (Marshall, J.). Although inappropriate in this case, there are times when the violation of the right is, itself, an injury. In such cases, damages could be awarded for the violation of the constitutional right.

XII. DEFAMATION

A. INTRODUCTION

At common law, every element of the prima facie case of defamation was based on strict liability, except that of publication. The publication of the defamatory matter must have been intentional or the result of negligence. Substantial changes in the proof requirements have occurred due to modern constitutional decisions, which will be discussed later in the chapter.

B. PRIMA FACIE CASE UNDER COMMON LAW

1. **Introduction.** The prima facie case for defamation is as follows:

    a. The matter published must be capable of a defamatory meaning.

    b. It must be understood as referring to the plaintiff.

    c. It must be understood in a sense defamatory of the plaintiff.

    d. There must be a publication.

    e. There must be causation.

    f. There must be damages.

2. **Publication.** In order to hold the defendant liable, the plaintiff must show that the defamatory matter was intentionally communicated by the defendant to some third person who understood it, or that the communication to the third person was made through the defendant's failure to exercise due care (*i.e.,* done negligently).

3. **Form of Publication.** The scope of damages recoverable for defamation depends on the form of the publication—whether it is libel or slander. Special rules limit the recovery in slander actions.

    a. **Introduction.**

        1) **Libel** is defamation usually appearing in some written or printed form; *i.e.,* reduced to some permanent, physical embodiment, such as in newspapers, a letter, etc.

        2) **Slander** is usually oral defamation—representations to the ear rather than to the eye. The principal characteristic of slander is that it is in a less physical form.

            a) Defamation in the form of slander is not actionable without a showing of special pecuniary damages, unless the defamation is of a class which the law deems actionable "per se." [*See* 5.b., below, for a description of the four slander per se situations]

    b. **Difficult cases.** In some cases it is very difficult to determine whether the publication is slander or libel, *e.g.,* the defamations contained on a phonograph record. In these cases, the courts usually consider the following factors:

(i) The permanency or nonpermanency of form.

(ii) The area of dissemination.

(iii) Whether the publication is deliberate or premeditated.

The Restatement (Second) of Torts, section 568A, provides that radio and television broadcasting of defamatory matter is libel.

4. **Matter Must be Taken as Referring to Plaintiff.** Any *living* person or other legally recognized entity may sue for defamation.

a. Ordinarily an unincorporated association cannot sue. However, some recent cases allow such suits. Further, even if the unincorporated association cannot sue, individual members thereof may sue if it is clearly defamatory of them.

b. The defamation of a deceased person may also be defamatory of a living person and hence actionable.

5. **Damages.**

a. **Slander in general.**

1) **Nominal damages.** At least nominal damages must be given where the words are actionable per se.

2) **Compensatory damages.** Compensatory damages are of two types:

a) **General compensatory damages.** General compensatory damages are available where the words are actionable per se and the plaintiff prevails. They are presumed by law to be the natural or probable consequence of the defendant's conduct, so the plaintiff need not show actual damages.

b) **Special compensatory damages.** Special compensatory damages must be alleged in the pleading and proven by the evidence.

3) **Punitive damages.** Punitive damages are given only when claimed in the pleadings and the evidence shows malice.

b. **Slander per se.** Damages are presumed by law in four (and only four) situations:

1) Where the defendant charges that the plaintiff has committed a serious, morally reprehensible crime, or that the plaintiff has been incarcerated for such a crime.

2) Where the defendant imputes to the plaintiff conduct, characteristics, etc., incompatible with the proper performance of the plaintiff's business, trade, office, or profession.

3) Where the defendant imputes to the plaintiff a presently existing, loathsome, communicable disease (venereal disease, leprosy, etc., but not tuberculosis, insanity, etc.).

4) Where the defendant imputes unchastity to a female plaintiff.

c. **Libel.** Most jurisdictions presume general damages from the fact that the defamation was published. However, if the plaintiff shows special damages, he can recover those, too.

1) **Minority view.** To mitigate the strict liability imposed on publishers, general damages will not be presumed in libel per quod cases in about a third of the states. Libel per quod refers to a statement published that is not defamatory on its face, but becomes so when the matter is linked up with certain extrinsic facts, which must be alleged in the pleading (called colloquium).

C. PRIVILEGES AND DEFENSES

1. **Absolute Privileges.** Absolute privileges are a complete defense to any action for publication of a defamation. They are not affected by the showing of malice, excessive publication, or abuse.

   a. **Governmental privileges.**

   1) **Judicial.** Witnesses, attorneys, judges, jurors, and the parties in an action are privileged to utter defamations which have some relevancy with the matter at hand.

   2) **Legislative.** All federal and state legislative members are absolutely privileged to utter defamations while on the floor or in committee. The utterances need not be relevant.

   3) **Executive.** Top cabinet-grade executives of state or federal government are absolutely privileged. This includes the President, his cabinet, and department heads. Relevancy is a requirement, however.

   b. **Domestic.** A spouse may utter defamations of third persons to the other spouse. Some courts extend this privilege to utterances among members of the immediate family.

2. **Liability of Original Publishers, Republishers, and Disseminators.**

   a. **Original publishers.** Anyone who has any part in the original publication is liable.

   b. **Republishers.** Every repetition of a defamation is another publication. Republishers are held to the same standards as original publishers, since every repetition of the matter can cause harm. They are not, however, strictly liable. The plaintiff must show that a republisher published the matter intentionally (with knowledge) or negligently.

c. **Disseminators.** A disseminator is someone who deals in the physical embodiment of defamatory matter (*e.g.*, a bookstore). Disseminators are not liable if they are unaware of the libelous contents.

3. **Defenses.**

   a. **Consent.** Consent is a defense to defamation under the same rules that consent is a defense to any intentional tort. [*See* I.C., *supra*]

   b. **Truth.** Truth is a complete and absolute defense. The burden of proving truth or falsity depends on whether the constitutional protections apply. If these protections apply, the plaintiff must prove that the statement was false.

4. **Conditional Privileges.**

   a. **Introduction.** A conditional privilege is recognized in situations where the public is concerned in the matter directly (*e.g.*, zoning hearings, statements made to law enforcement officers) or indirectly (*i.e.*, the public is concerned through its agent, the press). Also, the protection of certain private interests is condoned through the granting of a conditional privilege; this privilege applies to statements in the speaker's interest or the recipient's interest (*e.g.*, a statement from a former employee to a prospective employer about a job applicant).

   b. **Loss of privilege.** A conditional privilege may be abused by excessive publication or by acting with "malice," defined below.

D. **CONSTITUTIONAL ISSUES**

1. **Public Figures.** In *New York Times v. Sullivan*, 376 U.S. 254 (1964), the United States Supreme Court imposed constitutional restrictions on defamation actions. Where a public figure or public official sues, the plaintiff must prove more than merely that the statement was defamatory. In addition to all of the common law elements, the plaintiff must prove "actual malice." "Actual malice" was defined by the Court to mean that the defendant either knew that the statement was false or acted in reckless disregard of the truth of the statement.

Gertz v.
Robert
Welch, Inc.

2. **Private Figures--Gertz v. Robert Welch, Inc.**, 418 U.S. 323 (1974).

   a. **Facts.** Gertz (P), a reputable attorney, represented the family of a youth, who had been shot and killed by a police officer, in a civil action against the officer. Robert Welch, Inc. (D) published an article in its magazine accusing P of participation in a Communist conspiracy against the police and membership in two Marxist organizations. P sued D for libel and the trial court directed a verdict on the liability issue in his favor because the statements were admittedly false and libel per se. The jury returned a verdict of $50,000 but the trial judge entered judgment n.o.v. for D on the ground that the article was about a matter of public interest and protected by the *New York Times* rule absent a showing of malice. An appeals court affirmed. P appeals.

b. **Issues.**

    1) Is there a constitutional privilege to publish defamatory falsehoods about an individual who is neither a public official nor a public figure?

    2) May a private individual who sues for defamation be awarded punitive damages when liability is not based on knowledge of falsity or reckless disregard for truth?

c. **Held.** 1) No. 2) No. Judgment for D reversed and case remanded for a new trial.

    1) The erroneous statement of fact is not worthy of constitutional protection but it is inevitable in free debate. Some falsehood must be protected in order to protect important speech and avoid media self-censorship, which results when the media are required to guarantee the accuracy of their factual assertions.

    2) Nevertheless, there is a legitimate state interest underlying the law of libel, which is the compensation of the victims of defamation.

    3) The balance of freedom of speech and the state's interest in protecting its citizens from libel requires that a different rule be applied to private individuals than that stated in *New York Times*.

    4) A private individual does not have the access to the media available to public officials and public figures to contradict the libel and minimize its impact.

    5) Public officials and public figures by their involvement in public affairs accept the risk of close public scrutiny. Private individuals who are defamed are thus more deserving of recovery.

    6) As long as they do not impose liability without fault, the states may define the appropriate standard of liability for defamation of a private individual.

    7) P, although he had been active in civic and professional organizations, was not a public figure. He had not sought public notoriety. Furthermore, he never discussed the case with the media.

    8) Because of the competing interest of the First Amendment, state remedies for defamation must only compensate for actual injury unless "actual malice" is proved.

    9) The awarding of punitive damages must necessarily be carefully limited; otherwise, juries have the power to punish the expression of unpopular views.

d. **Dissent** (White, J.).

    1) The right of the ordinary citizen to recover for damage to his reputation has been almost exclusively the domain of the state courts. The majority opinion federalizes these important aspects of these defamation laws. These sweeping changes ignore the past court history of defamation.

2) The private person should not have to bear the heavy burden of proving that his reputation has actually been injured (damages should be presumed).

3) The majority is overly concerned with the potential for immoderate damage assessments by juries. Appellate courts can protect against that.

4) The Court wrongly rejects the punitive damages (express malice) test in favor of a test requiring P to show intentional falsehood or wrongful disregard ("actual malice"). There is nothing so constitutionally wrong with requiring a publisher to adhere to those standards of care ordinarily followed in the publishing industry.

e. **Comment.** In *Dun & Bradstreet, Inc. v. Greenmoss Builders, Inc.*, 472 U.S. 749 (1985), the Court indicated that the *Gertz* damages rules only apply when the statement involves a matter of public concern; presumed and punitive damages are permissible in purely private defamation actions.

Milkovich
v. Lorain
Journal Co.

3. **No Constitutionally Protected Opinion--Milkovich v. Lorain Journal Co.,** 497 U.S. 1 (1990).

a. **Facts.** Milkovich (P) was the coach of a high school wrestling team that was involved in a brawl with a competing team and placed on probation by the Ohio High School Athletic Association. Parents of some team members sued to enjoin the association from enforcing the probation. At a court hearing, P and the school superintendent denied that P had incited the brawl. A sports columnist wrote a column indicating that P had lied under oath, thereby preventing the team from receiving just punishment. P and the superintendent sued the newspaper (D) separately. After 15 years of litigation, the court held that the column was constitutionally protected opinion and granted D's motion for summary judgment. The Ohio Court of Appeals affirmed. The United States Supreme Court granted certiorari.

b. **Issue.** Is there a First Amendment-based protection for defamatory statements categorized as "opinion"?

c. **Held.** No. Reversed.

1) At common law, the privilege of "fair comment" developed as an affirmative defense to an action for defamation, affording immunity for the honest expression of opinion on matters of legitimate public interest when based upon a true or privileged statement of fact.

2) Here, D argues that we should establish another First Amendment-based protection for defamatory statements that are characterized as "opinion" as opposed to fact, relying on dictum in *Gertz v. Robert Welch, Inc.*, (*supra*). However, we do not think that *Gertz* was intended to create such a privilege. To do so would ignore the fact that an expression of "opinion" may often imply an assertion of objective fact.

3) Under our current law, a statement on matters of public concern must be provable as false before there can be liability for defamation, at

least where a media defendant is involved. Next, statements that cannot reasonably be interpreted as stating actual facts are protected. Thus, we are not persuaded that an additional separate constitutional privilege for "opinion" is required to ensure freedom of expression.

4) The dispositive question in this case then is whether a reasonable fact finder could conclude that statements in D's column imply that P perjured himself. We think the answer is yes. The language in the article is not the loose, figurative, or hyperbolic language that would negate the impression that the writer was seriously maintaining that P committed the crime of perjury. Also, the connotation that P committed perjury is sufficiently factual to be proved true or false.

XIII. INVASION OF PRIVACY

A. INTRODUCTION

The gist of the tort of invasion of privacy is not injury to reputation, but interference with the "right to be let alone" that results in injury to feelings, without regard to any effect on property, business, or reputation. Most states recognize this tort by case law; some do by statute. Some states do not recognize it at all.

B. PRIMA FACIE CASE

1. **Introduction.** The elements of the cause of action are:

   a. **Act by the defendant.** The act may consist of words or any type of affirmative conduct.

   b. **Serious and unreasonable invasion of plaintiff's privacy.** This is the crux of most invasion of privacy suits.

   c. **Intent, negligence, or strict liability.** Most invasion of privacy suits involve intentional acts, but this is not essential. Liability may be imposed for negligent invasions and even for invasions based on strict liability. Constitutional privileges established in *New York Times v. Sullivan*, *supra*, may affect this element of the case.

   d. **Causation.**

   e. **Damages.**

2. **Invasion of Plaintiff's Privacy.**

   a. **Four types of conduct held actionable:**

      1) *Unreasonable intrusion* upon the seclusion of another;

      2) *Appropriation* of another's name or likeness;

      3) *Publicity* which unreasonably places the other in a *false light* before the public; and

      4) *Public disclosure of private facts.*

   b. **Requirements for public disclosure of private facts.** If a reasonable person would find the disclosure of private facts highly objectionable, then the plaintiff has a cause of action for disclosure of them. The facts must be private; matters of public record are not actionable (since anyone has access to them), nor are public occurrences, since anyone present would have observed the same thing.

   c. **Stating cause of action--Hamberger v. Eastman,** 106 N.H. 107, 206 A.2d 239 (1964).

      1) **Facts.** D placed a listening device in the bedroom of a dwelling house which he rented to Ps, husband and wife. The device

Hamberger
v. Eastman

gave D the capability to listen to and record any conversation in Ps' bedroom from his nearby home. After Ps discovered the device, they each brought suit alleging that D had maliciously invaded their privacy, which had caused them humiliation, embarrassment, and intense mental suffering that had manifested itself in nervous upset and required expensive medical care. Further, the husband alleged that he had been rendered unable to properly perform his duties for his employer. D moved for dismissal on the ground that no cause of action was stated. The trial court transferred the cases to the supreme court without ruling.

2) Issue. Is a cause of action maintainable for intrusion upon one's physical and mental solitude?

3) Held. Yes. Motion to dismiss denied and the case remanded.

    a) Liability exists where a person unreasonably and seriously interferes with another's interest in not having his affairs known, to the extent that the interference is offensive to persons of ordinary sensibilities.

    b) D's alleged conduct is actionable even though there is no allegation that anyone listened.

    c) Whether actual or potential, such publicity with respect to private matters of purely personal concern is an injury to personality.

    d) The tort of intrusion on Ps' solitude requires no publicity or communication to third persons, although this would affect damages.

d. Electronic surveillance as intruding on right to privacy--Nader v. General Motors Corp., 25 N.Y.2d 560, 255 N.E.2d 765 (1970).

Nader v. General Motors Corp.

1) Facts. Nader (P), an author and lecturer on automotive safety and a critic of General Motors (D), brought suit alleging that D conducted a campaign of intimidation against him in order to suppress his criticisms and prevent his disclosure of information about its products. Among other things, P alleged that D had tapped his phone, electronically eavesdropped on private conversations, and kept him under surveillance. D moved to dismiss P's complaint. Two courts upheld the legal sufficiency of P's cause of action. The appellate court certified the question to the New York Court of Appeals as to whether the alleged conduct would constitute a tort for invasion of privacy.

2) Issue. Does the gathering of confidential information through wiretapping, electronic eavesdropping, and surveillance constitute an actionable invasion of privacy?

3) Held. Yes. Order appealed from affirmed.

    a) There is a cause of action for invasion of privacy based on the right to be free from intrusions in private matters.

    b) To constitute an actionable intrusion, there must be more than a mere gathering of information. The information sought must be of a private nature.

c) Conduct which merely harasses or attempts to uncover information which P has already revealed to others is not an actionable invasion.

b) "Overzealous" surveillance designed to obtain private information may be actionable to the same extent as wiretapping and electronic eavesdropping. Such is the case here.

Diaz v. Oakland Tribune, Inc.

e. **Matters of public interest--Diaz v. Oakland Tribune, Inc.,** 139 Cal. App. 3d 118, 188 Cal. Rptr. 762 (1983).

1) **Facts.** Diaz (P) had been born in Puerto Rico as a male. Later in life, P had a sex change operation to become a female. P sought to hide this information and told only her close friends and family. While a student in college, P was elected student body president. While serving in that position, a dispute arose with the administration concerning finances. During the course of the dispute, a newspaper reporter was informed of P's past. The reporter, Jones (D), wrote an article revealing this information and making jokes about it. *The Oakland Tribune* (D) published the article. P sued Ds for disclosure of the true but private facts. The jury returned a verdict of $250,000 in compensatory and $500,000 in punitive damages. Ds appeal.

2) **Issue.** Can Ds be held liable for the publication of true private facts?

3) **Held.** Yes, but judgment was reversed on other grounds.

a) A news media defendant may be held liable for the publication of private facts. The jury must be instructed, however, that the plaintiff must prove that the article was not newsworthy.

b) Although P was a public figure, she was not public for all purposes. Her sex change operation was not public information.

c) The publication of the information without prior notice to P and with the attempt to make a joke was evidence of malice, from which the jury could award damages.

d) The jury heard all of the evidence and there is no indication that the award was excessive.

e) The case must be reversed in order to allow the jury to properly determine the issue of newsworthiness.

The Florida Star v. B.J.F.

f. **State-protected privacy interests--The Florida Star v. B.J.F.,** 491 U.S. 524 (1989).

1) **Facts.** *The Florida Star* published the full name of B.J.F. (P), a rape victim, that it had obtained from a publicly released police report. P sued both the newspaper (D) and the sheriff's department for violation of a Florida statute making it unlawful to "print, publish, or broadcast . . . in any instrument of mass communication" the name of the victim of a sexual offense. The latter settled for $2,500. D's motion to dismiss was denied. At trial, P testified that she had suffered emotional distress stemming from telephone calls that her mother had received from a man who had said he

would rape P again. D moved for directed verdict and was denied. P was awarded $75,000 in compensatory and $25,000 in punitive damages. The court of appeals affirmed. The Florida Supreme Court denied discretionary review. D appeals.

2) **Issue.** May the state impose sanctions on the accurate publication of the name of a rape victim obtained from judicial records, that are maintained in connection with a public prosecution and which themselves are open to public inspection?

3) **Held.** No. Judgment reversed.

    a)   This case should be analyzed with reference to the limited First Amendment principle we articulated in *Smith v. Daily Mail Publishing Co.*, 443 U.S. 97 (1979): "[I]f a newspaper lawfully obtains truthful information about a matter of public significance then state officials may not constitutionally punish publication of the information, absent a need to further a state interest of the highest order." Although rape is a highly significant interest, imposing liability for publication is too precipitous a means for advancing this interest, because of the following reasons:

        (1)   D obtained the information through a government news release, issued without qualification, which conveyed that the government considered dissemination lawful;

        (2)   The Florida statute requires no case-by-case finding that the disclosure of a fact about a person's private life was one that a reasonable person would find highly offensive but rather imposes strict liability without regard for scienter or degree of fault; and

        (3)   The underinclusiveness of the statute raises serious doubts about whether Florida is in fact serving significant interests because it prohibits publication of identifying information only in an "instrument of mass communication" and does not prohibit the spread of such information by other means.

    b)   We hold only that where a newspaper publishes truthful information which it has lawfully obtained, punishment may lawfully be imposed, if at all, only when narrowly tailored to a state interest of the highest order, and that no such interest is satisfactorily served by imposing liability under the facts of this case.

4) **Dissent** (White, J., Rehnquist, C.J., O'Connor, J.). None of the three reasons relied on by the majority require setting aside a verdict for P.

    a)   By amending its statute to exempt rape victims' names from disclosure, Florida took virtually every step imaginable to prevent what happened here. Even when rape victims' names are mistakenly disclosed, the press should respect standards of decency and refrain from publishing them.

    b)   The majority's concerns about the damages resting on strict liability are irrelevant here where the jury found that D acted with "reckless indifference toward the rights of others." In addition, the legislature has found that disclosure of the fact that a person was raped is categorically a revelation that people find offensive.

    c)   Florida enacted a statute that evenhandedly covers all instruments of mass communication, no matter their form, media, content, nature, or purpose, but excluded neighborhood gossips because they do not pose the same danger and intrusion to rape victims.

Godbehere v. Phoenix Newspapers, Inc.

g.   False light distinguished--Godbehere v. Phoenix Newspapers, Inc., 162 Ariz. 335, 783 P.2d 781 (1989).

1)   Facts. Godbehere, a sheriff, and several deputies and civilian employees of the sheriff's office (Ps) were the subject of more than 50 articles published by Phoenix Newspapers (D). The articles claimed Ps engaged in illegal activities, staged arrests, misused public funds, committed police brutality, and were generally incompetent, among other things. Ps sued D for libel and false light invasion of privacy, alleging that the publications were false, damaged their reputations, harmed them in their profession, and caused them emotional distress. The trial court granted D's motion to dismiss the false light invasion of privacy claims, but refused to dismiss the libel claim. The court of appeals affirmed. The Arizona Supreme Court granted review.

2)   Issues.

    a)   Should a separate tort for false light invasion of privacy be eliminated because the action overlaps the torts of defamations and outrage?

    b)   Can a public official sue for false light invasion of privacy if the publication relates to performance of his public life or duties?

3)   Held. a) No. b) No. Affirmed.

    a)   To recover for invasion of privacy, where the damage resulting from invasion of privacy is emotional, Arizona applies a stricter standard than other states: to recover for invasion of privacy, Arizona requires a plaintiff to prove the tort of outrage, *i.e.,* that the defendant's conduct was extreme and outrageous. Ds argue that there is no need for an independent tort of false light invasion of privacy because the action overlaps two other recognized torts: defamation and intentional infliction of emotional distress.

    b)   To recover for the tort of outrage, the plaintiff must show that the defendant's conduct was extreme and outrageous, exceeding "all bounds usually tolerated by decent society." False light invasion of privacy protects against knowingly or recklessly publishing false information or innuendo that a reasonable person would find highly offensive. Just because the two torts provide redress for the same injury, *i.e.,* emotional distress, does not mean that the actions are merged. Both torts should be kept because each tort protects against a different type of conduct.

    c)   Likewise, defamation and false light invasion of privacy serve different objectives. Defamation protects against damage to reputation or good name caused by the publication of false information. Privacy protects mental and emotional interests, even in the absence of reputational damage; an action may arise when untrue information is published or when true information is published and creates a false implication. The publication must involve a "major misrepresentation of [the plaintiff's] character, history, activities or beliefs," not merely minor or unimportant inaccuracies. Thus, a plaintiff may bring a false light invasion of privacy action even where the publication is not defamatory, and the facts stated are true. Although defamation and false light may overlap, they serve different objectives and redress different wrongs.

d) The manner in which law enforcement officers perform their duties is a matter of great public interest. Thus, we adopt the following standard: A plaintiff cannot sue for false light invasion of privacy if he is a public official and the publication relates to performance of his public life or duties. However, if the publication presents the public official's private life in a false light, he can sue, but he must show actual malice under *Hustler Magazine, Inc. v. Falwell,* 485 U.S. 46 (1988).

h. **Rights of privacy and publicity--Carson v. Here's Johnny Portable Toilets, Inc.,** 698 F.2d 831 (6th Cir. 1983).

1) **Facts.** Entertainer Johnny Carson (P) host of *The Tonight Show* since 1962, is associated with the phrase "Here's Johnny." Here's Johnny Portable Toilets, Inc. (D) rented and sold "Here's Johnny" portable toilets. P sued D, alleging unfair competition, trademark infringement, and invasion of privacy and publicity rights. The district court dismissed P's complaint. On the right of privacy and right of publicity theories, the court held that these rights extend only to a "name or likeness" and "Here's Johnny" did not qualify. P appeals.

2) **Issue.** Does D's use of the phrase "Here's Johnny" violate the common law right of privacy and the right of publicity?

3) **Held.** Yes. Judgment vacated; case remanded.

a) Prosser delineated four types of the right of privacy, the last of which has become known as the "right of publicity." These rights protect: (i) intrusion upon seclusion; (ii) public disclosure of embarrassing private facts; (iii) publicity that places one in a false light; and (iv) appropriation of one's name or likeness for the defendant's advantage.

b) The first three types protect the right to be let alone. We do not think P's claim that this right has been invaded is supported by the law or its facts.

c) The right of publicity protects the commercial interest of celebrities in their identities. The district court dismissed P's claim based on the right of publicity because D does not use P's name or likeness. P's identity may be exploited, however, even if his name or picture is not used. D admitted that he had selected the phrase because he knew it was identified with P; hence, P is entitled to judgment.

4) **Dissent.** While I agree that there may be impermissible exploitation of an individual's identity, I do not believe that the common law right of publicity may be extended beyond an individual's name, likeness, achievements, identifying characteristics or actual performances, to include phrases or other things merely associated with the individual.

XIV. COMMERCIAL TORTS

A. MISREPRESENTATION

A misrepresentation may be defined as a false representation of a material fact to the plaintiff, made by the defendant, either intentionally, negligently, or under circumstances of strict liability, upon which the plaintiff justifiably relies to his damage.

1. **As a Basis for Other Torts.** Obviously, misrepresentation can be the mechanism by which the defendant accomplishes various kinds of tortious conduct, such as battery, false imprisonment, conversion, and trespass; and it may form the basis of a negligent act or omission, such as a failure to warn of a dangerous condition. However, the injured plaintiff often will seek relief under other tort actions, such as interference with contractual relations, malicious prosecution, negligence, battery, etc., or under nontort remedies such as breach of contract, rescission, constructive trust, estoppel, etc.

2. **As a Tort by Itself.** Misrepresentation has also served as a basis for development of a distinct cause of action in tort, which has been limited in practice to the invasion of interests of a pecuniary nature in the course of business dealings. While it is this type of action that will be dealt with here, it should be kept in mind that a misrepresentation may simply be the mechanism by which other tortious acts are accomplished, and that the plaintiff may have alternative remedies.

B. ELEMENTS OF MISREPRESENTATION CAUSE OF ACTION

1. **Basic Elements for Fraud.** The basic elements for fraud (intentional misrepresentation) are:

    a. A false representation of a material fact;

    b. Scienter or knowledge that the statement is false;

    c. Intent to induce reliance;

    d. Justifiable reliance on the statement; and

    e. Damages.

2. **Oral Representations in Connection with Written Contracts.** If fraud can be shown, the contract can be set aside.

    a. **Application--Adams v. Gillig,** 199 N.Y. 314, 92 N.E. 670 (1910). Adams v. Gillig

    1) **Facts.** Gillig (D) offered to purchase part of a vacant lot in a residential area from Adams (P) and represented that he would build dwellings on it. D actually intended to build an automobile garage on the land and began plans to do so the day after the sale. When P discovered this, she offered to return the purchase price and pay all the expenses D had incurred if he would reconvey the land to her. D's intended use of the land

would decrease the value of the rest of the lot by one-half and the value of two adjoining lots owned by P by one-fourth. D refused to reconvey. P sued and the trial court entered judgment upon a referee's report which directed reconveyance. An appellate court affirmed. D appeals.

2) **Issue.** Is a contract voidable which is induced by fraud as to a matter material to the party defrauded?

3) **Held.** Yes. Judgment for P affirmed.

   a) A contract may always be set aside for fraud affecting the transaction as to an existing material fact.

   b) A statement as to an existing material fact which is false and made to induce execution of a contract, and which does induce the contract, constitutes fraud.

   c) An oral statement that is fraudulent is grounds for setting aside a written contract that is deemed to be the complete agreement of the parties.

   d) Had D intended to use the land for dwellings, he could later have changed his mind in good faith, but the jury was justified in finding that D always intended to use the property for a garage. Therefore, D's false representation induced P to enter into a contract that she would not have otherwise.

4) **Comment.** Some courts refuse to find a separate tort of misrepresentation where there is a written contract. The theory here is that to do so would subvert the Statute of Frauds and the Parol Evidence Rule.

3. **Opinion vs. Material Fact.** For a cause of action to exist, there must be a misrepresentation of a material fact.

   a. **Performance, value, and quality.** Usually a person is not justified in relying on misrepresentations (or opinions) as to value or quality. A misrepresentation must be of an existing fact, not the mere expression of an opinion. And, where a buyer and seller are on equal footing, and the buyer has ample opportunity to examine the goods to be purchased, general statements by the seller as to the performance (*e.g.*, "it performs well") or value of the goods that are false will not give rise to an action for fraud and deceit. A reasonable amount of "puffing" is tolerable and to be expected, especially where the parties stand on equal footing.

   b. **False representations in an action for deceit—"puffing"--Vulcan Metals Co. v. Simmons Manufacturing Co.,** 248 F. 853 (C.C.A.N.Y. 1918).

   1) **Facts.** Vulcan (P) purchased from Simmons (D) equipment to manufacture a type of vacuum cleaner which D represented would be "perfect" and "the only sanitary portable cleaner on the market." P challenges these representations and alleges that D further represented that, although it had developed the vacuum and machines to produce it, D had never sold the vacuums. Evidence showed that a few

Vulcan Metals
Co. v.
Simmons
Manufactur-
ing Co.

machines had been sold. P brought an action for deceit and D brought an action against P for failure to honor notes given by P as part of the purchase price. The trial court directed a verdict for D in both actions. P appeals.

2) Issues.

a) May an action for deceit be maintained upon the seller's opinion of the capabilities of his product?

b) May an action for deceit be maintained against a seller who falsely represents that his product has never been sold?

3) Held. a) No. b) Yes. Judgment for D reversed.

a) Where the parties bargain on an equal basis, it is to be expected that the seller will "puff" about his product. In this case P had a full opportunity to inspect and test the vacuum cleaner. This placed it on an equality with the seller. P should not have taken D's puffing seriously. False representations would not be permissible if P had been forced to rely on D's opinion of the vacuum.

b) Knowledge of the prior sales record of the product might have been critical to P's decision to buy the equipment. The jury would certainly have the right to accept P's statement that he did rely upon the representation that no vacuums had been sold. Although the sales contract stated that D had been engaged in selling the machines, it was an issue for the jury as to whether this was an adequate retraction of the prior fraudulent statements.

4) Comment. When analyzing "opinion" problems, one must look at the following:

a) The form of the statement;

b) The subject matter (is it common or specialized knowledge);

c) The relationship of the parties;

d) The margin of error (how big a misrepresentation); and

e) Whether the parties were on an equal footing.

4. Misrepresentations of Law.

a. **General rule.** Misrepresentations as to law or matters of law are not actionable under the general rule, since everyone is presumed to know the law and such misrepresentations are thus treated as opinions only.

b. **Exceptions.** There are two exceptions to the general rule: the first exception occurs where the party misrepresenting the law is more knowledgeable about the law and is exploiting the confidence placed in him; the second exception is where there is a fiduciary relationship between the parties.

5. **Concealment and Nondisclosure.** Sometimes the misrepresentation is not affirmative, but constitutes concealment or nondisclosure of an important fact. Normally a failure to disclose all one knows is not a misrepresentation.

Swinton v.
Whitinsville
Savings Bank

    a. **Traditional rule—no liability--Swinton v. Whitinsville Savings Bank,** 311 Mass. 677, 42 N.E.2d 808 (1942).

        1) **Facts.** Bank (D) sold to Swinton (P) a house which D, through its agent, knew was infested with termites. The condition was not readily apparent by inspection and P did not ask about termite infestation. After purchasing the house, P discovered the defect and was required to spend large sums to correct the termite damage. P brought suit for fraudulent concealment. The trial court sustained D's demurrer. P appeals.

        2) **Issue.** Is a seller liable who fails to disclose a nonapparent defect about which he has not been asked by the buyer?

        3) **Held.** No. Order sustaining the demurrer affirmed.

            a) There is no liability for bare nondisclosure of defects.

            b) If D is held liable, every seller is liable who fails to disclose a known but nonapparent defect which is material and which the buyer fails to discover. Similarly, a buyer would be liable for nondisclosure of a nonapparent virtue known to him. The law does not impose so idealistic a standard.

        4) **Comment.** It is interesting to note that termites were rare in this locality. Presumably no prospective house buyer would have thought to ask about termites. The court here found that D had no duty of good faith to disclose material, nonapparent defects.

Ingaharro v.
Blanchette

    b. **Nondangerous conditions--Ingaharro v. Blanchette,** 122 N.H. 54, 440 A.2d 445 (1982).

        1) **Facts.** The Blanchettes (Ds) had owned a house for 10 years. During that period, they experienced a water shortage problem during the summer months. When they sold the house to Ingaharro (P), Ds made no statements concerning the water. P also asked no questions about the water. After the sale to P, P experienced water shortage problems and sued Ds for negligent misrepresentation. The master determined that Ds knew of the defect in the property, that the defect was material to the contract, and that there was a duty to disclose the defect. The trial court approved the master's recommendation, and Ds appeal.

        2) **Issue.** Is there a duty to disclose information?

        3) **Held.** No. Judgment reversed.

a) Some courts have held a duty to disclose defects in real estate transfers. These defects are usually those which are known to the owner, concealed and not knowable to the buyer, and dangerous to life or property.

b) These facts do not meet that rigid standard of requiring a duty to disclose.

6. Defendant's Standard of Conduct.

a. **Scienter.** Scienter refers to the defendant's knowledge of the falsity of the representation made, or knowledge that he had an insufficient basis for determining the truth of the representation.

b. **Proving scienter.**

1) P may be able to prove by inference that the defendant did not entertain an honest belief from the fact that the belief is unreasonable.

2) Motive does not play a part in an action for deceit, at least as far as liability is concerned. Therefore, an asserted good motive on the part of the defendant cannot provide a defense.

c. **Innocent misrepresentations.**

1) **Majority rule: no liability.** Under the majority rule, if a defendant innocently misrepresents a material fact by mistake, he will not be liable. The maker of the statement must have actual knowledge of its falsity, or no knowledge as to its truth or falsity.

2) **Minority rule: liability.** However, a growing minority position is that the good faith of the maker is immaterial. All that need be shown is that the statements were false, that the plaintiff relied on them, and that damages resulted therefrom. Most of the cases imposing strict liability arise in connection with the sale of land or chattels.

3) **Majority rule—application--Derry v. Peek,** 16 App. Cas. 337 (H.L. 1889).

Derry v. Peek

a) **Facts.** Peek (P) bought stock in a tramway company relying on false information in the prospectus that Parliament had authorized the use of steam power in the operation of the tramway. In reality, the Parliament's act required the consent of the Board of Trade before steam power could be used. This consent was refused and as a result the company was dissolved. P brought an action against Derry and four other directors of the defunct company (Ds) for deceit, claiming damages for the misrepresentations. The trial court dismissed P's action and held that Ds reasonably believed that they had the authority stated in the prospectus. A court of appeal reversed. Ds appeal.

b) **Issue.** May damages be recovered for deceit without proof of fraud?

c) **Held.** No. Judgment for P by the court of appeal reversed.

    (1) In order to recover for deceit, there must be proof of fraud. An action for deceit may not be based on misrepresentation alone.

    (2) Fraud is proven when it is shown that a false representation was made knowingly, without belief in its truth, or recklessly careless as to its truth.

    (3) An honest belief in the truth of a statement prevents it from being fraudulent, but the motive of the person is immaterial.

    (4) The maker must have reasonable grounds for his belief in a false statement.

d. **Negligence in making a statement.**

    1) **Introduction.** The English rule is that the plaintiff may have no relief from the defendant's negligently spoken or written word—negligence must be based upon an act. Many American courts, on the other hand, have adopted a contrary rule and allow recovery where there is a duty, if one speaks at all, to give correct information. However, for this rule to apply, there must be knowledge (or its equivalent) that:

        (i) The information is desired for a serious purpose;

        (ii) The recipient will rely on it; and

        (iii) The recipient will be injured in some way if it is false.

    In addition, there must be a relationship between the parties such that one has a duty to give the information with care and the other has a right to rely on it.

International Products Co. v. Erie Railroad Co.

    2) **Duty to give correct information--International Products Co. v. Erie Railroad Co.,** 244 N.Y. 331, 155 N.E. 662 (1927).

        a) **Facts.** International (P) imported certain goods for resale which Erie (D) agreed to store in D's warehouse. On August 17, P, in order to obtain insurance on the goods, inquired where the goods were stored and was informed that they were at Dock F. He told this to the insurer. In fact, the goods had not yet arrived and when they did arrive part of them were stored in Dock D. Several months later, when the goods in Dock D were destroyed by fire, P was unable to collect from the insurer because of the misdescription in the policy. P successfully sued D for the insurance it would have been entitled to but for D's negligent misinformation. D appeals.

        b) **Issue.** May damages be recovered for negligent misrepresentation, where there is a duty to give correct information?

        c) **Held.** Yes. Judgment for P affirmed.

(1) Where there is a duty to give correct information, the negligent giving of false information is actionable.

(2) Although the English rule as given in *Derry v. Peek* (*supra*) is that no cause of action is maintainable for a mere statement unless the maker knows it to be false, American courts have found liability for negligent statements where there is a duty to be correct.

(3) For the misrepresentation to be actionable, the maker must have known that the information was requested for a serious purpose and would be relied upon, and that damage would result if it was incorrect. Furthermore, the relationship between the parties must justify reliance upon the information.

(4) D, who was about to become bailor of P's goods, and knowing that P sought to insure its goods, owed a duty to P to provide accurate information.

3) **Scope of duty in negligence cases.** Where the action is one in negligence, the defendant must have contemplated the reliance of a particular plaintiff or group of persons to which the plaintiff belongs, whereas in a deceit action liability extends to all those whose reliance was reasonably foreseeable.

4) **Innocent misrepresentation--Johnson v. Healy,** 176 Conn. 97, 405 A.2d 54 (1978).

Johnson v. Healy

a) **Facts.** Johnson (P) bought a house from Healy (D). D, who built the house, had represented that there was nothing wrong with it. Over the subsequent six years, the house settled unevenly, due to improper fill, and extensive damage resulted. D bought the lot after the fill had been placed on it and was unaware of the instability. The trial court held D liable for misrepresentation, and both parties appeal.

b) **Issue.** Is a seller liable for innocent misrepresentations?

c) **Held.** Yes. Judgment set aside for a new trial on damages.

(1) Traditionally there was no action for innocent misrepresentation (except for rescission of the contract), although strict liability in the sale of goods was recognized. Warranty theories have affected the development of the law, and now tort liability even for innocent representations has become available in commercial transactions. D's representation was sufficient to induce P's reliance, and D is properly liable.

(2) The general measurement of damages for breach of warranty is whatever is necessary to put P in the position he would have been in if the property had been as warranted. However, this measure is tempered by a limit on damages to the diminished value whenever the cost of repair is dramatically larger than the difference in value. Since fully restoring the house would be more expensive than the original price P paid, the proper measure of damages should be the difference in value between the property had it been as represented and the property as it actually was.

7. Reliance.

a. **Reliance must be justified--Pelkey v. Norton,** 149 Me. 247, 99 A.2d 918 (1953).

1) **Facts.** D bought a car from P and, as part of the purchase price, traded in a truck which he represented to be two years newer than it was. P misread the auto's serial number, which would have revealed the true year of manufacture. P allowed D $700 more for the truck than it was worth. P then sold the truck to a third party who discovered the truck's true age and sued P. P, in turn, sued D for deceit. The trial court directed a verdict against P and P appeals.

2) **Issue.** May one who makes an intentional misrepresentation escape liability if the other party is negligent in relying thereon?

3) **Held.** No. Direction of verdict for D reversed.

   a) Generally, an action for deceit may not be maintained by one who knew the representation to be false or could have ascertained its falsity by exercising reasonable care. Nevertheless, one guilty of actual fraud may not excuse his own wrongful acts by claiming that the defrauded was guilty of contributory negligence.

   b) The law dislikes negligence but it abhors fraud. A court of justice is quite as much bound to stamp out fraud as to foster reasonable care.

b. **Contributory negligence--Corva v. United Services Automobile Association,** 108 A.D.2d 631, 485 N.Y.S.2d 264 (1985).

1) **Facts.** Corva (P) had a traffic accident with Sabia. P hired law firm Mangiatordi & Corpina ("M & C") to represent her. M & C contacted United Services Automobile Association ("USAA") to try to reach a settlement. When USAA indicated that the limit of the policy was $15,000, M & C believed this information and settled for that amount. It was later determined that USAA had misrepresented the policy limits and P sued USAA for damages. USAA sued M & C for contribution and indemnity should USAA be held liable. M & C moved to dismiss and the trial court granted the motion. USAA appeals.

2) **Issue.** Can a party who relies upon a misrepresentation be held liable for its own negligence in such reliance?

3) **Held.** Yes. Judgment reversed.

   a) Although M & C may have justifiably relied upon the statement, they may have still been negligent to P. M & C may have owed a higher duty of care to P than the duty to merely rely upon another party. Although M & C may still prevail on the merits, they are not entitled to be dismissed as a matter of law.

8. **Damages.**

   a. **Introduction.** Unlike most intentional torts, proof of actual damages must be shown in order to obtain recovery.

   b. **Measure of damages.** The courts have divided over the measure of damages to be awarded.

      1) **Benefit of the bargain rule.** The majority position is that the plaintiff should be given the "benefit of the bargain"—*i.e.,* the benefit he would have received if the misrepresentation had been true.

      2) **Out-of-pocket rule.** The minority position awards the plaintiff the price paid less the value of the property received.

9. **Causation.**

   a. **Introduction.** The plaintiff must show that the misrepresentation was not only material, and that a reasonable person in the plaintiff's position would have been justified in relying on it, but that the plaintiff actually did rely on the representation and that entering into the transaction caused the loss.

   b. **Proximate cause.** A plaintiff can recover any consequential damages resulting from the misrepresentation over and above the "normal" measure of damages. But the damage must have been proximately caused by the misrepresentation; hence, the foreseeability of the damages caused may be an important issue.

10. **The Ambit of Responsibility—Who Can Rely?**

    a. **Intentional misrepresentation.**

       1) **Old view.** Under the former view there was insufficient connection between the person who misrepresented the facts and the subsequent purchaser to allow the subsequent purchaser to recover for the misrepresentation.

       2) **Modern view.** The modern view is that the defendant is liable to anyone who he intended would rely on the misrepresentation, or who it was reasonably foreseeable would rely. For example, if the manufacturer of a product mislabels the product, it is not necessary that the reliance of a particular plaintiff be intended. Anyone who acquires the product may sue.

    b. **Negligent performance of duties.**

       1) **Scope of liability.** The scope of liability for negligent misrepresentation is much more limited than the scope of liability for deceit. Where the action is for deceit, the defendant will be liable to any person whose reliance on his representation was intended by him, and he will be deemed to have intended the reliance of all those who were substantially certain to be exposed to the information. However, where the action is for negligent misrepresentation, the defendant will be liable only if the defendant intended or contemplated that the par-

ticular plaintiff (or a class of persons to which the plaintiff belongs) would rely.

2) Applications.

a) Liability to third persons. It is not essential that the plaintiff be in privity of contract with the defendant. Liability may be found where the defendant makes a negligent representation to a third person with knowledge that that person intends to communicate it to a specific individual plaintiff for the purpose of inducing reliance thereon. For example, a public weigher who issued an erroneous certificate to a particular seller was liable to a purchaser who purchased in reliance on the certificate. [Glanzer v. Shephard, 233 N.Y. 236, 135 N.E. 275 (1922)]

b) Foreseeability not sufficient. Mere reasonable anticipation that a misrepresented statement will foreseeably be communicated to others, or even knowledge that the recipient intends to make a commercial use of it in dealing with unspecified strangers, may be sufficient to impose liability for deceit (if it is made without knowledge of the subject and is represented as one's own knowledge) but generally not for negligent misrepresentation.

Ultramares Corp. v. Touche

c) Limited scope of duty--Ultramares Corp. v. Touche, 255 N.Y. 170, 174 N.E. 441 (1931).

(1) Facts. Touche (D) a firm of public accountants, was hired by Fred Stern and Co. to prepare and certify a balance sheet exhibiting the condition of the business. Stern was involved in the importation of rubber, which required extensive credit. D knew that the sheet would be used by banks and creditors who dealt with the company, and presented it with 32 certified copies. Although it showed a net worth of $1.07 million, the business was actually insolvent. Further, D certified that in its opinion, the balance sheet presented a true view of the financial condition of Stern and Co. Ultramares (P) loaned Stern and Co. money in reliance upon the audit certified by D and suffered losses when Stern and Co. went into bankruptcy. P brought suit against D for negligence and fraud. A jury awarded P damages but the trial judge granted D's motion to dismiss without entering the judgment. An appellate court reversed and reinstated the verdict. D appeals. P cross-appeals the dismissal by the trial court of the cause of action for fraud.

(2) Issue. May damages be recovered by a person who is injured by the negligent misstatement of another with whom he has no contractual relationship?

(3) Held. No. Judgment for P reversed.

(a) Liability for negligent misstatement extends only to the other parties to the contract pursuant to which the statement was given.

(b) To allow recovery without privity would expand liability for negligent speech to that of liability for fraud.

(c) Stern and Co. sought D's services primarily for its own benefit and only collaterally for the benefit of those to whom the balance sheet might be exhibited.

(d) *Glanzer v. Shephard* is distinguishable because in that case transmission of information to the third party was the sole reason for the transaction and not merely a possibility.

(e) This holding does not limit liability for misstatements which are reckless or insincere but means only that liability for honest blunders is bounded by contract.

    d)   **Changing view.** Recent cases suggest that courts may now be more willing to expand the scope of duty in *Ultramares* types of cases.

C. INTERFERENCE WITH CONTRACT

1.   **Inducing Breach.** A cause of action will lie against a person who maliciously procures a breach of contract. In *Lumley v. Gye*, 118 Eng. Rep. 749 (Q.B. 1853), the plaintiff contracted for the exclusive services of a certain opera singer. The defendant, knowing of the contract, induced the singer to break the contract and perform for him. In finding a cause of action for breach of contract, a court for the first time set out the general principle of liability based upon interference with contract. Subsequent cases have extended this principle to cover interference with advantageous relations of pecuniary value.

2.   **Interfering with a Contract Right--Wilkinson v. Powe,** 300 Mich. 275, 1 N.W.2d 539 (1942).   Wilkinson v. Powe

    a.   **Facts.** Wilkinson (P) contracted with farmers to haul their milk to Powe's (D's) creamery. D and P had a disagreement and D informed all local farmers that it would not accept milk unless it was delivered by D's own carriers. P could not find another market for the milk he hauled and was forced to abandon his routes. P sued D for procuring a breach of his contract with the farmers. The trial court directed a verdict for D, finding that D had no obligation to accept the milk and that without D's acceptance of the product the delivery routes had no value. P appeals.

    b.   **Issue.** May damages be awarded against one who interferes with another's rights under a contract?

    c.   **Held.** Yes. Judgment for D reversed.

        1) The right to perform a contract and to reap the profits resulting therefrom is a property right.

        2) D interfered with P's property rights in the contract by active solicitation of a breach of the farmers' contract.

       3)   D had a right not to accept delivery of the farmers' milk; however, in continuing to accept the milk but imposing the requirement that the milk be delivered by D's own trucks, D actively interfered with P's property right to profits under the contract.

       4)   D's purpose was unlawful, *i.e.,* to bring about a breach of contract. Although D might have accomplished the same result by merely refusing to accept the milk, D may not be freed from liability for injury caused by unlawful acts merely because it could have caused the same injury lawfully.

3.   Illegal Contracts. Illegal contracts are not protected from interference.

4.   Negligent Interference. Liability based upon negligent interference with contract has for the most part been denied.

5.   Protection of Defendant's or a Third Party's Interest. Where the defendant has an existing legitimate interest to protect, courts usually recognize a privilege in the defendant (similar to that of defense of property) to interfere with the performance of a contract which would threaten his interest. Also, interference may be justified where a contract imposes intolerable conditions upon one of the parties. Such interference is not actionable. For example, in *Brimelow v. Casson*, 1 Ch. 302 (1924), it was held that a contract by which a young girl was employed as a chorus girl for such a low wage that she had to reinforce her earnings by resorting to prostitution could be interfered with without incurring liability. Similarly, interferences to protect the public at large may also be justified.

D.   INTERFERENCE WITH PROSPECTIVE ADVANTAGE

In torts involving interference with prospective advantage, the gravamen of the wrong is not interference with an existing contract, but interference with the potential or prospective economic relations of another.

Tuttle
v. Buck

1.   Predatory Practices--Tuttle v. Buck, 107 Minn. 145, 119 N.W. 946 (1909).

    a.   Facts. D set up a rival barber shop and operated it at a loss with the sole design of putting P out of business. P brought suit.

    b.   Issue. Does P have a cause of action?

    c.   Held. Yes.

       1)   The complaint states a cause of action.

       2)   When a person starts a place of business not for the sake of profit to himself, but regardless of loss to himself, and for the sole purpose of driving his competition out of business, he has engaged in an actionable tort.

    d.   Comment. There may also be liability where the purpose is a lawful one but where the means employed to accomplish that purpose are unlawful.

2. **Competitive Tactics.** The mere fact that the methods employed by a competition may be ruthless or morally unfair does not make them unlawful, and any detriment to business which is incidental to lawful competition is not actionable.

3. **At Will Contracts.** Where a contract for business services is terminable at the will of either of the parties, one cannot bring an action for interference with that contract by a competitor. But an action will lie for interference with such contract if done without legal or social justification, out of pure malice or spite, or for some other improper reason.

4. **Statute of Frauds.** Where the plaintiff had an oral agreement to supply widgets to a buyer and is prevented from performing the contract by the defendant; the fact that the contract came under the Statute of Frauds will not constitute a defense for the defendant. Only parties to contracts and those in privity with them can attack a contract on the basis that it is unenforceable under the Statute of Frauds.

5. **Intentional Conduct--Baker v. Dennis Brown Realty, Inc.,** 121 N.H. 640, 433 A.2d 1271 (1981).

> Baker v.
> Dennis Brown
> Realty, Inc.

   a. **Facts.** Baker (P) had her real estate agent contact Brown Realty (D) to show P a house that D had an exclusive listing on. P liked the house and issued an offer to purchase at the full asking price. An agent of D required P to add additional conditions that P did not want to add. The agent of D then showed the house to his own clients and they wrote an offer for $300 more than P's offer. D's agent then showed both offers to the sellers and they accepted the higher offer. If D's agent had arranged to sell the house to P, D would have had to split the commission with P's real estate agent. By selling the house to its own client, D got to keep the whole commission. During the transaction, no one told P that a higher offer had been made. P ultimately bought another house, but had to pay $3,100 more than the price of the original house. P sued D and won a verdict. D appeals.

   b. **Issue.** Is the intentional interference with a prospective contract actionable?

   c. **Held.** Yes. Judgment affirmed.

      1) It is clear that D acted intentionally and purposely to prevent the seller from entering into a contract with P. There was no privilege for this action, and in fact, D did this only to increase his share of the commission. The appropriate measure of damage is the additional amount of money it took P to obtain a similar house.

TABLE OF CASES

(Page numbers of briefed cases in bold)

Notes

Notes

Notes

Notes

Notes

Notes

Notes

Publications Catalog

Gilbert Law Summaries are the best selling outlines in the country, and have set the standard for excellence since they were first introduced more than twenty-five years ago. It's Gilbert's unique combination of features that makes it the one study aid you'll turn to for all your study needs!

Accounting and Finance for Lawyers
TBA
Basic Accounting Principles; Definitions of Accounting Terms; Balance Sheet; Income Statement; Statement of Changes in Financial Position; Consolidated Financial Statements; Accumulation of Financial Data; Financial Statement Analysis.
ISBN: 0-15-900382-2   Pages: 136 $16.95

Administrative Law
By Professor Michael R. Asimow, U.C.L.A.
Separation of Powers and Controls Over Agencies; (including Delegation of Power) Constitutional Right to Hearing (including Liberty and Property Interests Protected by Due Process, and Rulemaking-Adjudication Distinction); Adjudication Under Administrative Procedure Act (APA); Formal Adjudication (including Notice, Discovery, Burden of Proof, Finders of Facts and Reasons); Adjudicatory Decision Makers (including Administrative Law Judges (ALJs), Bias, Improper Influences, Ex Parte Communications, Familiarity with Record, Res Judicata); Rulemaking Procedures (including Notice, Public Participation, Publication, Impartiality of Rulemakers, Rulemaking Record); Obtaining Information (including Subpoena Power, Privilege Against Self-incrimination, Freedom of Information Act, Government in Sunshine Act, Attorneys' Fees); Scope of Judicial Review; Reviewability of Agency Decisions (including Mandamus, Injunction, Sovereign Immunity, Federal Tort Claims Act); Standing to Seek Judicial Review and Timing.
ISBN: 0-15-900000-9   Pages: 300 $19.95

Agency and Partnership
By Professor Richard J. Conviser, Chicago Kent
Agency: Rights and Liabilities Between Principal and Agent (including Agent's Fiduciary Duty, Principal's Right to Indemnification); Contractual Rights Between Principal (or Agent) and Third Persons (including Creation of Agency Relationship, Authority of Agent, Scope of Authority, Termination of Authority, Ratification, Liability on Agents, Contracts); Tort Liability (including Respondeat Superior, Master-Servant Relationship, Scope of Employment). Partnership: Property Rights of Partner; Formation of Partnership; Relations Between Partners (including Fiduciary Duty); Authority of Partner to Bind Partnership; Dissolution and Winding up of Partnership; Limited Partnerships.
ISBN: 0-15-900327-X   Pages: 142 $16.95

Antitrust
By Professor Thomas M. Jorde, U.C. Berkeley, Mark A. Lemley, University of Texas, and Professor Robert H. Mnookin, Harvard University
Common Law Restraints of Trade; Federal Antitrust Laws (including Sherman Act, Clayton Act, Federal Trade Commission Act, Interstate Commerce Requirement, Antitrust Remedies); Monopolization (including Relevant Market, Purposeful Act Requirement, Attempts and Conspiracy to Monopolize); Collaboration Among Competitors (including Horizontal Restraints, Rule of Reason vs. Per Se Violations, Price Fixing, Division of Markets, Group Boycotts); Vertical Restraints (including Tying Arrangements); Mergers and Acquisitions (including Horizontal Mergers, Brown Shoe Analysis, Vertical Mergers, Conglomerate Mergers); Price Discrimination — Robinson-Patman Act; Unfair Methods of Competition; Patent Laws and Their Antitrust Implications; Exemptions From Antitrust Laws (including Motor, Rail, and Interstate Water Carriers, Bank Mergers, Labor Unions, Professional Baseball).
ISBN: 0-15-900328-8   Pages: 193 $16.95

Bankruptcy
By Professor Ned W. Waxman, College of William and Mary
Participants in the Bankruptcy Case; Jurisdiction and Procedure; Commencement and Administration of the Case (including Eligibility, Voluntary Case, Involuntary Case, Meeting of Creditors, Debtor's Duties); Officers of the Estate (including Trustee, Examiner, United States Trustee); Bankruptcy Estate; Creditor's Right of Setoff; Trustee's Avoiding Powers; Claims of Creditors (including Priority Claims and Tax Claims); Debtor's Exemptions; Nondischargeable Debts; Effects of Discharge; Reaffirmation Agreements; Administrative Powers (including Automatic Stay, Use, Sale, or Lease of Property); Chapter 7- Liquidation; Chapter 11- Reorganization; Chapter 13-Individual With Regular Income; Chapter 12- Family Farmer With Regular Annual Income.
ISBN: 0-15-900245-1   Pages: 356 $19.95

Business Law
By Professor Robert D. Upp, Los Angeles City College
Torts and Crimes in Business; Law of Contracts (including Contract Formation, Consideration, Statute of Frauds, Contract Remedies, Third Parties); Sales (including Transfer of Title and Risk of Loss, Performance and Remedies, Products Liability, Personal Property Security Interest); Property (including Personal Property, Bailments, Real Property, Landlord and Tenant); Agency; Business Organizations (including Partnerships, Corporations); Commercial Paper; Government Regulation of Business (including Taxation, Antitrust, Environmental Protection, and Bankruptcy).
ISBN: 0-15-900005-X   Pages: 295 $16.95

California Bar Performance Test Skills
By Professor Peter J. Honigsberg, University of San Francisco
Hints to Improve Writing; How to Approach the Performance Test; Legal Analysis Documents (including Writing a Memorandum of Law, Writing a Client Letter, Writing Briefs); Fact Gathering and Fact Analysis Documents; Tactical and Ethical Considerations; Sample Interrogatories, Performance Tests, and Memoranda.
ISBN: 0-15-900152-8   Pages: 216 $17.95

Civil Procedure
By Professor Thomas D. Rowe, Jr., Duke University, and Professor Richard L. Marcus, U.C. Hastings
Territorial (personal) Jurisdiction, including Venue and Forum Non Conveniens; Subject Matter Jurisdiction, covering Diversity Jurisdiction, Federal Question Jurisdiction; Erie Doctrine and Federal Common Law; Pleadings including Counterclaims, Cross-Claims, Supplemental Pleadings; Parties, including Joinder and Class Actions; Discovery, including Devices, Scope, Sanctions and Discovery Conference; Summary Judgment; Pretrial Conference and Settlements; Trial, including Right to Jury Trial, Motions, Jury Instruction and Arguments, and Post-Verdict Motions; Appeals; Claim Preclusion (Res Judicata) and Issue Preclusion (Collateral Estoppel).
ISBN: 0-15-900272-9   Pages: 447 $19.95

Commercial Paper and Payment Law
By Professor Douglas J. Whaley, Ohio State University
Types of Commercial Paper; Negotiability; Negotiation; Holders in Due Course; Claims and Defenses on Negotiable Instruments (including Real Defenses and Personal Defenses); Liability of the Parties (including Merger Rule, Suits on the Instrument, Warranty Suits, Conversion); Bank Deposits and Collections; Forgery or Alteration of Negotiable Instruments; Electronic Banking.
ISBN: 0-15-900367-9   Pages: 222 $17.95

Community Property
By Professor William A. Reppy, Jr., Duke University
Classifying Property as Community or Separate; Management and Control of Property; Liability for Debts; Division of Property at Divorce; Devolution of Property at Death; Relationships Short of Valid Marriage; Conflict of Laws Problems; Constitutional Law Issues (including Equal Protection Standards, Due Process Issues).
ISBN: 0-15-900235-4   Pages: 188 $17.95

Conflict of Laws
By Dean Herma Hill Kay, U.C. Berkeley

Domicile; Jurisdiction (including Notice and Opportunity to be Heard, Minimum Contacts, Types of Jurisdiction); Choice of Law (including Vested Rights Approach, Most Significant Relationship Approach, Governmental Interest Analysis); Choice of Law in Specific Substantive Areas; Traditional Defenses Against Application of Foreign Law; Constitutional Limitations and Overriding Federal Law (including Due Process Clause, Full Faith and Credit Clause, Conflict Between State and Federal Law); Recognition and Enforcement of Foreign Judgments.
ISBN: 0-15-900011-4   Pages: 260 $18.95

Constitutional Law
By Professor Jesse H. Choper, U.C. Berkeley

Powers of Federal Government (including Judicial Power, Powers of Congress, Presidential Power, Foreign Affairs Power); Intergovernmental Immunities, Separation of Powers; Regulation of Foreign Commerce; Regulation of Interstate Commerce; Taxation of Interstate and Foreign Commerce; Due Process, Equal Protection; "State Action" Requirements; Freedoms of Speech, Press, and Association; Freedom of Religion.
ISBN: 0-15-900265-6   Pages: 335 $19.95

Contracts
By Professor Melvin A. Eisenberg, U.C. Berkeley

Consideration (including Promissory Estoppel, Moral or Past Consideration); Mutual Assent; Defenses (including Mistake, Fraud, Duress, Unconscionability, Statute of Frauds, Illegality); Third-Party Beneficiaries; Assignment of Rights and Delegation of Duties; Conditions; Substantial Performance; Material vs. Minor Breach; Anticipatory Breach; Impossibility; Discharge; Remedies (including Damages, Specific Performance, Liquidated Damages).
ISBN: 0-15-900014-9   Pages: 326 $19.95

Corporations
By Professor Jesse H. Choper, U.C. Berkeley, and Professor Melvin A. Eisenberg, U.C. Berkeley

Formalities; "De Jure" vs. "De Facto"; Promoters; Corporate Powers; Ultra Vires Transactions; Powers, Duties, and Liabilities of Officers and Directors; Allocation of Power Between Directors and Shareholders; Conflicts of Interest in Corporate Transactions; Close Corporations; Insider Trading; Rule 10b-5 and Section 16(b); Shareholders' Voting Rights; Shareholders' Right to Inspect Records; Shareholders' Suits; Capitalization (including Classes of Shares, Preemptive Rights, Consideration for Shares); Dividends; Redemption of Shares; Fundamental Changes in Corporate Structure; Applicable Conflict of Laws Principles.
ISBN: 0-15-900342-3   Pages: 308 $19.95

Criminal Law
By Professor George E. Dix, University of Texas

Elements of Crimes (including Actus Reus, Mens Rea, Causation); Vicarious Liability; Complicity in Crime; Criminal Liability of Corporations;
Defenses (including Insanity, Diminished Capacity, Intoxication, Ignorance, Self-Defense); Inchoate Crimes; Homicide; Other Crimes Against the Person; Crimes Against Habitation (including Burglary, Arson); Crimes Against Property; Offenses Against Government; Offenses Against Administration of Justice.
ISBN: 0-15-900217-6   Pages: 271 $18.95

Criminal Procedure
By Professor Paul Marcus, College of William and Mary, and Professor Charles H. Whitebread, U.S.C.

Exclusionary Rule; Arrests and Other Detentions; Search and Seizure; Privilege Against Self-Incrimination; Confessions; Preliminary Hearing; Bail; Indictment; Speedy Trial; Competency to Stand Trial; Government's Obligation to Disclose Information; Right to Jury Trial; Right to Counsel; Right to Confront Witnesses; Burden of Proof; Insanity; Entrapment; Guilty Pleas; Sentencing; Death Penalty; Ex Post Facto Issues; Appeal; Habeas Corpus; Juvenile Offenders; Prisoners' Rights; Double Jeopardy.
ISBN: 0-15-900347-4   Pages: 271 $18.95

Dictionary of Legal Terms
Gilbert Staff

Contains Over 3,500 Legal Terms and Phrases; Law School Shorthand; Common Abbreviations; Latin and French Legal Terms; Periodical Abbreviations; Governmental Abbreviations.
ISBN: 0-15-900018-1   Pages: 163 $14.95

Estate and Gift Tax
By Professor John H. McCord, University of Illinois

Gross Estate Allowable Deductions Under Estate Tax (including Expenses, Indebtedness, and Taxes, Deductions for Losses, Charitable Deduction, Marital Deduction); Taxable Gifts; Deductions; Valuation; Computation of Tax; Returns and Payment of Tax; Tax on Generation-Skipping Transfers.
ISBN: 0-15-900019-X   Pages: 283 $18.95

Evidence
By Professor Jon R. Waltz, Northwestern University, and Roger C. Park, University of Minnesota

Direct Evidence; Circumstantial Evidence; Rulings on Admissibility; Relevancy; Materiality; Character Evidence; Hearsay and the Hearsay Exceptions; Privileges; Competency to Testify; Opinion Evidence and Expert Witnesses; Direct Examination; Cross-Examination; Impeachment; Real, Demonstrative, and Scientific Evidence; Judicial Notice; Burdens of Proof; Parol Evidence Rule.
ISBN: 0-15-900020-3   Pages: 359 $19.95

Federal Courts
By Professor William A. Fletcher, U.C. Berkeley

Article III Courts; "Case or Controversy" Requirement; Justiciability; Advisory Opinions; Political Questions; Ripeness; Mootness; Standing; Congressional Power Over Federal Court Jurisdiction; Supreme Court Jurisdiction; District Court Subject Matter Jurisdiction (including Federal Question Jurisdiction, Diversity
Jurisdiction); Pendent and Ancillary Jurisdiction; Removal Jurisdiction; Venue; Forum Non Conveniens; Law Applied in the Federal Courts (including Erie Doctrine); Federal Law in the State Courts; Abstention; Habeas Corpus for State Prisoners; Federal Injunctions Against State Court Proceedings; Eleventh Amendment.
ISBN: 0-15-900232-X   Pages: 310 $19.95

Future Interests & Perpetuities
By Professor Jesse Dukeminier, U.C.L.A.

Reversions; Possibilities of Reverter; Rights of Entry; Remainders; Executory Interest; Rules Restricting Remainders and Executory Interest; Rights of Owners of Future Interests; Construction of Instruments; Powers of Appointment; Rule Against Perpetuities (including Reforms of the Rule).
ISBN: 0-15-900218-4   Pages: 219 $17.95

Income Tax I - Individual
By Professor Michael R. Asimow, U.C.L.A.

Gross Income; Exclusions; Income Splitting by Gifts, Personal Service Income, Income Earned by Children, Income of Husbands and Wives, Below-Market Interest on Loans, Taxation of Trusts; Business and Investment Deductions; Personal Deductions; Tax Rates; Credits; Computation of Basis, Gain, or Loss; Realization; Nonrecognition of Gain or Loss; Capital Gains and Losses; Alternative Minimum Tax; Tax Accounting Problems.
ISBN: 0-15-900266-4   Pages: 312 $19.95

Income Tax II - Partnerships, Corporations, Trusts
By Professor Michael R. Asimow, U.C.L.A.

Taxation of Partnerships (including Current Partnership Income, Contributions of Property to Partnership, Sale of Partnership Interest, Distributions, Liquidations); Corporate Taxation (including Corporate Distributions, Sales of Stock and Assets, Reorganizations); S Corporations; Federal Income Taxation of Trusts.
ISBN: 0-15-900024-6   Pages: 237 $17.95

Labor Law
By Professor James C. Oldham, Georgetown University, and Robert J. Gelhaus

Statutory Foundations of Present Labor Law (including National Labor Relations Act, Taft-Hartley, Norris-LaGuardia Act, Landrum-Griffin Act); Organizing Campaigns, Selection of the Bargaining Representative; Collective Bargaining (including Negotiating the Agreement, Lockouts, Administering the Agreement, Arbitration); Strikes, Boycotts, and Picketing; Concerted Activity Protected Under the NLRA; Civil Rights Legislation; Grievance; Federal Regulation of Compulsory Union Membership Arrangements; State Regulation of Compulsory Membership Agreements; "Right to Work" Laws; Discipline of Union Members; Election of Union Officers; Corruption.
ISBN: 0-15-900340-7   Pages: 243 $17.95

Legal Ethics
By Professor Thomas D. Morgan, George Washington University

Regulating Admission to Practice Law; Preventing Unauthorized Practice of Law; Contract Between Client and Lawyer (including Lawyer's Duties Regarding Accepting Employment, Spheres of Authority of Lawyer and Client, Obligation of Client to Lawyer, Terminating the Lawyer-Client Relationship); Attorney-Client Privilege; Professional Duty of Confidentiality; Conflicts of Interest; Obligations to Third Persons and the Legal System (including Counseling Illegal or Fraudulent Conduct, Threats of Criminal Prosecution); Special Obligations in Litigation (including Limitations on Advancing Money to Client, Duty to Reject Certain Actions, Lawyer as Witness); Solicitation and Advertising; Specialization; Disciplinary Process; Malpractice; Special Responsibilities of Judges.
ISBN: 0-15-900026-2   Pages: 252 $18.95

Legal Research, Writing and Analysis
By Professor Peter J. Honigsberg, University of San Francisco

Court Systems; Precedent; Case Reporting System (including Regional and State Reporters, Headnotes and the West Key Number System, Citations and Case Finding); Statutes, Constitutions, and Legislative History; Secondary Sources (including Treatises, Law Reviews, Digests, Restatements); Administrative Agencies (including Regulations, Looseleaf Services); Shepard's Citations; Computers in Legal Research; Reading and Understanding a Case (including Briefing a Case); Using Legal Sourcebooks; Basic Guidelines for Legal Writing; Organizing Your Research; Writing a Memorandum of Law; Writing a Brief; Writing an Opinion or Client Letter.
ISBN: 0-15-900305-9   Pages: 162 $16.95

Multistate Bar Examination
By Professor Richard J. Conviser, Chicago Kent

Structure of the Exam; Governing Law; Effective Use of Time; Scoring of the Exam; Jurisdictions Using the Exam; Subject Matter Outlines; Practice Tests, Answers, and Subject Matter Keys; Glossary of Legal Terms and Definitions; State Bar Examination Directory; Listing of Reference Materials for Multistate Subjects.
ISBN: 0-15-900246-X   Pages: 210 $19.95

Personal Property
Gilbert Staff

Acquisitions; Ownership Through Possession (including Wild Animals, Abandoned Chattels); Finders of Lost Property; Bailments; Possessory Liens; Pledges, Trover; Gift; Accession; Confusion (Commingling); Fixtures; Crops (Emblements); Adverse Possession; Prescriptive Rights (Acquiring Ownership of Easements or Profits by Adverse Use).
ISBN: 0-15-900360-1   Pages: 69 $14.95

Professional Responsibility
(see Legal Ethics)

gilbert
LAW SUMMARIES

Property
By Professor Jesse Dukeminier, U.C.L.A.

Possession (including Wild Animals, Bailments, Adverse Possession); Gifts and Sales of Personal Property; Freehold Possessory Estates; Future Interests (including Reversion, Possibility of Reverter, Right of Entry, Executory Interests, Rule Against Perpetuities); Tenancy in Common; Joint Tenancy; Tenancy by the Entirety; Condominiums; Cooperatives; Marital Property; Landlord and Tenant; Easements and Covenants; Nuisance; Rights in Airspace and Water; Right to Support; Zoning; Eminent Domain; Sale of Land (including Mortgage, Deed, Warranties of Title); Methods of Title Assurance (including Recording System, Title Registration, Title Insurance).
ISBN: 0-15-900032-7   Pages: 496 $21.95

Remedies
By Professor John A. Bauman, U.C.L.A., and Professor Kenneth H. York, Pepperdine University

Damages; Equitable Remedies (including Injunctions and Specific Performance); Restitution; Injuries to Tangible Property Interests; Injuries to Business and Commercial Interests (including Business Torts, Inducing Breach of Contract, Patent Infringement, Unfair Competition, Trade Defamation); Injuries to Personal Dignity and Related Interests (including Defamation, Privacy, Religious Status, Civil and Political Rights); Personal Injury and Death; Fraud; Duress, Undue Influence, and Unconscionable Conduct; Mistake; Breach of Contract; Unenforceable Contracts (including Statute of Frauds, Impossibility, Lack of Contractual Capacity, Illegality).
ISBN: 0-15-900325-3   Pages: 375 $20.95

Sale and Lease of Goods
By Professor Douglas J. Whaley, Ohio State University

UCC Article 2; Sales Contract (including Offer and Acceptance, Parol Evidence Rule, Statute of Frauds, Assignment and Delegation, Revision of Contract Terms); Types of Sales (including Cash Sale Transactions, Auctions, "Sale or Return" and "Sale on Approval" Transactions); Warranties (including Express and Implied Warranties, Privity, Disclaimer, Consumer Protection Statutes); Passage of Title; Performance of the Contract; Anticipatory Breach; Demand for Assurance of Performance; Unforeseen Circumstances; Risk of Loss; Remedies; Documents of Title; Lease of Goods; International Sale of Goods.
ISBN: 0-15-900219-2   Pages: 222 $17.95

Secured Transactions
By Professor Douglas J. Whaley, Ohio State University

Coverage of Article 9; Creation of a Security Interest (including Attachment, Security Agreement, Value, Debtor's Rights in the Collateral); Perfection; Filing; Priorities; Bankruptcy Proceedings and Article 9; Default Proceedings; Bulk Transfers.
ISBN: 0-15-900231-1   Pages: 213 $17.95

Securities Regulation
By Professor David H. Barber, and Professor Niels B. Schaumann, William Mitchell College of Law

Jurisdiction and Interstate Commerce; Securities Act of 1933 (including Registration Requirements and Exemptions); Securities Exchange Act of 1934 (including Rule 10b-5, Tender Offers, Proxy Solicitations Regulation, Insider Transactions); Regulation of the Securities Markets; Multinational Transactions; State Regulation of Securities Transactions.
ISBN: 0-15-9000326-1   Pages: 415 $20.95

Torts
By Professor Marc A. Franklin, Stanford University

Intentional Torts; Negligence; Strict Liability; Products Liability; Nuisance; Survival of Tort Actions; Wrongful Death; Immunity; Release and Contribution; Indemnity; Workers' Compensation; No-Fault Auto Insurance; Defamation; Invasion of Privacy; Misrepresentation; Injurious Falsehood; Interference With Economic Relations; Unjustifiable Litigation.
ISBN: 0-15-900220-6   Pages: 439 $19.95

Trusts
By Professor Edward C. Halbach, Jr., U.C. Berkeley

Elements of a Trust; Trust Creation; Transfer of Beneficiary's Interest (including Spendthrift Trusts); Charitable Trusts (including Cy Pres Doctrine); Trustee's Responsibilities, Power, Duties, and Liabilities; Duties and Liabilities of Beneficiaries; Accounting for Income and Principal; Power of Settlor to Modify or Revoke; Powers of Trustee Beneficiaries or Courts to Modify or Terminate; Termination of Trusts by Operation of Law; Resulting Trusts; Purchase Money Resulting Trusts; Constructive Trusts.
ISBN: 0-15-900039-4   Pages: 268 $18.95

Wills
By Professor Stanley M. Johanson, University of Texas

Intestate Succession; Simultaneous Death; Advancements; Disclaimer; Killer of Decedent; Elective Share Statutes; Pretermitted Child Statutes; Homestead; Formal Requisites of a Will; Revocation of Wills; Incorporation by Reference; Pour-Over Gift in Inter Vivos Trust; Joint Wills; Contracts Relating to Wills; Lapsed Gifts; Ademption; Exoneration of Liens; Will Contests; Probate and Estate Administration.
ISBN: 0-15-900040-8   Pages: 310 $19.95

Gilbert Law Summaries FIRST YEAR PROGRAM

Includes Five Gilbert Outlines:

■ **Civil Procedure**
By Professor Thomas D. Rowe, Jr. Duke University Law School, and Professor Richard L. Marcus U.C. Hastings School Of Law

■ **Contracts**
By Professor Melvin A. Eisenberg U.C. Berkeley School Of Law

■ **Criminal Law**
By Professor George E. Dix University Of Texas School Of Law

■ **Property**
By Professor Jesse Dukeminier U.C.L.A. Law School

■ **Torts**
By Professor Marc A. Franklin Stanford University Law School

Plus—

■ **Gilbert's Pocket Size Law Dictionary**
Published By Harcourt Brace

■ **The 8 Secrets Of Top Exam Performance In Law School**
By Professor Charles H. Whitebread USC Law School

All titles are packaged in a convenient carry case with handle. $120 if purchased separately. $95 if purchased as a set. Save $25.
ISBN: 0-15-900254-0   Set $95

Gilbert's Pocket Size Law Dictionary
Gilbert

A dictionary is useless if you don't have it when you need it. If the only law dictionary you own is a thick, bulky one, you'll probably leave it at home most of the time — and if you need to know a definition while you're at school, you're out of luck!

With Gilbert's Pocket Size Law Dictionary, you'll have any definition you need, when you need it. Just pop Gilbert's dictionary into your pocket or purse, and you'll have over 4,000 legal terms and phrases at your fingertips. Gilbert's dictionary also includes a section on law school shorthand, common abbreviations, Latin and French legal terms, periodical abbreviations, and governmental abbreviations.

With Gilbert's Pocket Size Law Dictionary, you'll never be caught at a loss for words!

Available in your choice of 5 colors
■ **Brown** ISBN: 0-15-900252-4 $7.95
■ **Blue** ISBN: 0-15-900362-8 $7.95
■ **Burgundy** ISBN: 0-15-900366-0 $7.95
■ **Green** ISBN: 0-15-900365-2 $7.95

Limited Edition: Simulated Alligator Skin Cover
■ **Black** ISBN: 0-15-900364-4 $7.95

The Eight Secrets Of Top Exam Performance In Law School
Charles Whitebread

Wouldn't it be great to know exactly what your professor's looking for on your exam? To find out everything that's expected of you, so that you don't waste your time doing anything other than maximizing your grades?

In his easy-to-read, refreshing style, nationally recognized exam expert Professor Charles

Whitebread will teach you the eight secrets that will add precious points to every exam answer you write. You'll learn the three keys to handling any essay exam question, and how to add points to your score by making time work for you, not against you. You'll learn flawless issue spotting, and discover how to organize your answer for maximum possible points. You'll find out how the hidden traps in "IRAC" trip up most students… but not you! You'll learn the techniques for digging up the exam questions your professor will ask, before your exam. You'll put your newly-learned skills to the test with sample exam questions, and you can measure your performance against model answers. And there's even a special section that helps you master the skills necessary to crush any exam, not just a typical essay exam — unusual exams like open book, take home, multiple choice, short answer, and policy questions.

"The Eight Secrets of Top Exam Performance in Law School" gives you all the tools you need to maximize your grades — quickly and easily!
ISBN: 0-15-900323-7 $9.95

Call 1-800-787-8717 or visit our web site at http://www.gilbertlaw.com for more information.

LAW SCHOOL LEGENDS SERIES

America's Greatest Law Professors on Audio Cassette

Wouldn't it be great if all of your law professors were law school legends? You know — the kind of professors whose classes everyone fights to get into. The professors whose classes you'd take, no matter what subject they're teaching. The kind of professors who make a subject sing. You may never get an opportunity to take a class with a truly brilliant professor, but with the Law School Legends Series, you can now get all the benefits of the country's greatest law professors...on audio cassette!

Administrative Law

Professor Patrick J. Borchers
Albany Law School of Union University

TOPICS COVERED: Classification Of Agencies; Adjudicative And Investigative Action; Rule Making Power; Delegation Doctrine; Control By Executive; Appointment And Removal; Freedom Of Information Act; Rule Making Procedure; Adjudicative Procedure; Trial Type Hearings; Administrative Law Judge; Power To Stay Proceedings; Subpoena Power; Physical Inspection; Self Incrimination; Judicial Review Issues; Declaratory Judgment; Sovereign Immunity; Eleventh Amendment; Statutory Limitations; Standing; Exhaustion Of Administrative Remedies; Scope Of Judicial Review.
3 Audio Cassettes
ISBN 0-15-900189-7 $45.95

Agency & Partnership

Professor Richard J. Conviser
Chicago Kent College of Law

TOPICS COVERED: Agency: Creation; Rights And Duties Of Principal And Agent; Sub-Agents; Contract Liability–Actual Authority: Express And Implied; Apparent Authority; Ratification; Liabilities Of Parties; Tort Liability–Respondeat Superior; Frolic And Detour; Intentional Torts. *Partnership:* Nature of Partnership; Formation; Partnership By Estoppel; In Partnership Property; Relations Between Partners To Third Parties; Authority of Partners; Dissolution And Termination; Limited Partnerships.
3 Audio Cassettes
ISBN: 0-15-900351-2 $45.95

Bankruptcy

Professor Elizabeth Warren
Harvard Law School

TOPICS COVERED: The Debtor/Creditor Relationship; The Commencement, Conversion, Dismissal and Reopening Of Bankruptcy Proceedings; Property Included In The Bankruptcy Estate; Secured, Priority And Unsecured Claims; The Automatic Stay; Powers Of Avoidance; The Assumption And Rejection Of Executory Contracts; The Protection Of Exempt Property; The Bankruptcy Discharge; Chapter 13 Proceedings; Chapter 11 Proceedings; Bankruptcy Jurisdiction And Procedure.
4 Audio Cassettes
ISBN: 0-15-900273-7 $45.95

Civil Procedure

By Professor Richard D. Freer
Emory University Law School

TOPICS COVERED: Subject Matter Jurisdiction; Personal Jurisdiction; Long-Arm Statutes; Constitutional Limitations; In Rem And Quasi In Rem Jurisdiction; Service Of Process; Venue; Transfer; Forum Non Conveniens; Removal; Waiver; Governing Law; Pleadings; Joinder Of Claims; Permissive And Compulsory Joinder Of Parties; Counter-Claims And Cross-Claims; Ancillary Jurisdiction; Impleader; Class Actions; Discovery; Pretrial Adjudication; Summary Judgment; Trial; Post Trial Motions; Appeals; Res Judicata; Collateral Estoppel.
5 Audio Cassettes
ISBN: 0-15-900322-9 $59.95

Commercial Paper

By Professor Michael I. Spak
Chicago Kent College Of Law

TOPICS COVERED: Introduction; Types Of Negotiable Instruments; Elements Of Negotiability; Statute Of Limitations; Payment-In-Full Checks; Negotiations Of The Instrument; Becoming A Holder-In-Due Course; Rights Of A Holder In Due Course; Real And Personal Defenses; Jus Teril; Effect Of Instrument On Underlying Obligations; Contracts Of Maker And Indorser; Suretyship; Liability Of Drawer And Drawee; Check Certification; Warranty Liability; Conversion Of Liability; Banks And Their Customers; Properly Payable Rule; Wrongful Dishonor; Stopping Payment; Death Of Customer; Bank Statement; Check Collection; Expedited Funds Availability; Forgery Of Drawer's Name; Alterations; Imposter Rule; Wire Transfers; Electronic Fund Transfers Act .
3 Audio Cassettes
ISBN: 0-15-900275-3 $39.95

Conflict Of Laws

Professor Richard J. Conviser
Chicago Kent College of Law

TOPICS COVERED: Domicile; Jurisdiction; In Personam, In Rem, Quasi In Rem; Court Competence; Forum Non Conveniens; Choice Of Law; Foreign Causes Of Action; Territorial Approach To Choice/Tort And Contract; "Escape Devices"; Most Significant Relationship; Governmental Interest Analysis; Recognition Of Judgments; Foreign Country Judgments; Domestic Judgments/Full Faith And Credit; Review Of Judgments; Modifiable Judgments; Defenses To Recognition And Enforcement; Federal/State (Erie) Problems; Constitutional Limits On Choice Of Law.
3 Audio Cassettes
ISBN: 0-15-900352-0 $39.95

Constitutional Law

By Professor John C. Jeffries, Jr.
University of Virginia School of Law

TOPICS COVERED: Introduction; Exam Tactics; Legislative Power; Supremacy; Commerce; State Regulation; Privileges And Immunities; Federal Court Jurisdiction; Separation Of Powers; Civil Liberties; Due Process; Equal Protection; Privacy; Race; Alienage; Gender; Speech And Association; Prior Restraints; Religion—Free Exercise; Establishment Clause.
5 Audio Cassettes
ISBN: 0-15-900319-9 $45.95

Contracts

By Professor Michael I. Spak
Chicago Kent College Of Law

TOPICS COVERED: Offer; Revocation; Acceptance; Consideration; Defenses To Formation; Third Party Beneficiaries; Assignment; Delegation; Conditions; Excuses; Anticipatory Repudiation; Discharge Of Duty; Modifications; Rescission; Accord & Satisfaction; Novation; Breach; Damages; Remedies; UCC Remedies; Parol Evidence Rule.
4 Audio Cassettes
ISBN: 0-15-900318-0 $45.95

Copyright Law

Professor Roger E. Schechter
George Washington University Law School

TOPICS COVERED: Constitution; Patents And Property Ownership Distinguished; Subject Matter Copyright; Duration And Renewal; Ownership And Transfer; Formalities; Introduction; Notice, Registration And Deposit; Infringement; Overview; Reproduction And Derivative Works; Public Distribution; Public Performance And Display; Exemptions; Fair Use; Photocopying; Remedies; Preemption Of State Law.
3 Audio Cassettes
ISBN: 0-15-900295-8 $39.95

Corporations

By Professor Therese H. Maynard
Loyola Marymount School of Law

TOPICS COVERED: Ultra Vires Act; Corporate Formation; Piercing The Corporate Veil; Corporate Financial Structure; Stocks; Bonds; Subscription Agreements; Watered Stock; Stock Transactions; Insider Trading; 16(b) & 10b-5 Violations; Promoters; Fiduciary Duties; Shareholder Rights; Meetings; Cumulative Voting; Voting Trusts; Close Corporations; Dividends; Preemptive Rights; Shareholder Derivative Suits; Directors; Duty Of Loyalty; Corporate Opportunity Doctrine; Officers; Amendments; Mergers; Dissolution.
4 Audio Cassettes
ISBN: 0-15-900320-2 $45.95

Criminal Law

By Professor Charles H. Whitebread
USC School of Law

TOPICS COVERED: Exam Tactics; Volitional Acts; Mental States; Specific Intent; Malice; General Intent; Strict Liability; Accomplice Liability; Inchoate Crimes; Impossibility; Defenses; Insanity; Voluntary And Involuntary Intoxication; Infancy; Self-Defense; Defense Of A Dwelling; Duress; Necessity; Mistake Of Fact Or Law; Entrapment; Battery; Assault; Homicide; Common Law Murder; Voluntary And Involuntary Manslaughter; First Degree Murder; Felony Murder; Rape; Larceny; Embezzlement; False Pretenses; Robbery; Extortion; Burglary; Arson.
4 Audio Cassettes
ISBN: 0-15-900279-6 $39.95

Criminal Procedure

By Professor Charles H. Whitebread
USC School of Law

TOPICS COVERED: Incorporation Of The Bill Of Rights; Exclusionary Rule; Fruit Of The Poisonous Tree; Arrest; Search & Seizure; Exceptions To Warrant Requirement; Wire Tapping & Eavesdropping; Confessions (Miranda); Pretrial Identification; Bail; Preliminary Hearings; Grand Juries; Speedy Trial; Fair Trial; Jury Trials; Right To Counsel; Guilty Pleas; Sentencing; Death Penalty; Habeas Corpus; Double Jeopardy; Privilege Against Compelled Testimony.
3 Audio Cassettes
ISBN: 0-15-900281-8 $39.95

Employment Guides

A collection of best selling titles that help you identify and reach your career goals.

The National Directory Of Legal Employers
National Association for Law Placement

The National Directory of Legal Employers brings you a universe of vital information about 1,000 of the nation's top legal employers— *in one convenient volume!*

It includes:
- Over 22,000 job openings.
- The names, addresses and phone numbers of hiring partners.
- Listings of firms by state, size, kind and practice area.
- What starting salaries are for full time, part time, and summer associates, plus a detailed description of firm benefits.
- The number of employees by gender and race, as well as the number of employees with disabilities.
- A detailed narrative of each firm, plus much more!

The National Directory Of Legal Employers has been the best kept secret of top legal career search professionals for over a decade. Now, for the first time, it is available in a format specifically designed for law students and new graduates. *Pick up your copy of the Directory today!*

ISBN: 0-15-900248-6 $39.95

Proceed With Caution: A Diary Of The First Year At One Of America's Largest, Most Prestigious Law Firms
William R. Keates

Prestige. Famous clients. High-profile cases. Not to mention a starting salary approaching six figures.

In *Proceed With Caution*, the author takes you behind the scenes, to show you what it's really like to be a junior associate at a huge law firm. After graduating from an Ivy League law school, he took a job as an associate with one of New York's blue-chip law firms.

He also did something not many people do. He kept a diary, where he spilled out his day-to-day life at the firm in graphic detail.

Proceed With Caution excerpts the diary, from his first day at the firm to the day he quit. From the splashy benefits, to the nitty-gritty on the work junior associates do, to the grind of long and unpredictable hours, to the stress that eventually made him leave the firm — he tells story after story that will make you feel as though you're living the life of a new associate.

Whether you're considering a career with a large firm, or you're just curious about what life at the top firms is all about — *Proceed With Caution* is a must read!

ISBN: 0-15-900181-1 $17.95

Guerrilla Tactics for Getting the Legal Job of Your Dreams
Kimm Alayne Walton, J.D.

Whether you're looking for a summer clerkship or your first permanent job after school, this revolutionary book is the key to getting the job of your dreams!

Guerrilla Tactics for Getting the Legal Job of Your Dreams leads you step-by-step through everything you need to do to nail down that perfect job! You'll learn hundreds of simple-to-use strategies that will get you exactly where you want to go. You'll Learn:
- The seven magic opening words in cover letters that ensure you'll get a response.
- The secret to successful interviews every time.
- Killer answers to the toughest interview questions they'll ever ask you.
- Plus Much More!

Guerrilla Tactics features the best strategies from the country's most innovative law school career advisors. The strategies in *Guerrilla Tactics* are so powerful that it even comes with a guarantee: Follow the advice in the book, and within one year of graduation you'll have the job of your dreams… or your money back!

Pick up a copy of *Guerrilla Tactics* today…and you'll be on your way to the job of your dreams!

ISBN: 0-15-900317-2 $24.95

Beyond L.A. Law: Inspiring Stories of People Who've Done Fascinating Things With A Law Degree
National Association for Law Placement

Anyone who watches television knows that being a lawyer means working your way up through a law firm — right?

Wrong!

Beyond L.A. Law gives you a fascinating glimpse into the lives of people who've broken the "lawyer" mold. They come from a variety of backgrounds — some had prior careers, others went straight through college and law school, and yet others have overcome poverty and physical handicaps. They got their degrees from all different kinds of law schools, all over the country. But they have one thing in common: they've all pursued their own, unique vision.

As you read their stories, you'll see how they beat the odds to succeed. You'll learn career tips and strategies that work, from people who've put them to the test. And you'll find fascinating insights that you can apply to your own dream — whether it's a career in law, or anything else!

From Representing Baseball In Australia. To International Finance. To Children's Advocacy. To Directing a Nonprofit Organization. To Entrepreneur.

If You Think Getting A Law Degree Means Joining A Traditional Law Firm — Think Again!.

ISBN: 0-15-900182-X $17.95

America's Greatest Places To Work With A Law Degree
Kimm Alayne Walton, J.D.

"Where do your happiest graduates work?" That's the question that author Kimm Alayne Walton asked of law school administrators around the country. Their responses revealed the hundreds of wonderful employers profiled in *America's Greatest Places To Work With A Law Degree*.

In this remarkable book, you'll get to know an incredible variety of great places to work, including:
- Glamorous sports and entertainment employers – the jobs that sound as though they would be great, and they are!
- The 250 best law firms to work for between 20 and 600 attorneys.
- Companies where law school graduates love to work and not just as in-house counsel.
- Wonderful public interest employers – the "white knight" jobs that are so incredibly satisfying.
- Court-related positions, where lawyers entertain fascinating issues, tremendous variety, and an enjoyable lifestyle.
- Outstanding government jobs, at the federal, state, and local level.

Beyond learning about incredible employers, you'll discover:
- The ten traits that define a wonderful place to work…the sometimes surprising qualities that outstanding employers share.
- How to handle law school debt, when your dream job pays less than you think you need to make.
- How to find – and get! – great jobs at firms with fewer than 20 attorneys.

And no matter where you work, you'll learn expert tips for making the most of your job. You'll learn the specific strategies that distinguish people headed for the top…how to position yourself for the most interesting, high-profile work…how to handle difficult personalities… how to negotiate for more money…and what to do now to help you get your next great job!

ISBN: 0-15-900180-3 $24.95

Presented by The National Law Journal

The Job Goddess column is a weekly feature of the *National Law Journal's Law Journal Extra*, and is written by Kimm Alayne Walton, author of the national best seller *Guerrilla Tactics For Getting The Legal Job Of Your Dreams*. View recent columns or e-mail the Job Goddess with your job search questions on the Internet at www.gilbertlaw.com

Call 1-800-787-8717 or visit our web site at http://www.gilbertlaw.com for more information.